Intimate Encounters

Intimate Encounters

Filipina Women and the Remaking of Rural Japan

Lieba Faier

UNIVERSITY OF CALIFORNIA PRESS
Berkeley · Los Angeles · London

A version of Chapter 6 was published as "Runaway Stories: The Underground Micromovements of Filipina *Oyomesan* in Rural Japan" in *Cultural Anthropology* 23, no. 4 (November 2008): 630–59.

University of California Press, one of the most distinguished university presses in the United States, enriches lives around the world by advancing scholarship in the humanities, social sciences, and natural sciences. Its activities are supported by the UC Press Foundation and by philanthropic contributions from individuals and institutions. For more information, visit www.ucpress.edu.

University of California Press
Berkeley and Los Angeles, California

University of California Press, Ltd.
London, England

Library of Congress Cataloging-in-Publication Data

Faier, Lieba.
    Intimate encounters : Filipina women and the remaking of rural Japan / Lieba Faier.
        p.   cm.
    Includes bibliographical references and index.
ISBN 978-0-520-25214-1 (cloth : alk. paper)
ISBN 978-0-520-25215-8 (pbk. : alk. paper)
    1. Women—Japan—Social conditions.
    2. Women—Philippines—Social conditions.
    3. Women—Japan—History.   4. Women domestics—Japan.   5. Women alien labor—Japan.   6. Alien labor, Philippine—Japan.   I. Title.

HQ1762.F25   2009
305.48'89921052163—dc22   2008050734

Manufactured in the United States of America

18   17   16   15   14   13   12   11   10   09
10   9   8   7   6   5   4   3   2   1

This book is printed on Cascades Enviro 100, a 100% post-consumer waste, recycled, de-inked fiber. FSC-recycled certified and processed chlorine free. It is acid free, Ecologo certified, and manufactured by BioGas energy.

*For my mother, in loving memory
of my father*

On all its various routes toward the object, in all its directions, the word encounters an alien word and cannot help encountering it in a living, tension-filled interaction.

Mikhail Bakhtin, *Discourse in the Novel*

I was struck with wonder that there had really been a time, not so long ago, when people, sensible people, of good intention, had thought that all maps were the same, that there was a special enchantment in lines; I had to remind myself that they were not to be blamed for believing that there was something admirable in moving violence to the borders and dealing with it through science and factories, for that was the pattern of the world. They had drawn their borders, believing in that pattern, in the enchantment of lines, hoping perhaps that once they had etched their borders upon the map, the two bits of land would sail away from each other like the shifting tectonic plates of the prehistoric Gondwanaland. What had they felt, I wondered, when they discovered that they had created not a separation, but a yet-undiscovered irony. . .

Amitav Ghosh, *The Shadow Lines*

Contents

Illustrations

Acknowledgments

This book is about the central role that relationships play in the production of cultural meanings—a fitting topic given the extent to which this book is itself a product of my relationships with others.

First and foremost, my gratitude goes to those I interviewed in Japan and the Philippines. In the interest of respecting their privacy, I refrain from mentioning them by name. However, I hope this book goes some small way toward expressing the respect and appreciation I feel for all who shared their lives and stories with me.

There are also those I met through my volunteer activities in Tokyo during the mid-1990s who introduced me to many issues facing Filipina and Filipino migrants in Japan. I am thankful to all and in particular to Carina Morita, who throughout the years has been a confidante, advisor, reader, and, above all, friend. Her support and input has been invaluable in countless ways. I also thank Sister Celine, Sister Celeste, Sister Lourdes, and Father Lari, four activist-clergy without whose introductions, trust, and support I would never have been able to conduct my research. I learned much from witnessing the love and commitment they extend to their communities.

Special thanks also go to Kamari Clarke and Kathy Chetkovich, who were wonderful interlocutors as I completed this book. Both offered feedback on multiple drafts and gave much appreciated encouragement. Jun Uchida, Jordan Sand, Miyako Inoue, Mariko Tamanoi, Jody Blanco, and Anjali Arondekar graciously read chapters and provided useful input.

Anne Allison, Vicente Rafael, and an anonymous manuscript reviewer pushed me with their savvy comments to develop my ideas. Jane Ward, Rachel Luft, Falu Bakrania, and Paul Frymer offered support, guidance, and friendship. Chase Langford created a terrific, imaginative map and allowed me to use his painting for my cover.

Many ideas in this book began in conversations with teachers, colleagues, and friends I met while I was a graduate student in anthropology at UC Santa Cruz. I thank especially Anna Tsing and Lisa Rofel for their intellectual and creative inspiration, ongoing encouragement and support, and invaluable feedback and advice. I could not have hoped to work with more brilliant or committed scholars. I also thank Neferti Tadiar, Alan Christy, Tim Choy, Joanie McCollom, Cathy Clayton, Falu Bakrania, Nina Schnall, Beth Callaghan, Scott Morgensen, Kale Fajardo, Yuko Okubo, Nelson Graburn, Gail Bederman, Patricia Pender, Paula Moya, Sibyl Schawarzenbach, and Ernesto Martinez for their comments and questions as I worked on the dissertation upon which this book is based.

I revised this manuscript while I was a postdoctoral fellow at UC San Diego's Center for Comparative Immigration Studies; a Mellon fellow at the Society for the Humanities and at the Feminist, Gender, and Sexuality Studies Program at Cornell University; and a research scholar at UCLA's Center for the Study of Women. At Cornell, I had the great fortune of being embedded in an intellectual community that included Amy Villarejo, Andrea Hammer, Hiro Miyazaki, Annelise Riles, Jody and Marivi Blanco, Andrew Williford, Brett de Bary, Dominic Boyer, Johanna Schoss, Rob Weiner, Sherry Martin, Bernadette Meyler, Victor and Nancy Koschman, Kristi Merrill, Kim Kono, and Helen Petrovsky. Our interactions were formative in the development of my ideas. At UCSD, I benefited from wonderful conversations with Gaku Tsuda, Esra Özyürek, Carolyn Turnovsky, Jon Fox, Xavier Escandell, Maria Tapias, Nadia Kim, Debbie Boehm, Tak Fujitani, and Lisa Yoneyama.

I am grateful too to those foundations and organizations that provided financial backing for different stages of my research and writing. Fulbright IIE and Wenner-Gren generously provided funding that enabled me to undertake ethnographic fieldwork in Japan and the Philippines between September 1998 and August 2000. Dissertation writing was partially funded by a women's studies dissertation fellowship from the Women's Studies Department at UC Santa Cruz.

During my doctoral fieldwork, I was affiliated with Tokyo University, where I was an advisee of Dr. Abito Itoh. His insight on rural Japan enabled my research to proceed smoothly. In addition, a heartfelt "thank you" goes to Dr. Shinji Yamashita, Dr. Teruo Sekimoto, and Dr. Take-fumi Terada for supporting my project. Fellow researchers—Dada Dacot, David Leheny, Peter Kirby, Leila Wice, Miriam Budner, Mika Miyoshi, Michiaki Okuyama, Sayuri Oyama, and Kenji Tierney—have made my stays in Japan both fun and intellectually exciting.

Members of my immediate and extended family have also directly and indirectly provided inspiration for this text by teaching me the importance of kinship. Above all, I thank my mother for her enduring love and support. I am also grateful to my aunt Sandra Luft who offered much guidance, counseling me on my writing process and introducing me to many texts that have been seminal to my thinking. I thank, too, my sister Michele, my late grandmother Betty Rudnick, Ethel Rest, Rufus Browning, Joseph, Josh, and Rachel Luft, and the Aaronson-Hickman-Murphy clan for their love, interest, and encouragement.

Last but by no means least, Ruben Hickman has provided creative inspiration and unwavering love and support throughout the years I have been working on this project. He has taught me much about the beauty and challenges of intimate worlds. I thank him for all he brings to my life and, especially, for our little Hirshl.

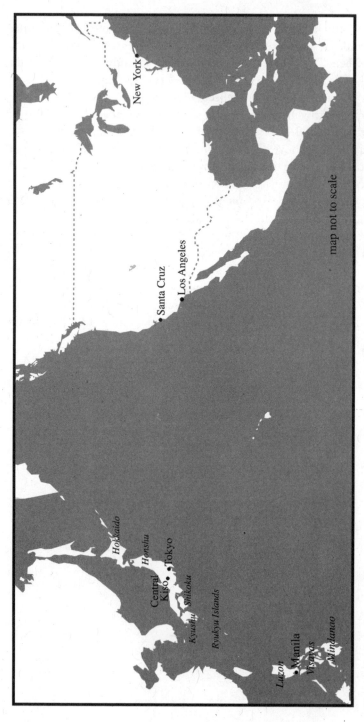

Zones of encounters are filamentary networks that include those relationships through which people construct lives and selves. This map shows some of the geographic places included in the zone of encounters ethnographically mapped in this book.

Relations of Cultural Production

This book is about the ways that cultural encounters make a difference in how people craft lives and selves in a globally interconnected world. It is about how paths converge in sometimes unexpected ways and the new forms of culture and identity that develop through their meeting. My approach to cultural encounters emphasizes the intimate and everyday dynamics of transnational cultural crossings. I describe how Filipina migrants and Japanese residents in a region of southwestern Nagano that I call Central Kiso create new meanings of Japanese and Filipino culture and identity through their shared daily lives.[1]

I use the expression cultural encounters to refer to the coming together of different discourses, genealogies of meaning, and forms of desire. Cultural encounters include interpersonal encounters, but they also involve historical interactions that extend beyond single individuals or cultural groups. Questions of encounter have been important in recent efforts to understand transnational formations of people, capital, and culture. While these studies make valuable use of ideas about flexibility and dynamics, as I discuss later, with few exceptions they tend to focus on the ways that such processes take shape *within* discursive, cultural, or political-economic formations. In contrast, I argue that the everyday dynamics of encounter constitute disparate meanings and subjects. I focus on quotidian sites of interaction where terms of culture and belonging get reworked on multiple sides. In this approach, the beginnings and endings of any encounter always lie somewhere in the middle of interactive, everyday social and historical processes.

Take, for example, how I met Corazon Nakamura, or *Ate* Cora as other Filipina women and I affectionately called her.[2] Cora was the first Filipina entertainer to marry a Japanese man in Central Kiso. She came to Japan in 1981 to work at Club Tomoko, a Filipina hostess bar in Kiso-fukushima, where she met her husband Kunihito. In 1984, Cora and Kunihito married, against his parents' wishes. Cora introduced herself to me the first day I attended the Mothers' Class for foreign wives, a Japanese-language course sponsored by the Kiso County public health center. It was a Thursday morning in early October, not long after I had moved to the region, and I had gone to the class in hopes of meeting Filipina wives in the area. So when, at the beginning of the period, the teachers called me up from my floor cushion to introduce myself to the class, I explained in my best Japanese that I was a student who had come to research the region and that I was particularly interested in the stories of Filipina women married to local Japanese men. Cora approached me during the break, when I followed a group of Filipina women out to the hallway while they had a smoke. She was an energetic woman who chain-smoked and spoke rapidly and expressively. I had noticed her during the class because she had read aloud in Japanese a short essay she had published in the community center newsletter about her participation in a local *taiko* (drum) circle and the Japanese class. I had sensed that she was a leader in the group. It was she who led us in the bows and greetings we recited to open and close the class, she spoke Japanese better and faster than the other students, and she had an air of self-assurance about her. I soon came to know Cora as a grassroots activist, a friend, and a generous supporter of my research, particularly my interest in the lives and perspectives of women. However, what I remember most about Cora from that day is the way that she approached me: with a confident smile and an outstretched hand, she presented herself in a mixture of English and Japanese as "Corazon Nakamura, the first *kokusai kekkon* in Kiso."

One could assume that this encounter was the beginning of my relationship with Cora. It was, of course, the first time we met. However, to assume that our lives were not in some ways connected would be to ignore long histories of unequal relationships among people in Japan, the Philippines, and the United States. These histories had led Cora and me along discrepant paths to our encounter, just as our relationship helped shape the paths that from that point on we decided to take.

Or consider Cora's use of the term *kokusai kekkon,* a Japanese expression that literally translates as "international marriage." Used in a sense similar to *intermarriage* or *interracial marriage* in the United States, the term refers to conjugal relationships between Japanese persons (Nihonjin) and persons from foreign countries *(gaikokujin)*. In Japan, a nation that has long imagined itself as ethnically and culturally homogeneous, kokusai kekkon has generally been perceived as something exceptional that goes against the social grain. The term itself reinscribes notions of Japanese ethnic and cultural homogeneity by marking nationality as the primary index of difference. Interestingly, however, given Cora's casual use of the term to identify herself, there is not a comparable indigenous word for kokusai kekkon in the Philippines. Not only are marriages among ethnolinguistic groups commonplace, but also people sometimes identify as members of a different group from their parents, based on where they grew up and the languages they speak most fluently. Even the word *intermarry*, awkwardly translated into Tagalog by my standard National English-Tagalog dictionary as *mangagkapangasawahan*, does not convey the sense that intermarriages are exceptional or assume that they transgress national or ethnic boundaries. Rather, it carries the nuance of *joining* families, tribes, or castes through marriage.

Cora had learned the term kokusai kekkon in Central Kiso. In Japan, marriages between Filipina migrants and Japanese men are widely identified as a new form of international marriage, which since the late nineteenth century has been almost exclusively associated with relationships between Japanese women and Euro-American men.[3] Central Kiso residents regularly used the expression to note the increasing numbers of Filipina-Japanese relationships in the area. In fact, Cora's in-laws, like those of many Filipina women in the region, initially protested her marriage to their son because they argued that kokusai kekkon was "too difficult." They claimed that a Filipina woman would never fit into a Japanese household. Based on Cora's employment in a hostess bar, they also questioned her sexual morals. When Cora's father-in-law first learned about his son's engagement to Cora, he begged the *mama-san* (proprietor, manager, Jpn.) at Club Tomoko to break up their relationship.[4] But that was years ago, Cora's mother-in-law would tell me. That was just in the beginning. Now the Nakamuras speak with pride of their respectful and hardworking daughter-in-law. On a number of occasions, I heard them and other Japanese community members describe Cora as an *ii oyomesan*, an ideal, traditional Japanese bride and daughter-in-law, and as "more typically Japanese *[nihonjinrashii]* than young Japanese women today." Cora's in-laws were encouraging Cora to become a Japanese citizen, something that would involve not only giving up her Philippine citizenship but also officially changing her name to a Japanese one. Cora had not yet decided whether or not she would, as she put it, "become a Japanese." But she was contemplating doing so, weighing the implications of such a decision for her sense of national and cultural identity, her relationships to people in both Japan and the Philippines, and her prospects for the future.

In its attention to the nitty-gritty of everyday social processes like these, this book is best characterized as an ethnography: a description of the ways people live and make sense of their worlds. However, it also stretches the parameters of this genre. Rather than focusing on Filipina migrants or rural Japanese residents as independent cultural groups, I explore the ways they together produce and transform meanings of Japaneseness and Filipinoness across relations of difference. Marriages between Filipina women and Japanese men in Central Kiso are one site of these unequal dialogues. In this book, I look to the ways these marriages create not only frustrations and limitations but also pleasures and possibilities for those involved. I suggest that these marriages can help illustrate the relational dynamics of culture making in a transnational world. That is, they can show us how cultural meanings and identities are shaped not only by structures of power and forms of human agency, but also by the mundane and sometimes surprising ways that discrepantly located agendas and forms of desire come into productive relation.

By *productive relation*, I am referring to those dialogic processes through which Filipina migrants and Japanese residents engaged what it meant to be an ii oyomesan in terms of sometimes resonant and other times conflicting discourses of gender, class, race, sexuality, nation, and locality.[5] I borrow the term *dialogic* from Mikhail Bakhtin, who tells us that any word (such as oyomesan) "lives . . . on the boundary between its own context and another, alien, context."[6] For Bakhtin, meaning making is an active process that involves borrowing from, anticipating, and relating to the discourses of others as one crafts meaning and a sense of self. As this book will show, this relational process of borrowing and self-definition does not happen in an abstract, symbolic, or structural realm of culture or a neutral space of cultural exchange or mixing. It occurs through intimate and interpersonal everyday relationships that are shaped by gender, desire, and affect and forged through unequal histories and relations of power.[7]

Over the past few decades, the unprecedented movement of people, capital, and cultural forms has brought different ideas and agendas into encounter all over the world, transforming the ways that people craft lives and selves in diverse and sometimes unexpected ways. However, dominant scholarly efforts to understand these cultural and subjective reconfigurations have tended to overlook the relational, day-to-day dynamics of these meetings and focus instead on questions of social structure and human agency on one side of them. In these studies, the term *encounters* is regularly invoked but the dynamics of cultural meetings are rarely explored. Instead, scholars focus on the ways that a given population negotiates global capitalism and transnational cultural flows, or that global processes or new regimes of citizenship and sovereignty shape the lives of members of different groups. They consider how novel cultural discourses, political-economic forces, and regimes of power inform a group's movement, and they consider how members of a group negotiate, accommodate, or resist these transnational formations of power. Even those approaches that manage to hold these processes in dialectical tension, or those that compare the experiences of two or more populations, pay little attention to interactions *between* different formations of desire and power as these play out in relationships among people, such as Filipina migrants and rural Japanese residents, who bring discrepant and unequally situated dreams and agendas to their daily meetings.

In contrast, a focus on cultural encounters asks us to consider the messy, interactive, and sometimes surprising ways that people create cultural meanings and identities through everyday relationships with others. It explores the reformulation of cultural meanings and identities on all sides: the relational dynamics through which people build lives and senses of self. In this book I develop an ethnographic methodology of cultural encounters to explore how Filipina migrants and Japanese residents in Central Kiso transformed meanings of culture and identity through their day-to-day interactions. I tack between stories of variously situated Filipina women and Central Kiso residents, of the distinctive stakes and desires they brought to their encounters, and of the possibilities and frustrations they found in their relationships. One might say that I offer a storm's-eye (as opposed to a bird's-eye) view: I start from the thick of things (including my relationship to what is going on), and I allow my inquiry to spin out from and around sites of engagement. In doing so, I focus not only on the ways that people's discrepant stakes and desires articulate, but also on what doesn't link up, what isn't said, what is misunderstood, left out, doesn't happen, or falls apart.[8] I consider how relationships form not on the basis of shared experience, but in spite of identified differences, and I examine those processes through which new lines of inclusion and exclusion are drafted.

Recent relationships between Filipina migrants and rural Japanese residents offer an especially rich site for ethnographically exploring the cultural dynamics of encounters. While a long history of political-economic relations links Japan and the Philippines, people in these two countries imagine their cultural identities in markedly different ways. The story that many Filipinos/as tell themselves about the origins of their nation begins outside the Philippines—in Europe, in fact—and continues through ongoing struggles to resist or reclaim the already internal presence and influence of outsiders or to bring outside money and power in. Take *Noli Me Tángere,* the novel credited with fomenting the first wave of Philippine nationalism and the first Philippine revolution.[9] This book was written in Spanish by a Chinese mestizo and first published in Berlin. Indeed, the majority of the *ilustrados,* the first to declare themselves Filipinos, were recognized as Chinese mestizo. Or consider the role constitutive *outsides* play in the contemporary Philippines. For instance, drawing on her fieldwork in Bicol during the 1980s and 1990s, Fennella Cannell explains that people in the Philippines "see the imagined 'outside' as one source of power, and as a key source of wealth. Making the voyage to America as a migrant worker is thought of as one of the only ways in which one can transform one's life *at home."*[10] These are some of the contradictions that Vicente Rafael evokes when he provocatively asks, "how does it happen that the very notion of 'Filipino' takes on a sociological density only in and through that history of displacement, conquest, resistance, and in relation to an always elusive outside?"[11]

Interestingly, however, questions like these are rarely asked in studies of things Japanese. In fact, a considerable body of literature, stretching back over a century, describes how Japaneseness and Japanese culture and people have developed through a constitutive interiority. From the end of the Second World War through at least the 1980s, theories of Japanese uniqueness (Nihonjinron) widely circulated in popular literary and media forms. Even today, scholars and mass media reference the Tokugawa government's national isolation *(sakoku)* policy or Japan's self-contained island geography to explain Japanese culture.[12] The calm, controlled, efficient, orderly, and homogeneous image often projected of Japan is strikingly at odds with representations of the Philippines' raucous political scene, disorder and inefficiency, proclivity toward performance and spectacle, and embrace of hybridity. If anything, the Philippines might be described as Japan's antithesis, or alter ego. People from the Philippines are usually imagined as anything *but* Japanese.

This book, then, undertakes a somewhat counterintuitive project. Rather than assume that Filipina women exist *outside* the constitutive interiority of Japaneseness, or focus on the role Japan plays *inside* the Philippines, I explore the active and material ways that Filipina migrants and Japanese residents together remake meanings of Japaneseness and Filipinoness through their shared daily lives. In particular, I focus on Filipina women's roles as *yome* (the informal form of oyomesan) in rural Nagano. As I discuss in chapter 4, the term *yome*, or bride and daughter-in-law, commonly refers to the role of a Japanese woman within an *ie*, a multigenerational corporate household that many believe still persists only in rural areas.[13] The Japanese countryside has long been considered the last bastion of a traditional and essentially Japanese way of life and, for many in Japan, Japaneseness is based on biological descent.[14] How is it possible, then, that Filipina migrants have come to be described as ideal oyomesan? How are Central Kiso residents able to maintain their commitment to notions of traditional Japaneseness despite the increasing presence of Filipina brides?

For their part, nearly every Filipina woman I met in Central Kiso told me that she had never planned to marry a rural Japanese man when she first came to the region to work in a hostess bar. Like many migrant laborers around the world, these women had been motivated by a lack of opportunity at home and by dreams of a modern, middle-class life—or what they called "a better life"—for themselves and their families in the Philippines. Most of these women also said that they had imagined working in glamorous and exciting cities such as Tokyo when they applied to work as entertainers in Japan. Some had worked multiple contracts in other parts of the country before being assigned by their promoters to work at bars in Central Kiso, or in between meeting and marrying their husbands. Many found life in the countryside boring, isolating, and marginalizing. Why, then, did many Filipina women in Central Kiso, despite their feelings of boredom and isolation, experiences of discrimination, and commitments to their lives and families in the Philippines, perform—and sometimes even embrace—their roles as oyomesan? What did being oyomesan mean to these women? What were the conditions under which these women performed this role?

These questions, I argue, cannot be answered solely by examining the dreams, motivations, prejudices, or even transnational culture of either Filipina migrants or their Japanese communities. Instead we must consider how these dreams and objectives come into productive relation. Filipina women's past experiences, ongoing relationships with their families in the Philippines, vulnerable positioning in Japan, and desires for their futures certainly informed their performances of their roles as oyomesan. However, these performances also depended on the intimacies of their day-to-day interactions with members of their Japanese communities. Similarly, Japanese residents' perceptions of these women as ideal brides were not informed only by dominant notions of tradition or by stereotypes of Filipina women that widely circulate in Japan. They were also shaped by the roles these women played in everyday life in the region.

To answer these questions, then, I look to the encounter: to the sometimes unforeseen and often transformative ways that Filipina migrants' and their Japanese communities' desires and agendas aligned and misaligned, and the possibilities and frustrations, hope and violence, that emerged among them. While I use the terms *Filipina/o* and *Japanese* throughout this text, I do not refer to fixed categories of identity. Rather, I use these terms to evoke contingent and relational formations of meaning and practice that are constantly being made and remade. I mean to draw attention to the uneven ways that these collective identities are made meaningful in different moments, as well as the inconsistencies and tensions among people within these groups. Marriage has long been understood as an institution that reproduces, reflects, or maintains a social order.[15] However, here I explore how being the perfect oyomesan is a relational site of subjectification through which meanings of Japaneseness and Filipinoness are not only reproduced but also transformed in everyday practice. By putting marriage at the center of my analysis, I do more than examine subjectification as part of the internal, psychological development of an individual or as a straightforward effect of relationships between individuals and formations of power. Rather, I focus on subjectification as a dialogic process that occurs through intimate and everyday encounters among discrepantly situated people, and I consider the ways different formations of desire, affect, gender, sexuality, class, kinship, race, religion, and nationalism interact to shape these dynamics.

THE CONTINGENCIES OF ENCOUNTERS

My interest in the relational ways that meanings of Japanese and Filipino culture and identity are produced through encounters builds on a tradition of scholarship in the social sciences and humanities that has challenged notions of essential, territorially bounded, national cultural communities. Much of this work follows from Benedict Anderson's *Imagined Communities*.[16] Anderson argued that nations are not natural, timeless entities but historically contingent political communities that are imagined as at once limited and sovereign. This argument drew scholarly attention to the diverse and unequal ways that nationalisms are produced, maintained, and experienced throughout the world. Following Anderson, scholars began to explore the technologies and forms of knowledge through which nation-states and national cultures and identities are produced and sustained. Thongchai Winichakul demonstrated the roles that mapping techniques and geographical knowledge play in the delineation of national territories.[17] S. Paige Baty, Purnima Mankekar, and Lisa Rofel looked to how mass media figure in the production of gendered nationalist selves.[18] Members of the Subaltern Studies group demonstrated the ways different historiographic methods legitimated and subverted nationalisms in postcolonial nations.[19] Marilyn Ivy looked to the role of discourses of a vanishing traditional national past in the making of national cultural modernity.[20]

While these studies focused on the ways hegemonic forms of knowledge and practice figure in the production of nationalisms and national subjects, others illustrated the creative and sometimes surprising ways that people craft lives in spaces within and between dominant national cultures. Gloria Anzaldúa, Renato Rosaldo, and Anna Tsing illustrated the hybrid and sometimes irreverent identities and cultural forms that develop in, respectively, borderlands, border zones, and national margins.[21] Kathleen Stewart drew attention to an "other America" by exploring the production of cultural meanings in an Appalachian "space on the side of the road."[22]

Still other studies looked to transnational spaces to explore how communities are lived and imagined across national borders. Paul Gilroy mapped the Black Atlantic, showing us the centrality of music in the making of a Black diasporic double-consciousness.[23] Arjun Appadurai drew attention to new forms of collective imagination and deterritorialized transnational communities created by recent movements of people and popular media.[24] Aihwa Ong demonstrated that national citizenship itself becomes a strategic and flexible resource for elite transnational actors.[25]

Together, these studies of nationalisms and transnationalisms challenged widespread and taken-for-granted notions that culture is tied to national territories, or even territorially bound.[26] Rather, they showed us that cultural meanings emerge within complex deterritorialized formations, and they offered new transnational languages for mapping national imaginaries. They also brought questions of power and politics to how we understand nationness, culture, and identity. Yet because work on nationalisms aimed to draw attention to the ways that hegemonic forms of culture and identity were deployed through powerful nationalist discourses, it tended to focus on the internal logics of these discourses within nation-states and the ways that national subjects negotiated them. Because studies of people living in borderland and transnational worlds were committed to demonstrating that members of these groups had culture, much of this work focused on the fact of their collectivity and the internal cultural logics of their practices.

More recently, feminist and queer studies of migration and diaspora have explored how relations of gender, sexuality, class, and citizenship lie at the heart of transnational cultural formations. Studies by Jacqueline Nassy Brown, Kamari Clarke, Yen Le Espiritu, and Gayatri Gopinath have drawn attention to how migrant and diasporic identities, like nationalisms, are forged across relations of inequality and difference.[27] However, while this work shows the ways these relations of power play out within a given migrant or diasporic formation, they tell us less about the everyday ways that individuals associated with these groups interact with members of the communities where they settle and the transformative roles they play within them. As a result, we still know little about how forms of migration bring discrepant genealogies of meaning and desire into unequal encounter in ways that transform understandings of culture and identity on all sides. We have not yet considered the relational formation of national and cultural identities and subjectivities in a world at once forged through transnational connections and divided among nation-states.

My aim is to open a conceptual space for understanding how new cultural meanings and identities take shape through the *contingencies of encounters:* the contingent, improvisational, and transformative ways that the convergence of people's paths in space and time brings different stakes and desires into relational everyday practice. I use the word contingency here in both of its senses: as the unexpected and open-ended *and* the dependent and conditional.[28] As I have suggested, most social theory today focuses on questions of structure and agency, by exploring how cultural discourses, ideologies, and political-economic logics inform the ways members of a group move through the world, and by considering how people manage these formations of power. Such frameworks leave little space for discussing the intimate and unplanned dynamics of everyday cultural crossings.

Paying ethnographic attention to the contingencies of encounters means recognizing that interactions between Filipina migrants and Japanese townsfolk are never entirely shaped by chance—they are always dependent upon specific histories and unequal organizations of power. However, they also cannot be understood apart from the everyday and sometimes unexpected ways that different dreams and understandings of the world come into productive relation. When we pay attention to the contingencies of encounters we can see how human agency and national and transnational formations of power shape social relationships. However, we also open up room for considering the messy and improvisational dynamics through which different stakes, desires, and genealogies of meaning interact in day-to-day life.

ENCOUNTERS AT THE CROSSROADS OF LOCAL/GLOBAL IMAGINATIONS

What happens at crossroads of imaginations, at those everyday sites where different national registers and genealogies of meaning and desire collide? Even in a globalized world, national borders matter. They still figure significantly in the distribution of rights, privileges, and vulnerabilities that shape people's daily lives.[29] How do people's understandings of relationships among nations and cultures—and themselves as national cultural subjects—inform their interactions with others? How do their dreams and attachments shape these relationships? How are new forms of identity and belonging, as well as new cultural values, made through them?

In this book, I focus on those intimate and quotidian sites of encounter through which people remake national cultures and identities across unequal relations of power. I suggest that these cultural encounters create dialogic spaces that are structured not only by history and geopolitics but also by everyday and gendered formations of affect and desire: love, antagonism, longing, resentment, competition, hate, honor, and prejudice. In these dialogic spaces, discrepantly formed dreams and agendas engage. They remake each other in sometimes predictable and other times unforeseen ways through the personal, temporal, spatial, and relational contingencies of everyday practice.

In focusing on these processes, I join two bodies of literature that have in different ways explored how meanings of culture and identity are produced through forms of cultural contact across difference. First, I draw on historical studies that have explored the role colonial encounters played in shaping colonial cultures and identities.[30] These studies illustrate the intricate workings of colonial power, as well as its fractures and the forms of resistance that emerged within it. Rafael's work on conversion in the Spanish colonial Philippines explores the role that language, and particularly processes of translation, played in creating the conditions of colonial domination. He demonstrates that just as language could enable conversion it could also "run amuck, rendering translation impossible, exploding the contract between ruler and ruled, and thereby obscuring politics and history altogether."[31] Mary Louise Pratt has argued for the active role colonial subjects played in shaping metropolitan cultures. She shows us the hybrid cultural forms that took shape in contact zones between these subjects and their rulers.[32] Ann Laura Stoler directly builds on Anderson's notion of imagined communities to explore how European colonists established and policed colonial identities among themselves. In doing so, Stoler demonstrates that in colonial discourse racialized boundaries of sameness and difference were expressed in terms of affective dispositions, cultural literacies, and sentiment.[33]

These historical retellings have been more than empirical corrections: they are political interventions that explore the intimate workings, fragilities, and contingencies of colonial power. They demonstrate that colonized subjects are agents (as opposed to symbolic Others) who have their own desires and agendas. In doing so, they draw attention to the intimate and dependent relationships that developed between colonizers and colonized.

I share with this literature a stake in exploring the ways relations of power shape worlds of cultural meeting, worlds that are sometimes violent, usually messy, and often surprising. In some sense, I pick up where these studies left off to explore the dynamics of contemporary postcolonial engagements. However, the encounters I describe do not involve powerful colonial elites who can turn their dreams into political structures. They involve members of discrepantly marginalized groups who have long struggled with inclusions and exclusions from nationalist and global capitalist projects. While the relationships I discuss are certainly informed by colonial legacies, they are also shaped by different and novel configurations of power—new organizations of nationalisms, capitalisms, sovereignties, and modernities "at-large."[34] In the case of colonial encounters, relationships between colonizers and colonized were the direct product of colonial occupation. The positions of members of these groups were formalized and to some degree fixed on this account. In contrast, Filipina migrants and Japanese residents in Central Kiso described their relationships in terms of personal desires, emotional attachments, flexibility, cosmopolitanism, independence, and choice—key tropes tied to recent discourses of neoliberal capitalist modernities. Members of these groups saw themselves as engaging in mutually, if unequally, dependent relationships as they attempted to craft lives and realize their dreams in a globalized world.

Thus, in contrast to studies of colonial encounters, I do not focus on the production and subversion of colonial, national, and capitalist regimes. I look to vernacular imaginings of culture and identity that emerge in the intimate and overlapping margins of an interconnected world, and I track how racial and national boundaries are destabilized and reworked within them. I examine cultures and identities as fields of interactive processes that emerge *in-relation,* that is, through the contingent formation of relationships and narratives (the ethnographic included) among people variously situated in global circulations of meaning and power. In other words, I focus on culture as a relational process and a contingent product—at once a set of practices and an object of knowledge—that is performatively made and unequally transformed through global crossings.

Second, I build on recent studies of global processes that explore how contemporary economic, political, and social formations emerge in sites of local/global contact. In her later work, Ong shows us how neoliberal governmentalities play out in East and Southeast Asia, reconfiguring conditions of work and life, establishing new relationships between governance and knowledge, and creating new and unequally situated subjectivities.[35] Anna Tsing explores how global political-economic processes take shape through diverse and conflicting forms of on-the-ground social engagement.[36] She demonstrates that "universals" such as global capitalism and environmentalism are made through "friction," the "sticky engagements" that occur at sites of local/global interaction.[37] Kamari Clarke is also interested in sites of local/global contact. Her work explores how tensions between African nation-states and an international human rights regime shape people's lives in sub-Saharan Africa, western Europe, and the United States.[38] By tracing such processes, she illustrates the unequal development of liberal subjectivities in relation to the expansion of political-economic human rights networks.

These scholars move elegantly between global, national, local, and subjective scales of analysis. They illustrate how global configurations of political-economic power take shape through on-the-ground practices, the everyday effects of these forms of power on differently situated populations and nation-states, and the ways various people and national governments negotiate them. However, studies such as these tend to focus on how big global formations—capitalism, neoliberalism, the universal, human rights, justice, nationalism writ large—get made in situated, localized settings. As a result, they tell us little about encounters as everyday and affective cultural processes through which discrepantly situated people relationally remake their worlds. They leave open the question of the how the very conditions of both national belonging and transnational connection are not only reproduced but also sometimes surprisingly transformed through intimate and quotidian engagements.

I am interested in encounters as ongoing cultural processes through which people rework national and transnational forms of culture and belonging through intimate everyday interactions. I use the word *intimate* to refer to the social and spatial proximities that define the relationships among Filipina migrants and Central Kiso residents that I discuss in this book. These relationships take shape through extended, if unequal, day-to-day engagements. I also use *intimate* because these interactions involve relational self-making practices that engage gendered and sexualized forms of affect and desire, often in the realm of what is considered the private (e.g., the home and family). Finally, I use it to suggest the mutual, although unequal, dependencies that these relationships entail and the ways that genealogies of meaning and desire are intertwined through them.[39] The intimate encounters I describe show us the everyday, dialogic practices through which Filipina migrants and Central Kiso residents remade their worlds through their daily lives. Through these practices, members of these groups developed new identities and subjectivities, such as *Filipina oyomesan*. They developed new financial patterns and ways of speaking. They created new political strategies for coping with their everyday realities, new daily habits, and new learning mechanisms. They created new conditions of cultural inclusion and exclusion—on all sides.

As I demonstrate in this book, we cannot fully grasp larger-scale cultural and political-economic processes without understanding the intimate and relational dynamics through which encounters such as these play out. Yet understanding these processes means paying attention to more than the ways people's everyday lives relate to large-scale global formations of power. Rather, we must also focus on that "in-between" space where relationships form among people, discourses, stakes, nation-states, capitalist practices, and desires.[40] We must ask how and why discrepant forms of meaning and desire align and misalign and consider the implications of such dynamics for people's understandings of their lives and the choices they make. As I will show, doing so means starting in the middle. A story about cultural encounters is a story that cannot be traced to a single point of origin or causal framework. It is a story of cultural meetings that follows multiple and deferred points of departure, a partial story that can be told only in terms of what lies between here and there and there again.

CULTURAL ENCOUNTERS AND HISTORICAL CONVERGENCES

The Kiso Valley winds serpentlike down the southwestern portion of Nagano Prefecture. Hedged by steep mountains, which press upon narrow strips of land flanking the Kiso River, the valley is a thin stretch of glen running the border between the Kiso and the Hida mountain ranges. The rugged, sylvan landscape both provides a measure of geographic isolation (only a few perilous roads dare to cross it) and, to the dismay of locals, marks the region as remote and backwards. One tourist from Nagoya illustrated this point with an offhand comment that Kiso was "a place where the sun doesn't shine." He was at once invoking the mountain topography, which often allows just a few unpredictable hours of sunlight each day, the socioeconomic problems of local communities, and the prevailing notion that a place like Kiso must be behind the times.

In the years following the Second World War, the towns and villages of Central Kiso were home to a thriving forestry industry. For a time during the 1970s—a brief but nevertheless proud period for local residents— they were a destination for domestic tourists interested in the history of the post towns (shukuba-machi) that had flourished along the Kisoji (Kiso Highway, also called the Kiso Kaidō or Nakasendō) under the Tokugawa Shogunate. Today, however, this part of Kiso County faces many of the problems that have become pronounced throughout rural Japan: the absence of lucrative industry and, correspondingly, of sufficient employment; depopulation resulting from increasing urban migration and resulting in an aging local community (and shrinking tax revenues for regional schools); and a "bride shortage" (yome busoku), a phrase widely used to refer to the dearth of Japanese women interested in marrying local men, a significant number of whom are eldest sons responsible for caring for their elderly parents. Related to these trends, and again not unlike many parts of rural Japan, over the past two decades Central Kiso has also become home to a growing number of women from other parts of Asia, in this case overwhelmingly the Philippines, who have married local men. During my primary fieldwork, about sixty Filipina women married to Japanese men lived in the region I call Central Kiso, many in the towns of Agematsu and Kisofukushima, which had a combined population of around fifteen thousand. As I discuss in chapter 6, several additional Filipina women had married local men and later "run away" from their Japanese husbands and families.[41]

The overwhelming majority of Filipina wives in Central Kiso—upward of 90 percent—initially came to the region on three-to-six month entertainer visas *(kōgyō biza)*. The Japanese government issues work visas only to foreign nationals who can perform a kind of "skilled" labor that is unavailable in the Japanese workforce. Entertainer visas are skilled labor visas issued to licensed or experienced performers. As I discuss in chapter 1, Filipina women who entered Japan on these visas were technically hired to work as cultural dancers and singers. However, many of these women were employed (in violation of their residence status) as "companions" *(konpanion)* or "hostesses" *(hosutesu)* in Filipina bars, pubs, cabarets, and clubs throughout Japan.[42]

The migration of Filipina women to Central Kiso as entertainers is connected to a larger influx of both documented and undocumented labor migration to Japan that started in the 1980s as the value of the yen rose and Japan began facing labor shortages. Small numbers of foreign professionals have come to Japan, but most migrants have filled those jobs described by the "three K's" *(kitsui, kitanai,* and *kiken;* in English, the "three D's": difficult, dirty, and dangerous). These labor niches have also been segmented by gender and ethnicity. Some groups of migrant laborers, such as Japanese-Brazilians, have tended to work in factories or the service sector. The overwhelming majority of Filipina migrants, like migrant women from Rumania, Thailand, Russia, Korea, and China, have worked in the *mizu shōbai* (literally, the water trades; the sex industry).[43]

As I discuss in chapter 1, Filipina women began working at bars in Japan as early as the mid-1970s, and the numbers of those coming over on entertainer visas began to increase dramatically in the early 1980s, peaking in the early 1990s. In 1980, slightly more than 8,500 Filipina women entered Japan on entertainer visas; by 1991 the number had jumped to more than 57,000. In both 2003 and 2004, more than 80,000 Filipina women entered Japan on such visas.[44] Many of them worked in major metropolitan centers or regional cities. However, some also worked in rural areas such as the Kiso Valley.

Small numbers of Filipina women first came to Central Kiso to work in bars alongside Japanese women in 1978, and the first Filipina hostess bar opened in the town of Kisofukushima in 1980. Other bars in Central Kiso followed suit, and by the mid-1980s most hostess bars in the area employed solely Filipina women. During my research between September 1998 and August 2000, there were at any one time between ten and fifteen Filipina bars open in the area.[45] When I first moved to Central Kiso, there were six Filipina hostess bars within a few blocks' radius of the house I rented in Kisofukushima, which was just off of what was once the main drag of town, and several more bars were or had been located above the town proper along Highway 19, the treacherous, two-lane national highway running the length of the region. There were a number of other bars in Agematsu, the neighboring town. Some of these bars had been around for a long time; others had more recently opened. I also heard about bars that had closed and then later reopened under new names by different owners. (In chapter 1, I discuss how and why a number of Filipina hostess bars became concentrated in Central Kiso.)

Although all these bars were in plain view of the road, I noticed that they moved in and out of focus depending on the person to whom I was speaking. For example, middle-aged Japanese women in the region never mentioned them when giving me directions, even if my destination was located next door to a Filipina bar. Although these longtime residents seemed aware of the bars when I mentioned them, they also did not seem to want to draw attention to them.[46] Thus, by making these bars an entry point for a story about the region, I risked upsetting those residents who would prefer to see the town noted instead for its post town history or natural landscape. However, for Filipina women I met in Central Kiso, hostess bars were landmarks by which one navigated through town. Moreover, stereotypes of Filipina women in Japan are tied to their work in these bars. These bars figure prominently in the ways many Central Kiso residents perceived Filipina women. Leaving these bars out of a story about the region, then, would also overlook a significant dimension of everyday life there.

In addition to fitting within a larger trend of labor migration to Japan, Filipina migration to Central Kiso can also be situated within a longer history of labor migration and emigration from the Philippines that began in the early twentieth century and is tied to U.S.-Philippine relations. Some scholars divide this migration history into periods or waves. The first period of Filipino/a migration (1906–1934) coincided with the U.S. colonization of the Philippines and included small numbers of government scholars and large numbers of laborers who were recruited to work on farms in California, Hawaii, and Washington. Between 1946 and into the late 1960s, a second wave of immigrants, most of whom were members of the U.S. armed forces or relatives of earlier immigrants, came to the United States from the Philippines. The U.S. Immigration Act of 1965 abolished national origin quotas and also opened the door for predominantly educated professionals—doctors, nurses, and engineers—who were invited to the United States to fill labor shortages. During this time, a number of Filipino men also settled in Europe, where they worked as sailors on international vessels. Beginning in the 1970s, the third wave is usually tied to the U.S.-backed Marcos regime, which, together with the World Bank and the IMF, encouraged overseas labor migration to bring much needed foreign currency into the Philippine economy. While this "labor export policy" was initially introduced as a temporary measure, it continues through the present and has made labor migration from the Philippines a global phenomenon. Filipinos/as are now one of the largest (im)migrant groups in the world, working throughout North America, the Middle East, and East and Southeast Asia. By 2005, close to 10 percent of the population of the Philippines—more than 7 million people—lived abroad.[47] Many (but not all) recent Filipina/o migrants are on temporary contracts and do not have plans (or cannot receive long-term visas) to settle in the countries where they are employed. Most send money to the Philippines on a regular basis. Filipina migration to Japan is generally identified as part of this third wave.[48]

However, we cannot simply situate Filipina migration to Central Kiso within larger migration flows from the Philippines or to Japan, attributing it to national trends or general shifts in capitalism and the global economy. Doing so does not help us understand the culturally specific forms Filipina migration has taken in the region. Why have some Filipina women come to be viewed as ideal, traditional Japanese brides in Central Kiso? How did political-economic forces figure in the intersecting decisions that Filipina migrants and Japanese residents made about their lives?

Early writings about Filipina migration to Japan stressed the roles that imbalances between Japan and the Philippines played in Filipina migration to the country.[49] Feminist scholars in Japan, the Philippines, and the United States built on these arguments to consider how interrelated "institutionalized oppressions" in Japan and the Philippines based on gender, race, class, and nationality also shape Filipina migration.[50] They also showed us that this migration trend is driven by some Filipina women's desires to improve their and their families' lives. These arguments are important. However, we also need to consider how Filipina migrants' and Japanese residents' desires came together in culturally, historically, and geographically specific ways to shape these women's migration experiences and the possibilities that emerged for them in Japan.

In the mid-1980s (several years after Filipina women began to work in hostess bars in Central Kiso), Filipino women also began coming to other parts of rural Japan through *kokusai ōmiai kekkon,* international mediated or "arranged" marriages (Jpn.). These marriages have garnered much popular and scholarly attention in Japan and have come to be viewed as paradigmatic of Filipina-Japanese marriages in rural areas. These marriages first attracted attention when a farming village in Yamagata Prefecture began to arrange group weddings between local bachelors and Filipino women. Local governments in this area initiated the programs as part of community-wide campaigns to counter depopulation and what they called "bride droughts." They claimed that these marriages were necessary to provide progeny to inherit farmland, ensure the future of the region, and maintain a traditional Japanese way of life. Before long, the pioneer programs in Yamagata had attracted representatives from over 250 municipal and agricultural organizations throughout Japan that were interested in learning whether similar arrangements would work in their own struggling communities. Over the next several years, groups of Japanese farmers from more than 100 villages paid large sums of money to marriage brokers who arranged international group marriage tours. Some of these men flew to the Philippines, selected wives from a significantly larger group of applicants, and invited them to their hometowns in Japan for group wedding parties.[51]

Similar sets of political-economic relations form the backdrops of government-sponsored international arranged marriages in Yamagata and of Filipina-Japanese marriages in Central Kiso. In addition, Filipina women living in both of these regions of Japan had been prompted to go abroad in part on account of their families' political-economic circumstances in the Philippines. Japanese men in rural regions throughout Japan have complained of a lack of marriageable women.[52] These men have similarly maintained that young Japanese women are unwilling to live in rural areas and marry rural Japanese men and have opted instead to move to urban areas to take pink- and white-collar jobs. Yet mountainous Central Kiso did not have a significant agricultural economy; for the most part, only older residents in the region did any farming, and it was small scale for household consumption. Moreover, unlike other cases of rural areas discussed by scholars and journalists in Japan, local men married to Filipina women in the region were not looking for heirs to maintain their ie, family land, or a family business. As I later discuss, many of these men worked in construction or in local *pachinko* parlors or bars.[53] Moreover, at the time of my fieldwork, few Filipina wives in Central Kiso had met their husbands through professional marriage mediators, which often require that the Filipina women they represent have never worked in bars. The overwhelming majority of Filipina women in Central Kiso met their spouses in one of the many hostess bars in the region. In this respect, these marriages more closely fit patterns of Filipina-Japanese marriages associated with urban Japan. Interestingly, too, the few Filipina women in the region who did meet their husbands through mediation services claimed that they would never consider working in hostess bars. Those who met their husbands when working in bars maintained that they could never imagine marrying a man to whom they had just been professionally introduced.

Thus, while I historically situate Filipina migration to Central Kiso within larger relevant national and global political-economic contexts, my argument does not focus on the ways Filipina-Japanese marriages in the region reflect overarching national or global migration trends or shifts in global capitalism.[54] Similarities and differences in how Filipina-Japanese marriages in Central Kiso relate to those in other regions of Japan or to other forms of Filipina migration need be carefully traced through the on-the-ground histories that both link and divide them.[55] Here my objective is to produce a fine-grained and geographically situated cultural analysis of the rhizomatic histories, political-economic networks, and day-to-day social engagements through which the lives of groups of people from the Philippines and Central Kiso have come to be connected. I map a particular set of cultural dynamics that has emerged through the specificities of current socioeconomic struggles in this region of rural Japan, the development of hostess bars in this area, and the experiences of Filipina women and Japanese men. In doing so, I join those feminist scholars who are trying to rethink the nature of global capitalism through careful attention to its multiple and contested nature as a messy and socially constructed process.[56] This approach maintains that we cannot understand capitalism as a fixed and unified system in which different local processes are slotted. Rather, it stresses the importance of considering the links among discrepant sets of social and political-economic practices as they play out in distinctive yet connected local sites. I am committed to this approach because it enables us to consider the intimate ways that culture, history, and political economics are intertwined. It points us to the uneven and disjunctive aspects of global processes and to the sometimes surprising forms of agency that emerge within them. And it enables us to develop locally specific, practical strategies for enabling change.

How, then, do we understand the ways that relationships between Filipina migrants and Japanese residents in Central Kiso are tied to larger political-economic forces and histories while not assuming that these forces wholly explain the shape of their engagements? How can we talk about interpersonal interactions while holding on to the ways that they are both formed through relations of power and have messy and unexpected outcomes? That is, how can we leave room for the contingent and not entirely predictable ways that discrepant sets of meanings and desires engage in such a way that new desires and understandings are produced through their encounter? A methodology of cultural encounters asks us to attend to the broader political-economic inequalities that shape relationships among Filipina migrants and their Japanese communities in specific sites. Yet it also leaves room for considering the distinctive quotidian forms these relationships can sometimes take. As I show in the first half of this book, to understand the context in which marriages among local Japanese men and Filipina migrants in Central Kiso are occurring, we must inquire into two discrepant, yet related, sets of political-economic processes. First, we must consider those processes through which Filipina women began migrating to Central Kiso as entertainers and then came to view Japanese men as appealing husbands; and second, we need to examine why hostess bars in the region began to hire Filipina women, and how local men became interested in these women as brides. Cultural encounters among Filipina migrants and Japanese residents in Central Kiso are enabled by the convergences among these discrepantly situated histories.

ZONES OF ENCOUNTERS

My focus on cultural encounters is a political project that offers a new way for understanding not only contemporary cultural processes but also cultural regions. This book is based on ethnographic fieldwork in Japan and the Philippines. I spent twenty-three months living in and around the town of Kisofukushima, the administrative hub of Kiso County.[57] During this time, I socialized with and interviewed both Japanese and Filipina people in the region: I participated in rural revitalization efforts sponsored by the local government, I attended local government-sponsored events for Filipina wives as well as prayer meetings and social gatherings the women organized for themselves, I regularly visited Filipina women's homes and the bars in which they worked, and I lived for several months with three Filipina-Japanese families. In addition, I made three trips to the Philippines to visit Filipina women's families and communities there. I also returned to Central Kiso in 2005, 2006, and 2007 and to the Philippines in 2007 to follow up with people about their lives.

Yet while this book is full of thick and textured descriptions of the central Kiso Valley, and of the lives of people who live in it and in places in the Philippines such as Metro Manila and Cavite, I caution against mistaking the sites of my research for the site of my inquiry. The field mapped in this book is a translocal web of relations spanning Japan, the Philippines, and the United States and a set of conceptual and practical spaces of interaction among people from these three countries: a zone of encounters.

Zones of encounters takes shape through "power-geometries" in which places emerge as "constellations of social relations."[58] They offer a different kind of geographical mapping than a nation-state or transnational space. They are filamentary networks that stretch to include those material and conceptual relationships through which people construct senses of self and live their daily lives. In this sense, zones of encounters are not cultural regions. They are areas that include people who share culture-in-relations: cultural formations forged through relationships across difference. When we locate ourselves within such zones, we recognize these relationships so that we can learn how to become more accountable to them.

Amitav Ghosh's novel The Shadow Lines is a book that evokes just such a world.[59] It focuses on the interconnected lives of three families in London, Calcutta, and Dhaka—cities more linked than divided by the shadow lines separating England and India, and dividing Bengal. In this novel, maps are not simply representations of places. They are also stories in which people live. The map/story Ghosh offers us is one of a hybrid in-between place, a "third space" forged through colonial histories, postcolonial politics, and family ties.[60] Yet if we read this novel slightly against the grain, we can see a world not only of hybridity, but also of the pain, messiness, and confusion of gendered, sexualized, and racialized cultural encounters. Ghosh's narrator strives to make sense of Bengal's partition, as it shapes the lives of members of his family. As he pieces together fragments of a story about his favorite relative Tridib's violent death in the context of communal violence, his narrative is punctuated, if not propelled, by his unrequited love for Tridib's niece Ila and his sexual desire for Tridib's English girlfriend, Mary Price. In this novel, national borders not only figure as shadow lines but also suggest "cartographies of desire" that delineate bodies and families across matrices of gender, sexuality, race, and kinship.[61]

It is such a set of relations that I aim to evoke in this book. Unlike studies of transnationalisms, which explore how people, ideas, identities, and capital transgress and transform national boundaries, here I assume an already translocally connected world of difference upon which sameness—in the form of, say, a national or diasporic culture or identity—is performatively grafted. In other words, I do not approach national borders between Japan and the Philippines as marking boundaries that are now being transgressed and reformed by recent migrations and cultural flows. Rather, I take those national borders as dynamics of translocal relationships among differently situated people with longstanding and intimate ties. In focusing on that in-between space among Filipina migrants, their Japanese communities, and me, my interest lies in the ways that the borders of the nation space figure as shadow lines—that "enchantment of lines"—that stand in the way of alternate chartings of contiguous relationships, communities, and regions.[62] We might, then, best understand zones of encounters as fields of inquiry for understanding where discrepant desires and genealogies of meaning come into relational practice, aligning in novel and unexpected ways and creating new cultural meanings. Focusing on such zones enables us to pay attention to more than hybrid forms of culture and identity. It also draws attention to "relational ontologies" and "co-constituitive relations of significant otherness," or what I think of more simply as the ways that subjectivities and meanings come into being through practices of relation.[63]

REMAPPING RELATIONS

Remapping relations among Filipina migrants and Japanese residents as part of a zone of encounters forces us to reconsider many assumptions about Japanese and Filipino culture and identity. In the zone of encounters I evoke in this book, "Japan" is not a nation of people or a geographic or cultural region, but ongoing practices of inclusion and exclusion negotiated among persons who are "Japanese" and "foreign."

In mapping this zone, I am fortunate to be able to draw from a growing literature within Japan studies that has challenged cultural nationalisms that have since the late nineteenth century perpetuated myths of Japanese racial, cultural, and class homogeneity.[64] These studies have drawn attention to Japan as a country crosscut by differences of class, ethnicity, geography, gender, sexuality, and able-bodiedness.[65] Over the past few decades, feminist scholars of Japan have set forth trenchant critiques of the homogenizing tendencies of androcentric approaches to contemporary Japanese culture and society that take gender and sexuality for granted.[66] Others have explored the ways discourses of race and ethnicity informed the production of Japanese national identity through an imperialist project.[67] Still others have maintained that we cannot so easily draw lines between Japan and the West but need to pay attention to the ways meanings of Japaneseness are produced on a global scale.[68] Here, I build on these challenges to notions of Japanese ethnic and cultural homogeneity by exploring the central role that Filipina women are playing in the production of meanings of Japanese culture and identity in contemporary rural Nagano.

In doing so, I also build on the work of scholars that have focused on the lives of other migrant and ethnic minority populations in contemporary Japan. These studies have argued that we must account for the ways that such groups have been marginalized by hegemonic discourses of Japaneseness and how they negotiate their status.[69] This literature offers rich and often moving descriptions of the lives of members of these populations. Yet most of these studies focus either on the fact of these groups' marginality or on them as subcultures, comparing their perspectives with those of their Japanese communities. Thus, we still do not have a clear understanding of the active, everyday, practical ways members of migrant groups in contemporary Japan contribute to the reproduction and transformation of Japaneseness.

In addition to drawing on recent studies of Japanese culture and society, my argument is also indebted to a growing literature about the Philippine diaspora.[70] This scholarship has demonstrated that Filipina migrants are agents and has insisted that we pay attention to the ways that inequalities based on race, class, gender, and citizenship shape these women's lives. It has also challenged stereotypes about Filipina migrants and their families.[71] However, while these studies have demonstrated that Filipina migrants have agency, they have not yet considered why it comes to take certain forms. As a result, we risk naturalizing Filipina migrants' agency either as wholly determined by the forms of political-economic marginality they confront at home and abroad or as an essential property of them as individuals (or as Filipina women).

Here I focus on the interactive historical and cultural contexts through which certain forms of agency and subjectivity become possible and preferable for Filipina migrants in rural Nagano. Rather than viewing the role of the yome as one these women might as free agents choose or challenge, I explore it as a site of encounter—a crossroads of desire—that unequally takes shape through Filipina women's everyday encounters. At such a crossroads, these women's desires for their futures, which are shaped by the vulnerabilities and possibilities of their lives in Japan *and* the Philippines, come into dialogic relation with those of their Japanese families and communities. As people borrow, resist, agree with, misunderstand, and ignore the desires and agendas of others, they articulate new cultural meanings, practices, subjectivities, and identities.

THE ETHNOGRAPHY OF ENCOUNTERS

Encounters cannot but change the ways people see the world and how they move through it. They interrupt, if even ever so slightly, the paths that brought us to them and set us in new directions. However, encounters rarely, if ever, happen on level ground. This book is also an ethnography of encounters in its attention to the politics of my encounters in Japan and the Philippines. The title of this introduction, "Relations of Cultural Production," refers not only to the new cultural meanings produced through relationships among Filipina women and Japanese residents in Central Kiso, but also to the ways that my relationships with the people I met shaped the stories about culture I tell in this book.

My ethnographic encounters did not always take the forms I had expected they would when I first came to Central Kiso. I prepared for fieldwork in the wake of critiques that challenged ethnographers to account for the colonial roots and contemporary politics of their research methods.[72] These critiques have inspired much rethinking of both the foci and form of ethnographic writing. I went into fieldwork self-conscious about the politics of my endeavor and my positioning vis-à-vis the people I would meet. However, I faced challenges not only in situating myself in relation to my Filipina and Japanese interlocutors but also in negotiating the ways I became a node in relationships *among* them. Many people I met were engaged in sincere and intimate relationships, but significant tensions also existed between and among members of these groups. Many Filipina women had experienced discrimination in Japan because they were from the Philippines, and they resented that some members of the Japanese community treated them with contempt on this account. Because, in contrast, most Japanese community members treated me with privilege and respect on account of my U.S. American nationality, whiteness, and education level, spending time with Japanese residents only highlighted my difference from Filipina women and made some of these women question how open they could be with me regarding their lives in Japan.

At the same time, most Japanese residents in Central Kiso were perplexed by my interest in Filipina women's lives. Many struggled to understand why a graduate student affiliated with prestigious universities in Japan and the United States would want to associate with women who had worked (and in some cases still worked) in hostess bars. As I later discuss, I was even cautioned against doing so. Both Filipina women and Japanese residents also expressed hesitation and sometimes competition regarding what members of the "other side" might be telling me (and also others in their own group). On more than one occasion a Filipina friend asked me outright, "Who do you feel more comfortable with: Filipinas or Japanese?" Sometimes when we were alone, Japanese community members would inquire in discrete tones about Filipina women's migration histories and how the women felt about their lives in Japan ("Are they happy?"). I soon learned that those whom I interviewed had stakes not only in how I represented them, but also in how I represented others. Kamala Visweswaran has suggested that feminist ethnography hinges on betrayal, and this insight proved especially true to my fieldwork.[73] Being accountable to some people in Central Kiso inevitably entailed betraying others. My focus on encounters developed in the context of my efforts to understand people's divergent perspectives and of my recognizing the ways that my relationships with them were not only reshaping my understanding of my world and myself, but also potentially affecting their relationships with each other.

I also take a point of departure, then, from James Clifford, who suggests that fieldwork is best understood as a series of travel encounters, and that the field should be seen as a fluid and situated network of relations between ethnographers and the people they meet—not as a place but a habitus: "a cluster of *embodied* dispositions and practices."[74] Yet I also contend that engaging questions of fieldwork solely on a personal level is insufficient. That is, to even mark the ethnographic encounter, as Clifford suggests, in terms of a personal break between pre- and postfield habituses only helps to reinscribe the field as someplace out "there." The very notion that the field is unfamiliar depends on what we consider familial: how we reckon notions of kinship and belonging, whom we consider kin and kind. In a globally interconnected world, our field is in some sense part of all of our homes and habituses before we ever enter it. We need an ethnographic practice that can help us understand these connections.

Visweswaran suggests one useful model when she proposes that anthropologists learn to do their homework, that is, to specify and claim their sites of enunciation. She builds on Mary John's suggestion that decolonizing ethnography requires enacting a politics of location that directs its gaze homeward toward a politics of arrival.[75] Here I extend Visweswaran's and John's arguments by suggesting that, for those of us living in the United States, doing our homework means not only recognizing the sites from which we speak, but also reflecting on how our lives in the United States are part of the stories we tell. In this sense, taking a storm's-eye view also means asking: How is my life over here tethered to their lives over there? How do I need to not only tell my story but also live my life to be accountable to that relationship?

One cannot begin to understand relations between people in Japan and the Philippines without considering the role of the United States in them. The U.S. colonial government first brought large numbers of Japanese men to the Philippines as laborers to build the road from Manila to Baguio, the "summer capital."[76] It was also on account of the U.S. military that Filipina women came to work in bars around U.S. bases in Japan when the yen rose and local Japanese and Okinawan women's labor became too expensive.[77] Today, U.S. foreign policy (from trade agreements to former and existing military bases) not only continues to shape the lives of people in Japan and the Philippines but also informs unequal relations among people in these countries. These histories enabled my research in Central Kiso, just as they shaped Filipina migration to the region. In this book, I begin the work of tracking the ways my field is—in very practical, historical, and material ways—part of my home. As I describe encounters between Filipina migrants and Japanese residents, I double back to reflect on how both the United States and I figure in them. In doing so, my aim is both to "provincialize" the United States and to draw attention to the ways it is produced through its very "dislocations."[78]

It is in this sense, too, that my interest in cultural encounters also reflects my commitment to contributing to a form of ethnography oriented to social justice: a practice that aims to understand how relations of marginality and privilege are maintained in this world and that imagines new possibilities for a planet in which inequalities do not grow and rigidify but diminish and exist in constant flux. The project of decolonizing ethnographic research is not simply a matter of arriving upon a prescriptive solution. Colonialisms, and their legacies of exploitation and racism, are ongoing processes.[79] Thus efforts to work against these legacies must not only continue but also take new forms. Again and again we must look for new answers to old questions: What does it mean to tell stories that "make a difference in a way that might itself begin to make a difference?"[80] How can we find more responsible, sustainable, and just ways to live in a brutally unequal world?

The politics of the stories we tell are tied to not only their content or the theoretical approaches we develop but also to the writing strategies we engage.[81] One strategy I engage here is a focus on personal narrative. I offer portraits of people I met. However, a careful reader will notice that my characterizations of people are sometimes inconsistent across several chapters. In this book, I am less interested in presenting people as consistent and coherent subjects than in asking why, at certain moments and for certain contingent historical, cultural, political-economic, and ethnographic reasons, they presented themselves as they did. I focus on pulling apart the layers of meaning and power through which people made various claims. I have written with the assumption that people change. We articulate ourselves in different ways in different contexts and to different audiences. Rather than policing the boundaries of selfhood, I have retained the self-contradictory ways in which people presented themselves to me, and I allow these descriptions to jostle against each other in my text. I also use the past tense throughout the book as a reminder that things said were things said in the moment, and that people's senses of themselves and the ways they narrate their lives are constantly changing.

Another narrative decision I made was to represent not only people's most honorable characteristics and behaviors, but also the uglier sides of even those about whom I care deeply–those acts of self-interest, narrow-mindedness, and even racism. There has been a tendency in ethnographic writing, and particularly feminist ethnography, to champion our informants' positions. This, in part, is why "studying up" has been such a challenging ethnographic enterprise.[82] In preparing for fieldwork, I had read the work of feminist writers who were counterbalancing widespread representations of women in the global south as abstract victims by stressing their diversity and agency in actively resisting and negotiating the discourses and structures that marginalized them.[83] When I arrived in Central Kiso, I expected to meet people who, by virtue of their marginalization within various patriarchies, nationalisms, and capitalisms, were steadfastly resisting these systems of inequality. However, those I met were not the "noble exploited" I expected to find but people who, like me, lived through contradiction and with ambivalence about themselves and their worlds. They were people, like me, who had been raised in societies structured through forms of racism, nationalism, classism, sexism, able-bodiedism, and heterosexism—people who were struggling to make lives in an unequal world, whose intentions were often admirable and sometimes not good enough.

The people whose lives I discuss did find creative ways to maneuver around the discourses and relationships that marginalized them. But they were often not the ways I would have chosen for them. And I believe that none would claim to be innocent. Representing them as such would deny them what Avery Gordon has described as "the right to complex personhood . . . that all people (albeit in specific forms whose specificity is sometimes everything) remember and forget, are beset by contradiction, and recognize and misrecognize themselves and others. . . . [T]hat people suffer graciously and selfishly too, get stuck in the symptoms of their troubles, and also transform themselves."[84]

Organizationally, I have approached relationships among Filipina migrants and Central Kiso residents as nodes of engagement among people who access discrepant histories, genealogies of meaning, and forms of agency and desire. In this sense, this book involves a kind of multidimensional mapping that charts a social landscape by relating archaeologies of social and political-economic pasts to the topographies of daily practice. I work radially inward and outward from sites of engagement among Filipina migrants and Japanese residents, moving backward and forward across time and space to track the emergence and effects of their encounters. Throughout this text, I maintain that to understand the terms through which cultural encounters involving Filipina migrants and Central Kiso residents take shape, we must inquire into both the different stakes and desires that members of these groups bring to their interactions and the ways that these stakes and desires are positioned within larger relationships and structures of meaning and power.

In the first half of this book, "Figures of Desires," I explore the ways that Filipina migrants and Central Kiso residents narrated the dreams and desires they brought to their relationships. I consider the discrepant historical processes through which these desires emerged: the establishment of hostessing in Central Kiso, the construction of cultural dance performance and the development of Japanese sex tourism in the Philippines, the socioeconomic marginalization of places like Central Kiso vis-à-vis places like Tokyo, and the linking of dreams of "America" and "a better life" in the Philippines. However, rather than weaving these histories together into a single and causal framework, I juxtapose them in ways that highlight both the awkward contingencies and the unequal collaborations through which different relationships take shape.

In chapter 1, "Sites of Encounter," I trace the establishment of Filipina hostess bars in Central Kiso through the intersection of two different, but related, historical processes: the development of Filipina migration to Japan as entertainers during the 1970s and 80s and the establishment of a hostess bar industry in the Kiso region beginning after the Second World War. I consider how the overlap between these histories enabled Filipina hostess bars in Central Kiso to become sites of encounter where Filipina migrants' and Japanese residents' discrepant, but similarly ambivalent, desires came together in ways that made new forms of relationships possible between them. Chapters 2 and 3 explore, respectively, how the United States and Japan became "figures of desires" for Filipina migrants and Japanese townsfolk. In chapter 2, "America and Other Stories of Filipina Migration to Japan," I focus on the narratives women told about the migration paths that brought them to their lives in Central Kiso. I consider how relational imaginings of Japan, the Philippines, and the United States informed both the ways they understood their migration decisions and their dreams for their futures. Chapter 3, "Japan in the Kiso Valley, the Kiso Valley in Japan," turns to the desires that Japanese-identified residents brought to their interactions with Filipina women. In this chapter, I suggest that these local residents made sense of the increasing numbers of Filipina women in the region through the matrix of their desires to be part of what they viewed as a cosmopolitan, affluent, and modern Japanese nation and their experiences of exclusion from it.

In "Terms of Relations," the second half of the book, I consider how the desires discussed in the first half of the text come into productive relation by exploring how marriage became a site of both possibility and frustration for Filipina migrants and Japanese residents. In particular, I look to the ways that oyomesan became a term of relations—part of both a language and a set of conditions through which interactions among members of these groups took shape. In chapters 4 and 5, I examine the resonances and dissonances that emerged among Filipina migrants' and their Japanese communities' understandings of Filipina women's roles as brides and daughters-in-law in their new households. Chapter 4, "Kindred Subjects," considers what identifying Filipina migrants as oyomesan meant to Japanese residents in Central Kiso. It examines how and why Filipina women's Japanese families and community members both reinscribed and transformed popular understandings of Japaneseness when they identified the women in this way. Chapter 5, "The Pressures of Home," reflects on Filipina women's perspectives toward being oyomesan. This chapter explores how these women both self-consciously and inadvertently performed this role by engaging discourses of gender and kinship that were sometimes resonant with, and sometimes different from, those of their Japanese families. In chapter 6, "Runaway Stories," I focus on stories about Filipina women who ran away from their Japanese husbands in Central Kiso. I consider how running away marked the unbridgeable gaps that emerged among Filipina women and their Japanese communities and how these gaps took on a runaway agency, becoming an unsettling social force in their lives.

DISORIENTING REMINDERS

If this book evokes a zone of encounters involving Filipina migrants, Central Kiso residents, and others in Japan, the Philippines, and the United States whose lives touch theirs, it also opens an ethnographic and analytical space that is its own such zone. On this account, some comments on language use and naming are in order. First, with most ethnographies, readers can easily determine which language was spoken by members of any given group. In this book, however, one cannot always assume a given language was being used. Most Japanese people in Central Kiso spoke to me in standard Japanese, a few used local dialects, and a small number used some English (for example, including English words and phrases they knew). Most Filipina women and I communicated in a mixture of Japanese, English, and Tagalog (sometimes using different languages in different contexts, and sometimes using all three languages within a single sentence). These women were accustomed to using a range of languages in their everyday lives: With Japanese family and community members, or when Japanese speakers were present, they spoke Japanese. Among themselves, they usually spoke Tagalog (or, in a few cases, other Philippine dialects), often mixed with Japanese and English words. Some women spoke English, both to develop their skills or because Japanese community members wanted to practice it. Because I do not undertake a linguistic analysis of these communication practices, I have chosen for the ease of reading to indicate language use in the text only where relevant to my argument or where words given in Japanese or Tagalog do not easily translate into English. I mention these language practices here because they reflect the kind of creolized worlds in which I found myself in Central Kiso.

Second, in an effort to be accountable to my ethnographic context, I have employed an unusual system for naming the people about whose lives I write. In Japan, Japanese names are conventionally given surname first, and outside of intimate relations (for example, among couples, parents and children, or childhood friends), people usually address each other by their last names followed by the suffix -*san* (Mr., Ms., Mrs.). I found, however, that some Japanese people in Central Kiso, aware of standard practice in the United States, requested that I address them by their given names (without a suffix) because it demonstrated their familiarity with

Western practice and hence suggested their cosmopolitanism. Moreover, all Filipina women in the region addressed each other by their first
names, and often with nicknames. Throughout this text I use pseudonyms
to refer to the people I discuss. However, while it is common in ethnographic writing to choose a consistent system for rendering names, I have
selected pseudonyms that reflect the different ways that I addressed
people. For example, rather than referring to my landlady by her surname
followed by -san (i.e., as Matsubara-san), I refer to her as "Emiko" because this was how I knew her. Other Japanese people in town, I refer to
by their last name followed by an appropriate suffix, for example, Murai-
san, the plumber's wife, and Iida-sensei (teacher), our Japanese teacher.
I addressed Filipina women by their first names or nicknames, and I have
selected names for them accordingly. While these inconsistencies may initially seem confusing, I also hope they will serve as productively dis-
orienting reminders of the different ways my presence figured for people
in the region, of the different people I become in my encounters with
them, and of how the ethnographic encounter shaped the terms of our relations.

PART ONE

Figures of Desires

WHERE DOES ONE BEGIN TO map a zone of encounters? Classic ethnographies began with stories of arrival that located the ethnographer and the reader in an unfamiliar world, a world that the text promised to render comprehensible. This "setting trope" at once delineated the object of ethnographic study as a fixed and bounded culture and established the ethnographer's territorial claims to it.[1] But when we focus on zones of encounters, the object of our analyses is not a culture or a people but sets of contingent, translocal relationships in which we are in different ways implicated. What different points of departure, and arrival, does such an analysis entail?

Understanding cultural encounters means paying attention to the affective commitments—the wishes, wants, objectives, dreams, goals, aspirations, and longings—that shape people's everyday lives and lead their paths to cross. It also means understanding the intertwined historical, social, and political-economic processes through which people come to articulate and act on their desires. I use the word *desires* here to refer to ways that cultural and political-economic processes play out at the level of the subject. I am building on Michel Foucault's argument that desires are products not of universal and subconscious human needs but of historical processes and social and political-economic relations of power.[2] They are, as Lisa Rofel suggests, key tropes through which people come to understand themselves as subjects in a neoliberal and globalized world.[3] They are thus useful theoretical tools for understanding the different subjective and located ways that people inhabit these processes.

To give a preliminary sense of the kinds of desires that guided Filipina women and Japanese men to their relationships in Central Kiso, I'll offer two ethnographic sound bites. The first is from a conversation I had in Manila with a woman named Marites, who is the younger cousin of a Filipina friend in Central Kiso. Twenty-four years old at the time, Marites was soon to return to Japan on her sixth six-month contract as an entertainer. She had agreed to an audio-recorded interview about her decision to go to Japan and her work experiences there.

"I just wanted to go," Marites told me in a mixture of Tagalog and Japanese when I asked her why she had first decided to work in Japan. We were sitting in the small house that her cousin had built for her mother. Marites told me that she had for some time wanted to go to "America," but after watching many young women from her neighborhood, including her older cousin, go to Japan as entertainers, she had also grown curious about what life was like there. She had wondered, "When they return to the Philippines, why are they so beautiful? Their hair is colored. They bring bracelets, necklaces. So I was curious. I wanted to go to Japan. Maybe I could be beautiful."

Marites suggested that other dreams had also prompted her to go abroad. She told me that after watching her cousin return from Japan and purchase a house and business for her family, she decided that she wanted to try to do the same. She explained, "I saw my cousin. She didn't need to work as a prostitute. But she had a brain. So she could build her own house. I thought to myself, why not me? Maybe I'm capable of that too. So I wanted to try, on my own, without help from anybody."

Now consider a conversation I had with the husband of a Filipina woman in Central Kiso, a man I'll call Tanaka-san, about his decision to marry his Filipina wife, whom he had met while she was working in a local hostess bar.

"I didn't marry her because she was beautiful," Tanaka-san explained in Japanese. "In Japan we have a saying: In three days you get sick of a beautiful woman and used to an ugly one."

I tried to mask my discomfort with his comments as he continued. "I dated a lot of women before I married my wife, a lot of Filipinas that I met in local bars."

"How many?" I asked.

Tanaka-san waved his fingers in the air and replied that he couldn't count them all on both hands.

"Why so many?" I pushed.

"I dated them to see if I liked them enough to marry them. You don't know if you want to marry someone until you date them."

"But why Filipinas?"

"After I hit thirty I started to like Filipinas."

"Why?" I pressed.

Tanaka-san paused. "I really couldn't say." He reflected for a moment and then replied, "They have the good characteristics of traditional Japanese women. I like that in a woman. They look up to their husbands. They respect them. They listen to what their husbands say."

"What attracted you to your wife out of all the Filipinas you dated?" I asked.

"I couldn't really say," Tanaka-san responded. "Part of it was that the timing was right. I also liked her because she was poor. Because I wanted to help her."

These two anecdotes suggest that both Filipina women and Japanese men crafted senses of self through their relationships. They also suggest that members of these groups brought desires for certain kinds of futures to their interactions. Yet, while their visions may have in some places overlapped, they were also strikingly different. Like many of the Filipina women I discuss in the pages that follow, Marites told me that she was inspired to go to Japan by dreams of glamour and travel that resonated with her image of "America." She also wanted to help her family while asserting her independence. In contrast, a number of Japanese men married to Filipina women in Central Kiso expressed nostalgia for traditional times and gender roles. They also suggested desires to craft a sense of masculinity based on feelings of both benevolence toward and superiority over Filipina women. As I later mention, some of these men also expressed cosmopolitan desires to travel and an interest in the Philippines.

In the second half of this book, I will explore the alignments, misalignments, and gaps that developed between Filipina migrants' and Japanese residents' desires. In this half, I first want to consider: How did these different forms of desire come to be in the first place? What gave them shape and force in Filipina migrants' and Central Kiso residents' lives? Filipina women's decisions to marry rural Japanese men, and Japanese men's interest in Filipina women as brides, cannot be understood within a singular top-down narrative of globalization. While their desires were in some sense linked by globally circulating discourses of modernity, cosmopolitanism, and capitalism, these discourses have taken a range of culturally and geographically specific forms in Japan and the Philippines. In the three chapters that follow, I explore how the desires that Filipina migrants and Central Kiso residents brought to their encounters took shape through discrepant, but not unconnected, sets of social and political-economic relations involving not only Japan and the Philippines but also the United States. Specifically, I focus on the ways these social and political-economic relations condensed dreams and life-worlds into recognizable, beckoning shapes: the beautiful and glamorous world of show business; "America"; the cosmopolitan; discourses of wealthy, urban Japanese masculinity; a modern Japanese nation. I call these charismatic cultural forms "figures of

desires." I take the idea of the "figure" from Donna Haraway and Claudia Castañeda, who stress the way that figures at once condense meaning
and give it form.[4] Unlike passive objects of desire, figures of desires give
shape to people's dreams, just as they emerge through the material relations that inform the very dreams people can imagine. The figures of desires invoked by Filipina migrants and Japanese residents in Central Kiso
were beacons that guided them along intersecting paths. How did these
figures come to define the dreams of Filipina migrants and Japanese residents and to mark the routes that led them to their relationships with each
other? How and why did these dreams take hold?

CHAPTER 1

Sites of Encounter

In my morning newspaper, I occasionally found fliers for local Filipina hostess bars. Printed in dark red ink on glossy white paper, one such ad featured a large eye-catching photograph of seven women: Four were smiling, two had serious expressions, and one seemed to be caught off guard by the camera. Five of the women, standing on a stage, were dressed in white spandex pantsuits with beaded detail and low-cut spaghetti-strap tops, posed in a line like Las Vegas showgirls, their hips sharply angled toward the camera, front knees cocked. The two women sitting in front, their crossed legs hanging off the stage, wore similar outfits in black. Printed in bold Japanese lettering, the caption read: "Cabaret Boracay's First Year Anniversary Gratitude Service. Thanks to you, we have made it through our first year. We would like to earnestly thank all for their support. We are trying to be even more 'inexpensive and friendly' so we hope you will increase your patronage. From the owner and employees together." And below the photograph: "One complimentary reserve bottle. Shows daily!"

The flier, sandwiched between local advertisements and announcements—town hall and community center notices about regional events, ads for sales at the local kimono store and the neighborhood shoe and sportswear shops, and fliers from grocers listing the week's specials: fuji apples, three for ¥200, or salmon, 200 grams for ¥500—reminded me that Filipina hostess bars were embedded in the mundane practices of everyday life in Central Kiso. The flyer from a local shoe shop had pictures of fashionable leather pumps and tennis shoes on sale, the latest arrivals from France and the United States. Alongside this ad, one could read the bar's flier as suggesting that its Filipina employees were analogous to new shoes, the latest commodities available for purchase. The objectifying gaze of the camera belied the ad's claim that the women, like the owner, are the bar's humble and gracious hosts. However, if one focuses on the sharpness of the women's poses and their smiles and stares, one could also glimpse in the photograph the dreams and goals that led these women to work in bars in Japan.

I contrast these two ways of reading the bar advertisement because they reflect familiar lines of feminist debate regarding women's experiences with forms of sexualized labor. Feminist scholars have long, and often fiercely, disagreed, over how to understand women's participation in areas such as prostitution, bar work, pornography, and correspondence marriages. Some have argued that these practices evidence the ways women are subject to exploitation and violence in patriarchal and capitalist worlds. Others, however, see in them women's struggles for self-determination and even forms of empowerment.[1] Debates over these issues today inform feminist positions on a range of issues, including not only prostitution but also marriage and human trafficking. At the heart of these debates lie questions of choice and individual agency, and specifically whether women can freely choose to do sexualized labor or whether they are always in some sense directly or indirectly forced into it.

In recent years, feminist ethnographers have complicated this binary argument. They have suggested that while women who engage in prostitution and correspondence marriages are agents, their agency is always configured within unequal relations of power.[2] Many of these scholars are drawing on practice theory, which maintains that human action does not simply reflect the autonomous will of an individual human subject, but is always situated within social, cultural, and political-economic structures of power.[3] This insight has complicated our understanding of what human agency means in relation to sexualized forms of labor. For example, feminist ethnographers have shown that women's choices and actions in sexualized economies are unequally shaped by gender ideologies, capitalist structures, and discourses of cosmopolitan modernity. However, these studies have paid less attention to how women's agency also takes shape through the everyday dynamics of social relationships. They have shown us little of these historical and cultural processes of encounter.

While still being mindful of the ways that formations of power shape people's lives and decisions, I want to shift the focus of these inquiries.

Every Filipina woman I met in Central Kiso told me that she did not intend to marry a Japanese man when she went to Japan to work in a hostess bar—most women told me that they had boyfriends in the Philippines at the time, and some also shared unflattering impressions of Japanese men. Japanese men married to Filipina women in the region similarly relayed that in their youth they could never have imagined marrying a Filipina woman, and particularly one who worked in a hostess bar. Yet in the 1980s and 1990s, Filipina hostess bars became important places in Central Kiso where marriages developed between members of these groups. In fact, many Filipina women in Central Kiso told me romantic and dramatic stories about "falling in love" with their husbands, whom they met in these bars. How, then, can we understand these bars as places in which their relationships developed?

In this chapter, I focus on Filipina hostess bars as *sites of encounter* in which Filipina migrants' and their Japanese customers' divergent, yet in both cases ambivalent, desires came into unequal yet productive relation in ways that transformed their senses of self and the possibilities they imagined for their lives. I use the expression *sites of encounter* to refer to the ways that these bars figured as nodes of social relationships where different histories, genealogies of meaning, and forms of desire coincided within unequal relations of power. Doreen Massey has argued that places are best understood as spatial-temporal events: power-laden processes that both include and stretch beyond local relations and that are full of internal differences and conflicts.[4] Here I consider how specific localized configurations of historical contingencies came to bear on Filipina women's and their Japanese customers' experiences in these bars and made new forms of relationships—such as romance and marriage—possible between them.

In what follows, I examine three factors that shaped these bars as sites of encounter and enabled them to become places where Filipina women and rural Japanese men met spouses: the coinciding histories through which Filipina hostess bars were established in Central Kiso, Filipina women's experiences of glamour and shame in their bar employment, and the ways these bars enabled Japanese customers to articulate themselves as wealthy and modern "Japanese men" while making them painfully aware of their exclusions from this category.

A NOTE ON BARS

Before I continue, I should note that I am using the term *hostess bars* to gloss a range of establishments that might otherwise be differentiated as snack bars *(sunakku)*, pubs *(pabu)*, cabarets *(kyabarē)*, and clubs *(kurabu)*. The basis of these distinctions generally lies in the prices an establishment charges (clubs are usually the most expensive) and the services it offers (for example, a cabaret might feature a show). However, I found that Filipina women in Central Kiso characterized their experiences working in these businesses less in terms of the type of establishment where they were or had been employed and more in relation to the specific expectations and personality of a given owner or mama-san.[5] Moreover, over the course of several contracts in Japan, a woman might work at a variety of these establishments. Some Filipina women told me that when they applied to go to Japan they were asked whether they wanted to work in a hotel or in a club, but others never spoke of having this option. (These women also had very little say regarding what part of Japan they would be working in; they were either requested by bar owners or assigned by their promotion agency.) Because these women described their job responsibilities and relationships with customers at all of the aforementioned types of establishments in very similar ways—they were expected to perform manual labor and entertain customers along lines that I describe later—I group them together and use the terms interchangeably.

I do, however, distinguish the bars I discuss from businesses that explicitly offer sexual services, such as pink salons *(pinku saron)*, soaplands *(sōpu rando)*, or brothels.[6] Although some women working in hostess bars develop sexual relationships with customers, prostitution is technically illegal in Japan and, as I discuss later, women working in hostess bars (including Japanese women) do not necessarily have sexual relationships with bar clients.[7] Based on her fieldwork in an elite hostess bar in Tokyo during the early 1980s, Anne Allison argues that in hostess bars, Japanese men are not paying for sex or for "the woman," but for the eroticization of the man, for his projection as a powerful and desirable male.[8] Thus while hostesses are performing sexualized labor, they do not necessarily offer sexual services. Rather, they are paid to make men feel special, at ease, and indulged, or to, as one customer explained to Allison, "feel like a man."[9] This distinction between bar work and prostitution was crucial to Filipina women I knew. Not one Filipina women in Central Kiso identified herself to me as a prostitute or sex worker (although they occasionally identified other Filipina women working at bars in such terms).

Hostess bars developed in Japan during the period of postwar economic growth as part of a set of stratified processes facilitating corporate capital accumulation. However, these bars also find precedents in a number of

different kinds of establishments, including prewar cafés and special coffee shops *(tokushu kissa)* and postwar cabarets that catered to U.S. American occupation forces.[10] Early hostess bars catered to elites—wealthy
businessmen, male politicians, and the like—and were important sites for
settai (business entertaining) during Japan's high-growth period between
the late 1960s through the 1980s.[11] Hostess bars are also ranked hierarchically according to the perceived quality of their service and the women
who work there and, correspondingly, to their cost. At the high-class hostess bar in Tokyo where Allison conducted fieldwork, elite corporate employees paid large sums of money to be flattered and served drinks by what
were considered to be very attractive and refined women. During my fieldwork, less expensive hostess bars, including those in rural areas and those
catering to working-class men, were generally acknowledged as "lower
ranked," and the women who worked at these bars were often considered
to be less attractive and refined.[12]

I use the expression *Filipina hostess bar* to refer to a bar that employs
Filipina women as hostesses. Beginning in the late 1970s and into the
1980s and 1990s, the range and numbers of bars employing women to
serve and entertain customers expanded. As the Japanese economy grew
in the 1970s and 1980s, young Japanese women began to move into
pink- and white-collar work, and women from places outside Japan—
including the Philippines, Korea, China, Taiwan, Thailand, Rumania,
and Russia—increasingly were hired to replace Japanese women in what
were usually considered to be lower-ranking bars throughout the country.[13] In some clubs, women from various countries (including Japan)
worked alongside each other; often, however, bars featured women of a
particular nationality. In the mid-1980s, women from the Philippines
came to be the largest group of foreign women employed in hostess bars
in Japan, and Filipina hostess bars came to occupy a particular niche
within the sex industry in Japan.

In this chapter I focus on Filipina hostess bars as they existed in Central Kiso from the early 1980s though the 1990s. As I discuss in the epilogue, these bars no longer exist quite as I characterize them. First, Sampagita, the bar I describe in this chapter, closed in 2002 on account of
"poor management" (or so I was told by some Filipina women in the region). Second, changes in Japan's immigration policies since 1999 have
made both being in Japan without a visa and procuring entertainer visas
to come to Japan considerably more difficult, and ultimately forced
many bars in the area to shut down.[14] In addition, the economies of both
Central Kiso and the Philippines have increasingly worsened over the

past ten years, making for more demoralizing and difficult working conditions for Filipina migrants. Recent decentralization policies initiated by
the national government have increasingly strained rural regions, reduc-
ing national economic support that provided jobs and pushing rural
areas to become economically self-sufficient.[15] As a result, men in rural
areas have considerably less money to spend at bars.

In the Philippines, economic policies have continued to benefit elites
and foreign corporations at the expense of workers.[16] These policies have
made people in the Philippines more desperate to find work abroad and
thus more vulnerable when they are overseas. During my fieldwork in the
late 1990s, Filipina women with whom I spoke in Central Kiso complained
that those working in bars were increasingly pressured to, in their words,
"do more" with customers to sustain their interest. While most of these
women were ambiguous about what this meant, some explained that
they were expected to wear more revealing clothes and that more customers now expected to be able to grope them, possibly leading to sexual relations. They spoke with frustration about how much more challenging the job had become in comparison to their earlier stints working
in bars in the 1980s and early 1990s. I discuss Filipina women's experiences in these bars in more detail later in this chapter. First, though, let
me trace the coinciding political-economic histories through which Filipina hostess bars came to be established in Central Kiso.

COINCIDING HISTORIES

As sites of encounter for Filipina migrants and local Japanese men,
Filipina hostess bars in Central Kiso emerged through the convergence
of two distinctly located, although not unconnected, sets of political-
economic histories: (1) the establishment of hostess bars, and later Filipina hostess bars, in the region, and (2) the development of overseas
labor migration, and particularly Filipina migration to Japan as entertainers, as an accumulation strategy in the Philippines. These two histories reflect the distinctive ways that people in rural Japan and the Philippines have been incorporated into larger national and global visions of
capitalist modernity, and have tried to manage their marginality within
them. These histories were also shaped by U.S. Cold War policy in Japan
and the Philippines; economic policies initiated by the IMF, World Bank,
and U.S.-backed Marcos regime; and Japanese and U.S. investment and
overseas direct assistance (ODA) to the Philippines. These bars, then, are
more than sites of encounter for Filipina migrants and Japanese towns-

folk. They also are nodes within broader geopolitical sets of relationships that in different ways involve not only Japan and the Philippines, but also those of us in the United States, who craft lives in the wake of such projects.

As I trace, in the pages that follow, the histories through which Filipina hostess bars developed in Central Kiso, I restrain from weaving my narratives together in a single causal framework. I also strive not to privilege one narrative over another and instead foreground the contingencies and unequal collaborations through which these bars have come into being in Central Kiso as sites of encounter.

History I: On Dams and Bars

One high-level employee of the Kisofukushima Town Hall told me that women working in hostess bars in Central Kiso were a modern-day derivative of geisha who once served both local elites and important travelers and officials passing through the area.[17] This man's comment was a pointed reminder of the region's location along important travel and trade routes during the Tokugawa period, a time that, as I discuss in chapter 3, some residents nostalgically contrasted with the economic struggles the region was facing at the time. Other middle-aged residents, however, suggested that hostess bars were introduced to the town in the late 1950s to provide entertainment for the construction workers who came to the area to build the Makio Dam in the nearby Mitake and Ōtaki villages. Funded by World Bank loans that stipulated that the heavy equipment necessary to build the dam be purchased from U.S.-based companies, the Makio Dam was part of the Aichi Waterworks Project (Aichi Yōsui Keikaku), jointly commissioned by regional and national Japanese governments (and clearly supported by the U.S. government) as part of a wave of modernization and development projects begun during the postwar years to rebuild the Japanese economy.[18] Specifically, the project was intended to supply water and electrical power to the growing industrial region in and around Nagoya, a major port, manufacturing center, and now the fourth largest city in Japan. To this day, automobile, steel, agricultural, and other manufacturing industries in this area depend on the Kiso River for at least part of their water and power needs.

The Aichi Yōsui Kōdan (Aichi Waterworks Corporation) oversaw construction of the dam, hiring contract laborers from across the country to do the work. These men resided in Central Kiso for the four years it took to complete the project (1957–1961), introducing large amounts of

Figure 1. A view of the Kiso River from a bridge in Kisofukushima, September, 1998.

money (with their disposable incomes) into the then desperate local economy. Providing for the workers' entertainment in a manner to which these often urban-based laborers were accustomed prompted the development of two movie theaters, a string of pachinko parlors, and the first hostess bars in Central Kiso. Friends who had been raised in the region reminisced about this period when "Kiso was so rich!" For these residents, the luxury of the movie theaters, now long closed (the pachinko parlors, like the bars, have survived), and the improved standard of living contrasted starkly with the poverty and deprivation of the years during and immediately following the Pacific War.

However, the Aichi Waterworks Project yielded for local residents not only the pleasures of incorporation into a modernizing Japan, but also dangers, frustrations, and unfulfilled desires. The damming of the river displaced entire hamlets, prompting local protests against the plans.[19] The construction project also made local women feel vulnerable. My friend Sachiko, who was a high school student at the time, remembered how her mother cautioned her not to walk alone at night out of fear that she might be raped by dam workers. Others commented about how envious they had been of the families of the construction companies' managers and engineers, whose incomes far surpassed those of most local residents. Sachiko recalled her wonder at the large amounts of food one construction manager's son consumed as a paying boarder in their home. His hearty appetite was a daily reminder of the luxury and indulgence of his father's position and the different standard by which her family lived. As Sachiko put it, shaking her head with both bitterness and wonder, "We were living quite different lifestyles!"

According to Sachiko, many bars closed shortly after the dam was finished and the workers left the area. However, other local residents maintained that just as many bars remained. Several residents explained that as local economies in the region became increasingly cash dependent, men (and women) from nearby villages that had previously been self-sufficient began seeking employment in logging and construction (building roads, bridges, and dams). As these industries flourished, people came to Central Kiso from other parts of Japan in search of work.[20] These laborers provided a new client base for local bars. I was told that some construction companies even began treating their workers to periodic evenings in them.

Between the late 1950s and the late 1970s, hostess bars in Central Kiso, like the majority of those throughout Japan, employed only Japanese women. The shift to employ Filipina women in these bars was part of a larger trend throughout Japan that can in part be linked to the U.S. military presence in Okinawa and other parts of Japan. Thus, the development of a labor niche for Filipina women in hostess bars has historical ties to both the occupation of Okinawa by Japan and to U.S. Cold War policy and its continued investment in maintaining a strategic military presence throughout the Pacific. In the 1960s, as the value of the Japanese yen continued to rise, the ability of U.S. military personnel to purchase Japanese commodities and labor diminished. The wages of Japanese and Okinawan women who had previously worked in bars around U.S. bases became too high to accommodate demand. After the Ryukyu Islands were transferred to Japan in the mid-1970s, owners of bars on Okinawa began to employ Filipina women, who because of their migration status were more vulnerable and would work for lower wages, to serve the U.S. military who remained on bases there. Soon, bars catering to local men and Japanese tourists also began to hire Filipina women, and the bar industry around U.S. bases broadened to include not only Filipina but also Thai women. Women from these two countries now make up the majority of foreign women working in sex industries on Okinawa, and Filipina hostess bars can be found around U.S. military bases across Japan.[21]

The first Filipina hostess bar in Kisofukushima was opened by a woman named Yamada Tomoko, who herself had worked in hostess bars in the Kiso region for many years. The daughter of a fisherman in Kumamoto, on the west coast of Kyushu, Yamada-san came to Kisofukushima in 1959, when she was nineteen. She had left Kyushu to work in a textile factory in Nagoya, but finding the work unsatisfactory, she proceeded to Kiso-fukushima, where her uncle was working in the logging industry and her aunt was working in a sushi bar in the area. Her aunt's employers also owned a hostess bar, and they soon employed Yamada-san there. Yamada-san recalled that at the time there were at least eight hostess bars in the town of Kisofukushima, and others in the nearby town of Agematsu and throughout the county, that catered primarily to men working on dam construction and in the lumber industry. Over the next few years, Yamada-san worked at a variety of bars in Kisofukushima, in regional cities such as Shiojiri and Matsumoto, and back in Kyushu, where she returned briefly. Then in 1966, a former boss in Kisofukushima offered her a job as a mama-san at a new bar he was opening. Twelve years later at this bar, Kurabu Yume (Club Dream), Yamada-san first hired Filipina women as hostesses.

Yamada-san explained that in 1978, while she was working as the mama-san at Kurabu Yume, a promoter based in Matsumoto approached her and proposed hiring Filipina women at her club. At the time, she recalled, promoter fees were high and hiring Filipina women was more expensive than employing Japanese women. Yamada-san told me that she decided to take the business risk because she was ambitious. The local economy, which was benefiting from a domestic tourism boom, was doing well and, she suggested, Filipina women would be something new and different in the town. Yamada-san was also increasingly having difficulty finding young Japanese women who were willing to work at bars in the countryside. At first, Yamada-san hired only two or three Filipina women who worked alongside an equal number of Japanese hostesses.[22] She recalled that customers would come into the bar just to see the Filipina women because they looked different than Japanese women. "They had dark skin and prominent features," she explained. A long-time denizen of local hostess bars also mentioned that men in the area were initially interested in the Filipina women, "because it was a first, because they were a novelty." He later explained that Japanese hostesses in the region tended to be in their thirties or forties (younger Japanese women had moved to the cities); in contrast, the Filipina women were in their early twenties, if not younger. Their youth also contributed to their popularity.

According to Yamada-san, some customers preferred to sit with the

Japanese women with whom they could more easily converse. However, others wanted to sit with the Filipina women. In the beginning, Yamada-san would seat a Filipina woman on one side of a customer and a Japanese woman on the other. She explained that sometimes the customer liked to just look at the Filipina woman and to talk to the Japanese woman. Based on her clients' favorable response, Yamada-san decided to hire more Filipina women. However, Kurabu Yume was too small to be eligible for work visas for more than three women. In 1980, another opportunity arose for Yamada-san: a large ramen shop up the highway went on sale at auction. Yamada-san purchased the property with the aim of fulfilling her dream of owning her own business. She converted the restaurant into a club—Club Tomoko—with the intention of running it as a Filipina hostess bar. A few years after Yamada-san started hiring Filipina women, another bar followed suit—it did not want to lose out to Club Tomoko, which was attracting more customers; Filipina women had become a selling point for the bar.

When I began my research in 1998, local residents whom I asked agreed that for nearly a decade all hostess bars in Central Kiso had employed Filipina women almost exclusively.[23] At the time, six of the nine bars in Kisofukushima were being run by Filipina mama-sans.[24] Club Tomoko was the oldest Filipina bar in the area. Relatively successful, Yamada-san hired ten Filipina women every six months, not infrequently rehiring women over several contracts. According to Yamada-san, most of her customers were men who lived nearby, many of whom had associations with the construction industry, which was by then financially suffering but still to some degree supported by national and regional public works projects. Sometimes truck drivers and men on business or staying in vacation homes (both company and privately owned) in the area also came in. One middle-aged Japanese friend explained that unlike white-collar workers, who have fixed monthly salaries, men in the construction industry received their relatively high salaries on a daily or weekly basis; thus, they regularly had large amounts of money to spend on entertainment. Although many bar customers worked in construction, I learned (despite the protests and denials of some of my middle-aged Japanese women friends in town), that many men employed at the town hall and from elite families also sometimes patronized Filipina hostess bars.

History II: Filipina Migration to Japan

Filipina migration to Central Kiso is part of a larger-scale migration of Filipina women to work at bars in Japan that began in the late 1970s, dramatically accelerated during the 1980s, and continued growing in the 1990s. Previous studies have linked this migration trend to Japanese and U.S. American sex tourism to the Philippines, which flourished after the onset of martial law there in 1972.[25] However, this explanation alone cannot explain why many Filipina women who work in hostess bars entered Japan legally on skilled-labor entertainer visas or the ways that many of these women associated work in hostess bars with the glamorous and desirable world of show business. Only by considering how a history of Japanese and U.S. American sex tourism in the Philippines converged with a tradition of Filipina cultural dance performance can we understand Filipina migration to Japan to work in hostess bars and the ways these women came to understand their relationships with the Japanese men they met in them.

Filipina women who came to work in clubs in Japan with government-issued entertainer visas were technically hired as cultural performers. The six-month visas these women received were the same visas issued to professional dance troupes and celebrities when they came to Japan to, for example, perform big shows. A tradition of cultural dance performance in the Philippines dates to the early twentieth century when Francesca Reyes Aquino, inspired by the U.S. colonial introduction of physical education and European folk dances in schools, founded the first Filipino folk dance company and began staging dances for U.S. colonial officers. Early dance troupes were tied to elite universities, such as the University of the Philippines. In 1958, the Bayanihan Folk Dance Company, associated with the Philippine Women's University, garnered international recognition when it performed at the World Expo in Brussels and then appeared on the *Ed Sullivan Show*.[26] Soon universities and private organizations throughout the Philippines began forming their own folk dance troupes, and cultural dancing became a popular recreational activity for elite youth throughout the country.[27] Beginning in the 1960s, large numbers of professional Filipino cultural dance troupes began performing on U.S. military bases in Saigon, Okinawa, Guam, Hawaii, and the Japanese mainland. During the 1970s, Filipina/o cultural dancers and performers were also increasingly hired as entertainment on U.S. cruise ships and in big hotels and tourist spots in Japan. This tradition of cultural performance offered a precedent for issuing entertainer visas to the growing number of Filipina women who entered Japan to work in clubs in the 1980s and 1990s.[28]

At the same time that growing numbers of Filipina/o cultural performers began performing abroad, the U.S.-backed Marcos administration, working in concert with the World Bank, the IMF, and the U.S.

government, began engineering a new economic order—what some have called "authoritative modernization"—to "integrate" the Philippines into the world economy.[29] These strategies were part of a larger process of liberalizing the Philippine economy that involved devaluing the peso, dismantling previous import-substitution protections that had slowed foreign investment during the 1950s and 1960s, and adopting an export-led industrial and agricultural economy.[30] The export-oriented economy, however, encouraged farmers to cultivate monocultural crops that relied on prices set in a global market, which declined drastically during the late 1970s.[31] Land reform and "Green Revolution" technologies initiated during this period also failed to give tenant farmers control over the land they worked and effectively concentrated control of agriculture in the hands of wealthy landowners.[32] The result was extreme poverty in many areas, coupled with the dispossession and deterritorialization of the bulk of rural laborers.[33] Many of these rural laborers went to Manila to look for work.[34]

Alongside these changes in rural areas, during the 1970s the Marcos government, again together with the IMF and World Bank, developed three strategies to bring foreign currency into the Philippines and thereby manage the country's growing external national debt: creating export-processing zones, encouraging overseas labor migration, and developing the tourism industry. These projects also tended to benefit wealthy elites and foreign nationals at the expense of workers. First, the development of export-processing zones was designed to attract foreign investment, in part by dissuading union organizing and keeping wages depressed.[35] Second, as development strategies continued to fail, the Marcos government increasingly encouraged overseas labor migration (in which migrants were expected to remit significant portions of their incomes home) as a national economic strategy to bring foreign currency into the Philippine economy.[36] Initially, primarily Filipino men went as contract workers to the Middle East to work in construction.[37] However, as I discuss later, by the early 1980s, growing numbers of Filipina women were looking for contract work abroad.

Third, the Marcos administration made developing the Philippines' tourism industry a central pillar of its economic plan. In 1973, Marcos created the Ministry of Tourism, which, over the course of the 1970s, saw to the development of fourteen first-class hotels, a luxurious conference center, and a cultural center.[38] A significant, although often unspoken, dimension of tourism development in the Philippines involved sex tourism, which had initially developed during the Vietnam War to capture the "rest and recreation" market of the U.S. military. Beginning in the early 1970s, the Philippines became a popular destination for Japanese men on sex tours.[39] Although prostitution was (and is) not legal in the Philippines, prohibitions against it were rarely enforced, and some have argued that the government in fact tacitly encouraged sex tourism because it brought money into the country.[40] By the end of the 1970s, the number of cocktail lounges in the Philippines where foreign men could purchase sexual services had more than doubled. However, Filipina and Japanese feminists soon began protesting Japanese sex tours.[41] A rally in Manila held by Filipina and Japanese feminists in 1981 drew significant media attention, and the number of Japanese sex tourist to the Philippines soon dropped by 25 percent.[42] As sex tourism to the Philippines declined, Japanese promoters began to recruit Filipina women to work not only in hotels, but also in clubs in Japan. As the Japanese economy had grown, Japanese women had been moving away from work in hostess bars, while Japanese men had more money to spend in them. The Japanese government began to issue a growing number of entertainer visas to Filipina women who came to work in hotel bars, cabarets, and hostess bars throughout Japan. Although Filipina women were granted entertainer visas to work as cultural performers, they were often expected to work as hostesses part or all of the time. Bar owners in Japan were rarely held accountable for their employment practices even when they were in clear violation of Filipina women's visa conditions.[43] Moreover, while increasing numbers of Filipina women began to come to Japan on entertainer visas, growing numbers also began to go through underground channels to work in other parts of the sex industry, often as prostitutes and in sex shows. As I later discuss, on account of these converging trends, Filipina entertainers in Japan came to be popularly associated with sex work.

If the beginning of a trend of documented Filipina migration to Japan to work in hostess bars is identifiable by the late 1970s and early 1980s, it gathered momentum over the 1980s and 1990s. By 1980, the employment situation in the Philippines had grown severe, and the debt crisis had reached a critical point. The IMF and World Bank issued an ultimatum to the Marcos government, calling for a restructuring of the Philippine economy that eventually entailed accepting a structural adjustment loan and further devaluation of the peso in the interest of making the country more profitable and accessible for foreign investment. In the years that followed, these efforts only increased unemployment, poverty, and unequal income distribution.[44] For example, between 1982 and 1985, GDP in the Philippines fell dramatically and, continuing a trend that had begun in the 1960s, real wages dropped 30 percent.[45] By 1986, real agricultural wages were below three-fourths of what they had been in 1962, and real wages of both skilled and unskilled laborers in urban areas were less than one-third of what they had been.[46] During this time, too, Japanese direct investment in and ODA to the Philippines began to grow, and by 1998 Japan was the single largest donor to the Philippines.[47] These political-economic trends established new linkages between the two countries. As I suggest in the next chapter, they formed a backdrop for Filipina migration to Japan, which began during the Marcos regime and gathered steam during the subsequent Aquino and Ramos administrations.[48]

On account of the converging histories through which a migration niche for Filipina entertainers developed—the blending of stigmatized work in the sex industry with a glamorous and elite performance tradition in the Philippines linked to the world of *showbiz* (show business, Tg.)—many Filipina women in Central Kiso expressed ambivalence about working in Japan. Cherie, a Filipina friend in Tokyo, explained that when small numbers of skilled Filipina/o performers were employed abroad, the work was considered quite prestigious.[49] For example, Cherie described a friend of her uncle's, a beautiful, college-educated office worker in her midtwenties, who impressed Cherie with stories about her experiences performing Filipino cultural dances at elegant hotels and resorts in Japan during the early 1970s. Cherie explained that the image of "dancing in Japan" changed in her mind during the mid-1970s—the height of Japanese sex tourism in the Philippines. Cherie described how soon thereafter promotion agencies in the Philippines that arranged for women to work in bars in Japan "sprouted up overnight, starting up here and there."

However, links between professional and university cultural dance troupes in the Philippines and Filipina entertainers in Japan remained strong even through the 1980s and 1990s. Filipina women who went to Japan on entertainer visas had to demonstrate they were trained as performers. Professional Filipino folk dancers worked as instructors, promoters, and licensing examiners for these women, and some former cultural dancers used capital acquired performing abroad to start businesses recruiting Filipina women to train to work in bars. One professional Filipino folk dancer I met, who was at the time a PhD student at an elite university in the United States, told me that he had helped put himself through college in the Philippines by working as an examiner for women going to Japan as entertainers. Moreover, many promoters had at one time worked as cultural dancers. Cherie recalled that her promoter, who ran one of the largest promotion agencies in the Philippines, had regaled her group with stories about his experiences performing on U.S. bases in Japan, Hawaii, and Guam. He had used the money he saved while performing to start his promotion company.

Because going to Japan as an entertainer was linked to professional Philippine cultural performance, many Filipina women in Central Kiso viewed it as a potentially glamorous and exciting opportunity even while the work became stigmatized and stories circulated in the Philippines about the tragic fates of some Filipina migrants in Japan. Many Filipina women in Central Kiso, who primarily came from urban and rural poor communities, described being treated like celebrities when they were recruited and trained to be entertainers. These women first signed with managers and promotion agencies that arranged their training and paperwork so that they could pass licensing exams as cultural performers and apply for entertainer visas. These agencies often gave the women cash advances to go shopping for clothes and makeup to take abroad. Several women explained that this was the first time they ever had such a luxury. As part of their training, they also had costume fittings and professional makeup applications. They were invited to photo shoots at which professionals took portfolio photographs of them in full costume and makeup under professional lighting. These photos were then sent to Japan by the Philippine promoter. In some ways, going to Japan as an entertainer offered these women an opportunity to live a life imagined only for models or movie stars. In fact, in an effort to professionalize (and thereby regulate and capitalize on) this migration trend, the Philippine state encouraged women to view their work in such a light. For example, the *Philchime Career Manual for Overseas Performance Artists*, the standard text used during the early 1990s in the Academic Training Program for Filipina women applying to work in Japan, asserts, "The honor, glamour, and privilege of this profession are only for those who can be considered as talented and beautiful according to standards of show business."[50]

SAMPAGITA

Through the convergence of two discrepant, but related, sets of histories— one of the establishment of hostess bars in Central Kiso and the other of the development of a trend of Filipina migration to Japan—Filipina hostess bars came to offer sites of encounter for Filipina women and Japanese men in the region. In this next section, I illustrate how the contradictory factors that shaped the development of hostess bars informed not only the capitalist organization of these establishments but also Filipina migrants' and their Japanese customers' ambivalent experiences in them. I'll begin with an evening I spent at a bar I call Sampagita.

Sampagita was a small bar nestled along the road that leads down from the Kisofukushima train station, which is perched on a hill above the town proper. The neon sign identifying the bar had already been turned on when I opened the front door and began to descend the dimly lit stairs that led into the club. The flight was steep and I watched my footing, staring down at the aged, dirty red carpet and working my way around the crates of large, empty bottles of Sapporo beer. It was Ruby's birthday, and I could hear music, a tape of Happy Birthday tunes, filtering through another door at the base of the stairwell. A bell went off as I continued my descent, notifying whoever was in the club that I was about to enter.

Ruby's birthday party marked the first time I had gone unaccompanied to a Filipina hostess bar while it was open for business, and I opened the door to the bar with a mixture of excitement and unease. Kisofukushima was a small town, and I had not yet lived there long. I worried that my landlady and other Japanese residents might question my character if they learned that I was spending time at these clubs. Just a few weeks earlier, I had mentioned to my landlady that I had attended a private gathering at Sampagita—a get-together with Sister Ruth and some Filipina friends and their husbands and children—and she had seemed troubled. As I have mentioned, my landlady was among the elite of the area. She prided herself on coming from and marrying into good local families, families that traced their descent from feudal officials or had historically owned land and important businesses, such as the area's miso shop. She told me that neither she nor anyone she knew had ever entered a Filipina bar. She qualified her comment by explaining that she was not prejudiced against Filipina women as a whole, telling me about a Filipina friend of hers, a "truly lovely person," who had come to Central Kiso through an *"omiai kekkon,"* a mediated marriage, as my landlady's own mother and many women of that generation had. However, she had maintained that Filipina women employed at clubs were working as prostitutes, and she had rationalized that they must be poor and desperate, as well as *keihaku* (shallow, frivolous, immodest), to do such work. When I had tried to protest, she had asserted that her parents would never have let her take such a job, even if they had been reduced to the direst of circumstances. She cautioned me, "People might think that one was *keihaku* if she associated with Filipinas who worked in bars."

I later learned that many local men, including those working at the town hall and Kiso County government offices, and even on occasion my landlady's assistants and son, sometimes patronized these bars. For many Japanese men in Central Kiso, Filipina clubs were a well integrated, although sometimes concealed, feature of the local social landscape. But my landlady's warning unsettled me, reminding me that many Japanese community members did not perceive these establishments as places for nice, well-bred women, which I—by virtue of my white U.S. Americanness, my education level and university affiliations, and my formal and polite Japanese—had, thus far, been assumed to be. It also painfully reinforced for me the premium placed on one's reputation in the small community and the fact that my actions would reflect not only on me but also on my landlady and her family, to whom I was greatly indebted. Despite myself, I could not help but feel self-conscious every time I entered a hostess bar.

But Ruby's birthday party was a research opportunity. And what was perhaps more important, Ruby considered me a friend, and because of both my status in the community and the low turnout expected at the event, my attendance meant a lot to her and to other Filipina women in the community. It had snowed unexpectedly that afternoon, and because of the weather, several women had to cancel plans at the last minute to come to the party; their husbands would not allow them to drive in the snow. Sorry for their absence, they had stressed the importance of my attendance at the celebration. So I had come bringing a birthday cake—a whipped cream and strawberry shortcake confection bought at a local bakery—and apologies and best wishes from Tessie, Cora, and others.

As I entered the club, Ruby's employees, Victoria, Gina, and Malou, looked up from what they were doing to offer big smiles and call out, "*irrashaimase,*" the standard, formal Japanese greeting to customers entering a business establishment. "Hello," I cried back, placing the cake and my backpack on the bar and removing my old down jacket, gloves, and scarf. It was nearly eight o'clock and the women were busy preparing the club for the evening ahead. They were wearing jackets over their strapless and sleeveless cocktail dresses, and they had not yet switched into their heels from the clogs and tennis shoes they wore to work. Malou and Gina were rolling up *oshibori* (small moistened hand towels) and placing them in the steamer for customers who were soon to arrive. The women were laughing and discussing a Tagalog soap opera that they had borrowed on video from another friend whose mother had sent it from the Philippines. I interrupted and asked where Ruby was, and they told me that "Mama," as they called her, would arrive later. "We are the ones who will clean and set up the bar."

Sampagita's facilities were modest. They included the club itself, a small kitchen sectioned off from the main room with colorful curtains, and a tiny washroom and toilet. The club itself was narrow and windowless. Always choked with cigarette smoke, the small, dimly lit space quickly became stuffy during the winter when Ruby turned the heater up high. A long, low bar with chairs curved along the right wall, and behind the bar were glass-doored cupboards filled with bottles of whisky and an assortment of glasses. At the far end of the club sat a small, crescent-shaped stage with a television monitor and a microphone for karaoke performances. The remainder of the space was filled with six short booth-like seats covered in mint green vinyl and three low marble-patterned plastic coffee tables. Neither the booths nor the tables were bolted to the floor, and Ruby was fond of rearranging the furniture and redecorating the club. On several occasions, she enlisted the women working for her, as well as me and several other Filipina friends, to help. We spent hours tacking colorful floral decorations and Philippine fans and flags up on the walls, hanging lace curtains from the Philippines around the stage, and putting up cross-stitched pictures of angels and figures of the Santo Niño.

The stage in Ruby's bar was too small for her to apply for visas for "talents" *(tarento),* what Japanese promoters and Filipina women often called those who entered Japan on entertainer visas. After 1991, in part as a response to the well-publicized death of a Filipina entertainer named Maricris Sioson and to corresponding protests in the Philippines over the sexual exploitation and abuse of women working in clubs, the Japanese government specified that only bars with stages large enough for cultural performances could qualify to hire foreign workers.[51] Because Ruby could not hire women on entertainer visas, she employed Filipina friends married to Japanese men—at least one-third of Filipina women married to Japanese men in the region continued to work in local bars— and other women who were, in Tagalog, *bilog* or *TNT,* that is, working in Japan without government-issued visas.[52] (As I discuss in greater detail in chapter 6, Filipina women in Japan without visas often find jobs through friends from earlier contract jobs or through relatives married to Japanese men.)

A number of Filipina women married to Japanese men wanted to work in hostess bars because the salaries there were considerably higher than in other work available to them in the region, such as factory work and piecework. Gina and Malou were two of what some Filipina women in the region referred to as the "lucky" ones, whose Japanese husbands and in-laws permitted them to continue working at night. The women had met their husbands several years back while working at bars in Kisofukushima and Agematsu, respectively. Both had stopped working while their children were young and had recently gone back to jobs in local bars to do *arubaito* (part-time work, Jpn.). Unlike talents, they were paid hourly rather than salaried wages, and they did not live in club-provided housing. Unusual in Central Kiso, Victoria was *TNT* (or, as she joked, an "OW: an OCW [over-seas contract worker], without the C, the contract"). Most undocumented Filipina women I met in Japan had stayed beyond the limit of visas that they initially received through a number of routes: jobs as entertainers that they had left because they did not like their work conditions or did not want to return to the Philippines when their visas expired; marriages with Japanese men whom they had left, often while they still had time remain-ing on temporary spousal visas, which then later expired; or visits paid to immediate relatives legally residing in Japan (one is not legally permitted to work while on a temporary visitor's visa, but some do anyway).[53]

Victoria had run away from her third contract job because she did not want to return to the Philippines and wait to come back to work in Japan. After a woman's contract was over, she was required to return to the Philippines and to wait several months before she was rehired and her pa-pers were reprocessed. The eldest daughter, Victoria was the breadwin-ner in her family, and the loss of income during this hiatus caused her family in the Philippines financial difficulty. Her father had diabetes and she was putting her siblings through school. Without her monthly remit-tances, her father could not afford insulin and other necessary medica-tions (which are sold, often by drug companies based in the United States, for prices that are relatively astronomical in the Philippines), and her sib-lings could not afford to remain in school. Moreover, because Victoria no longer had a promoter or manager taking a cut from her salary, her in-come was significantly higher than when she had worked as a talent—an additional attraction of going *TNT*. However, her situation was also much more precarious, and because of her undocumented status she was vulnerable in ways that many contract workers are not. (Again, see chap-ter 6 for a more complete discussion of these vulnerabilities.)

The evening of Ruby's birthday party, the seats at Sampagita were arranged around the tables to form three small private booths. In lieu of the usual Japanese snacks served from the kitchen, a buffet of Filipino

Figure 2. An entire piglet made for the dramatic centerpiece at Ruby's birthday party, March, 1999.

foods was spread along the bar. Ruby had specially prepared *lechon,* Filipino-style roasted pork: an entire piglet with an apple in its mouth formed a dramatic centerpiece for the spread.[54] Accompanying the roast pig were *lumpiang shanghai* (Filipino-style spring rolls), fruit salad in a sweet and heavy mixture of both fresh and whipped cream, a salad smothered with a mayonnaise sauce, and pieces of roast chicken, all of which Ruby, with Victoria's help, had made to serve to her friends and the paying customers she expected that night.

About half an hour after I arrived, just as the women had changed out of their casual shoes and jackets, the bell in the stairwell went off, and a few moments later the first customer entered. He was carrying a large bouquet of red roses wrapped in cellophane, presumably a gift for Ruby, who had yet to appear. The women greeted the man as he came into the bar, and Victoria ushered him into one of the mint green booths. She started talking with him as she finished arranging things, addressing him in Tagalog as *kuya* (big brother) and throwing other Tagalog words, such as *ako* (I) and *ikaw* (you), in with her Japanese. Meanwhile Malou came over with a warm hand towel for the man, and Gina brought him a beer. I made myself a drink and sat down at the bar. Having overheard Victoria and the man's exchange, I asked in Tagalog if the man understood. "A little," Victoria replied in Tagalog, turning back to the man and confirming in Japanese, "Right you understand some Tagalog?" "Not really," he responded in Japanese, looking rather embarrassed to be the focus of attention of so many women and relieved when a few minutes later another customer arrived.

The women sat the second customer at a different booth, and Malou brought him a hot towel and a beer before she joined him at his table. By this time, Victoria had sat down with the first customer, and she was chatting with him and squeezing his face in an affectionate and flirtatious manner. I turned back to Malou and Gina, who were sitting with the second customer in awkward silence. The three looked bored, as if they all were waiting for Ruby's arrival.

THE EVERYDAY PRACTICE OF HOSTESSING

Ruby's employees helped her clean up the bar after closing and on holidays, and they set up the club before it opened. They rolled hand towels, refilled napkin and toothpick holders, set out ice buckets, washed dishes, wiped down tables, prepared snack foods for customers, refrigerated beer, rearranged furniture and decorations, accompanied Ruby in buying supplies, and periodically vacuumed the carpet and cleaned the toilet and kitchen. Bars that employ foreign women on entertainer visas are required to provide housing for the women they employ, and many in Central Kiso had dorms or apartments that the women also were expected to keep clean. Ruby's employees also entertained customers at the club by pouring drinks, serving snacks, and making their male customers feel important, welcome, and comfortable. They were responsible for ensuring that customers were satisfied and had fun at the bar by talking, flirting, dancing, and singing with them, and sometimes by performing songs on the karaoke stage.

As I have mentioned, Filipina women on entertainer visas were technically hired as cultural performers, and they were not legally allowed to have sexual relationships with customers. Some bars expressly forbid hostesses from doing so—they had policies calling for immediate dismissal if discovered. Most bars in Central Kiso (at least as far as I was told) did not physically force, or even directly coerce, women to sleep with men. However, like all hostess bars (including those that hired Japanese women), Filipina hostess bars in Central Kiso encouraged Filipina women to develop intimate and affectionate relationships with their male clients so that the men would be inclined to patronize and spend money at the club. In other words, the bars expected these women to not only perform manual duties, but also, what Arlie Hochschild has called "emotional labor," to convince clients that the women cared for them and were having a good time so that the men would want to remain at their bar and increase their tabs.[55] This expectation structured not only the capitalist organization of the bars, but also the ways these women understood their jobs and the kinds of relationships that developed between them and Japanese men in Central Kiso.

To encourage the women to please and entertain customers, many Filipina hostess bars instituted quota systems that offered financial incentives, not unlike commissions. One of these was a "drink-back" system in which women received ¥100 (at the time about $0.88) for every drink a customer ordered above a weekly quota of, say, fifty. If women did not meet their quotas, not only did they not receive any drink-back money, but also they were sometimes penalized. Women developed different strategies to get customers to drink so that they could meet their drink-back quotas. For example, Ruby once explained with pride how she would apply subtle pressure on her customers, encouraging them to get drunk, being attentive to them, and cultivating their affections by making them feel special and cared for in the club.

Drink-back quotas were not the only incentive employed by the bars to encourage the women to develop personal connections with customers. Many bars had a "request" system through which customers could request that specific women sit at their tables and serve them. At these bars, women frequently had request quotas that they had to meet each week; that is, they had to have a certain number of customers request their presence at their tables. A particular woman might be known as the prettiest or most charming woman at a bar and the most popular with customers; this woman was the bar's number one request for a given period, and she might receive a bonus for this status. Although it was a source of pride for the women to be chosen the number one request, the request system sometimes fostered competition or tension among them. Moreover, Filipina women in Central Kiso sometimes became jealous if they liked a particular customer but he requested another woman.

To maintain relationships with customers and encourage them to patronize a bar and request them, Filipina women working in local bars often called their customers during daytime hours. Many of these women carried cellular phones that enabled them to do this, and they—even those who were married—would frequently get calls from their male customers. I would listen as they joked around with and flattered the men, asking why the men had taken so long to call, telling the men that they were missed, and encouraging them to come to the bar that night. Some of these relationships extended outside the region and even outside Japan. For example, Filipina women working at bars in Central Kiso sometimes were in contact with men who had visited their bars on business trips. These women would keep track of when the men would be in the area and encourage them to come visit again. Occasionally when a Filipina woman who had come on a six-month entertainer visa returned to a different region of Japan on a new contract, a customer she met at a previous job might travel across the country to pay her a visit. In the Philippines, I met and interviewed a Filipina woman who had been going back and forth between the two countries, working multiple contracts as an entertainer, over the course of several years. Even in Manila (during the course of a two-hour interview), she was receiving calls from admirers in Japan who were anxiously awaiting her return.

In addition to request quotas, many but not all bars had quotas on *dōhan,* which literally means "accompaniment" in Japanese, but in this context referred to dates in which a man took a woman out to dinner or shopping, after which she brought him back to her club. In some cases, men paid the club to take a woman on dōhan and women sometimes got a "dōhan-back," or a monetary bonus for each date they went on. One Filipina woman explained in Tagalog that what happened on these dates, *"depende sa babae"* (depends on the woman, varies from woman to woman). She told me that while some Filipina women might be willing to sleep with customers on dōhan, she and many Filipina women she knew were not. She clarified that with "ordinary customers" she only went out to dinner or sang karaoke. She told me that she would only ever be physically intimate with a customer, "if he is my boyfriend," that is, if she trusted him and had some kind of committed relationship with him.

As I mentioned, as the political-economic situation in Japan and the Philippines has worsened, Filipina women working in bars have become more vulnerable. Toward the end of my fieldwork, many lamented that they were increasingly expected to do more to satisfy customers. However, a number of Filipina women in Central Kiso who had worked in bars in the late 1980s and early 1990s when the Japanese economy was peaking and customers had relatively large disposable incomes, and who had felt some degree of security in their jobs and their visa status, described how they used the dōhan system to their advantage. When I asked one of these woman how she and other hostesses would get customers to take them on dōhan, she laughed and said, "Do you want to know our technique?" She recounted how she would tell the customer, "Oh, I want to buy such and such, do you know where I can find it?" And the customer would subsequently offer to take her shopping. Not only would he wind up buying her whatever she wanted, but he would also take her out to dinner and then to the club. She also described excitedly how she used to work in Chiba, close to Tokyo Disneyland, and how she would repeatedly tell customers (with feigned naïveté), "I've never been to Disneyland." She laughed as she told me that she had been there many times, but that when a customer took her she didn't have to pay for anything. Not only would he cover her admission and food, but he would also buy her souvenirs for the club and for herself. Knowing that women could be put in vulnerable positions on these outings, this woman told me that she and her friends would strategically avoid the *"sukebei"* (lecherous men, Jpn.) and asked only the *"majime"* (serious or sincere-intentioned, Jpn.) men or, as another woman put it, those men who could be satisfied "in a simple way." She added that if she were scared to go out alone with a man for the first time, she would bring one or two other friends from the bar as chaperones.

While these quotas put pressure on Filipina women to financially perform for the bar, they also encouraged the women to develop intimate and caretaking relationships with their male customers and, ultimately, to learn to frame some of these relationships in terms of dating, romance, and even love. Many Filipina women in Central Kiso described going on dōhan as fun and even, in some cases, as a form of courtship. One woman said that going on dates with customers who took her out shopping or to *yakiniku* (Japanese-style barbeque) was her favorite part of the job. She waxed nostalgic about her experiences hostessing when the Japanese economy was booming and customers would buy her expensive gifts. Another Filipina woman in Central Kiso told me that she preferred working at a bar with a dōhan system and a kind mama-san in lively and cosmopolitan Tokyo to working at those in the countryside that did not have dōhan quotas. She boasted that she had been to Mitsukoshi, an expensive department store in Tokyo, on a dōhan with a wealthy customer who was smitten with her and had bought her a coat worth more than ¥100,000 (about $885). He had bought it, she said, because he had wanted her to see her in those kinds of clothes. She told me that when she first came to Japan she didn't know anything about fashionable restaurants and expensive brand names, like Gucci, Versace, and Louis Vuitton. She soon learned about them from the other Filipina women with whom she worked, and also from Japanese customers who took her out on dōhan and bought her expensive, brand-name gifts. In this sense, dōhan served as an introduction into an elite, cosmopolitan, and bourgeois world that was new and exciting to this woman. Other Filipina women shared similar experiences, delighting not only in the gifts received, but also in the flattery of receiving them. These women expressed a sense of pride and accomplishment: expensive gifts symbolized not only one's participation in an elite capitalist world, but also one's popularity with men and one's skill at balancing and manipulating relationships with them.

Some women who had grown up in strict Catholic homes or who did not have money or time to care for their appearance in the Philippines told me that they enjoyed having admirers and receiving attention from men who, unlike the men they had known in the Philippines, had the means to take them out on dates and buy them gifts. Many of these women spoke with pleasure of the customers who vied for their affection and who wanted to marry them. One described having multiple "boyfriends" (her relations with whom, she reported, had not been sexual) who would take her out. She complained, with a deep sigh, of the difficulties of juggling these men and of staving off their jealousies, "because they know that you have other customers, so [each] one wants to think that he's your favorite." Another woman told me that Japanese men preferred Filipina women to Japanese women because Filipina women were so loving and affectionate; for her, the attention she received from male customers validated her sense of herself as an attractive and caring woman and as a Filipina.

These women's descriptions of the pleasures they found in receiving attentions from customers were only heightened in their discussions of the men they had decided to marry. Most married Filipina women I knew in Central Kiso had begun dating their husbands as part of their jobs, and many of them told romantic and exciting stories about their courtships, describing how their husbands had visited their bars every night and spent vast sums of money to help them avoid the attentions of other men. They spoke of exciting dates in which the men took them out driving and then for expensive dinners. Some of these women told stories of "love at first sight," describing how they had fallen for their husbands the minute the men had walked into the clubs where they worked and how they had maneuvered around the rules of their club, which usually allow only male customers to select hostesses, to arrange to sit with the men who became their husbands. Other Filipina women told me that, while they had not initially been romantically interested in their husbands, they had grown to have feelings for these men because they were so kind and persistent in their attentions.

In addition to the pleasures these women found in some of their interactions with male customers, Filipina women in Central Kiso also derived great satisfaction from their paychecks, sums of money that would have taken them years to accumulate in the Philippines and that enabled them to present themselves as dutiful daughters and responsible sisters, nieces, mothers, and friends to those back home. These women used their paychecks in a variety of ways. They purchased lots and built homes in the Philippines; bought jeepneys and opened *sari-sari* (general) stores; put siblings, nieces, or children through school; lavished expensive brand-name gifts on their friends and their families; treated friends and family members to meals at special restaurants when they went home; or simply, as Marites explained in Tagalog, used the money "for becoming beautiful" *(pagpapapaganda)*—to color their hair, purchase jewelry, and keep up with the latest makeup and fashions.

In fact, many Filipina women who had worked in local bars suggested that becoming beautiful was an exciting part of a hostess's job.[56] Married Filipina women in the region often displayed photographs in their homes of themselves dressed up and striking glamorous—and sometimes seductive—poses while at work in hostess bars. One day Victoria brought in a roll of photos she had taken of herself and her friends at a club in another prefecture where she had recently been employed. She proudly displayed photograph after photograph of herself in different outfits, lounging in booths, singing karaoke, and posing, like a fashion model, with friends. Many Filipina women in the region also enjoyed singing karaoke and took pride in their skill and talent, performing hits from U.S. American and Filipina artists: Mariah Carey, Celine Dion, Lea Salonga, and Zsa Zsa Padilla. As I mentioned earlier, when Filipina women came to Japan as talents they were hired as either singers or dancers. Competition to be a singer was fierce, and other women recognized those selected as singers as quite talented. For women in the Philippines with dreams of being professional performers, singing in clubs in Japan provided an opportunity to achieve some degree of celebrity. Even when customers were not around, these women would pay to use the karaoke box, singing solos, duets, and group numbers, applauding and encouraging each other, and acknowledging those women who were especially skillful performers.

Filipina hostess bars also provided spaces where Filipina women could exercise their entrepreneurial skills. One Filipina woman married to a man in a nearby village started a business giving facials to other women working at bars. Another sold fashionable hostessing outfits on commission. I remember one evening, before the club had opened for the night, when Rose appeared with a large plastic bag and started pulling clothes from it. An array of colorful outfits appeared—turquoise and purple miniskirts paired with jackets fastened by rhinestone-studded buttons; long red skirt-and-top sets in stretch rayon; shimmering gold and magenta evening dresses; and fitted black spandex tank tops covered with long pieces of black netting to wear over then fashionably bell-bottom, snakeskin-print pants. All the women were excited, taking the outfits from the bag one by one in their plastic covers and laying them on the booths to look at them. Victoria and Gina immediately selected outfits they liked and began trying them on in the bar, pulling the tops carefully over their heads so as not to smudge their makeup. Then they ran into the bathroom to see how they looked, while Rose yelled after them, "They're all made in Korea," a point of prestige.

In all of these ways, working in Filipina hostess bars made many Filipina women feel to some degree empowered as it shaped the ways that these women learned to relate to Japanese men, the forms of intimacy that they developed with their male customers, and ways these women came to understand these relationships. However, at the same time that hostess bars created opportunities for Filipina women to feel glamorous, fashionable, desirable, and in control of their relationships with customers, their work in these establishments was also based in deep political-economic inequalities between them and their Japanese customers, and also placed them in many vulnerable and undesirable positions as women.

Filipina women who had worked at bars in Central Kiso consistently said that their least favorite part of the job involved dealing with men who were lecherous, especially when they got drunk. These women distinguished between *sukebei* and men who were "respectful," those (often relatively few men) who were polite and treated women like people, not sexual objects. They shared how they would deal with lecherous customers who tried to grope them, either by politely telling the men that they were not "that kind of woman" or simply by saying that they did not like being touched. A few of these women said that when customers groped them they would respond by boldly grabbing the man's genitals, which caused the man to recoil in shock. However, these women also recognized that a woman's ability to maintain boundaries with customers depended both on her willingness to speak out and the support she could expect to receive from her bar management for a refusal.

Problems with lecherous customers were magnified when it came to dōhan. A number of Filipina women in Central Kiso suggested that going on dōhan could be risky, but if they had to meet a dōhan quota they had little choice in the matter. Moreover, the burden of getting a man to go on dōhan was on them. Some Filipina women relayed stories of friends who were raped when they went out on dōhan. Others spoke of consoling friends who were pressured into having sex with customers and were ashamed or distraught afterward. Dōhan was often riskiest for women who were undocumented. However, it was also risky for those on entertainer visas. In many ways, a Filipina woman's job requirements depended on the expectations of her mama-san or bar owner, who varied in their treatment of these women. If a Filipina woman did not have the support of her bar management, or if she were financially vulnerable (as most of these women, who were supporting their families in the Philippines, were to a range of degrees), she could easily find herself in uncomfortable or dangerous situations. As a result, the very pleasures these women derived from dōhan and from meeting quotas and being chosen as the number one request were also linked to their vulnerability as Filipina migrant laborers in Japan (and particularly to the limited—if any—assistance and protection the Japanese government offered them) and to anxiety surrounding the lack of complete control they had in these situations over what happened to their bodies.

Moreover, the excitement of articulating oneself as a glamorous, sexually attractive, successful, and cosmopolitan woman in bars was also tempered by these women's self-conscious feelings of anxiety and shame that bar work was immoral. The overwhelming majority of Filipina women in Central Kiso were Catholic, and religious ideas about women's sexuality informed how they viewed bar work. A number of Filipina women in Central Kiso told me that they had cried when they first came to Japan and learned what their jobs would actually entail. Even after working for many years in these bars, Filipina women in Central Kiso expressed reservations about the work.

For example, one evening before Sampagita opened, I stopped by to visit Elsa, Rose, and Victoria. The preparations for the night were complete, and we chatted as we waited for customers to arrive. I happened to notice that the statues of the Santo Niño decorating the bar had been moved to a new, more prominent spot, and that led me to ask if the statues were there to protect the bar. Elsa, who spoke English with confidence, explained that, no, the images were for decoration, "to remind us that God is with us." She added that, for protection, prayer was more important than images. She then expressed reservations about having the statues in the bar at all. "When I first came I didn't think that it was good they had them," she said, "It's like mocking God to have them in a place like this. I'm embarrassed to the Lord." Rose, who had been listening to our conversation, began to discuss her feelings with Elsa in Tagalog. She said that she too felt that "it's a sin to work in a place like this," and that she too was "embarrassed in front of God." Then Elsa started to assert in Tagalog that what was really important was having a pure heart. Anyone could go to church and go through the motions of praying, but God could see what was underneath; God knew if one's heart was pure. While Elsa and Victoria went to the bathroom to freshen up, I asked Rose what she thought. Rose had initially come to Japan as a drummer in a band. Now married to a Japanese man with a job in a construction company, she worked at a semiconductor factory during the day and occasionally at bars at night. She repeated, this time in a mix of Japanese and English, that she thought working in a bar was a sin. "Do you feel guilty about it?" I asked. "Not guilty," she maintained, "just embarrassed in front of God." "But," she added hesitantly, "it's OK to work in a place like this if you have a good reason." For example, she explained, more than 50 percent of her salary went to her family in the Philippines; that justified her working in a club. All three of the women agreed that one could justify working in a club if she were doing so for her family as opposed to for selfish reasons, for example just for oneself or to buy oneself expensive things.

RUBY'S ENTRANCE, OR THE PLEASURES AND CHALLENGES OF BEING MAMA-SAN

Ruby was known for being late, but on the night of her birthday she was uncharacteristically prompt. At exactly nine o'clock the bell in the stairwell went off, notifying us that someone was about to enter the club. A few moments later, the door to the bar slowly opened and Ruby made a grand entrance, pausing in the doorway for a moment with her left hand on her hip until she had captured our attention. Ruby was a vision in pink. She had told me a few days earlier that she had bought a new dress in Shiojiri for the party, but she had refused to describe it, telling me that it would be a big surprise. She was correct. Ruby, notorious for her flashy and outrageous clothing among other disapproving and embarrassed Filipina women in the region, had outdone herself that night in a floor-length, skin-tight, cotton candy pink, stretch-lace strapless gown with a ruffled pink lace choker attached to a revealing bustier top with four strands of white pearls that offset her cleavage. Beauty contests have a

Figure 3. Statues of the Santo Niño decorated Ruby's bar, October, 1999.

long and celebrated history in the Philippines, and I could not help but think that Ruby had crowned herself the queen of her own private pageant.[57] She sashayed into the club as we all watched, spellbound, and then she began her rounds. Her lips stretched into a wide smile as she approached the customer who had brought her the roses, now resting on the booth beside him. Greeting the man warmly with a hug, she accepted the flowers, cradling them regally in her arm. She then greeted the other customer, and finally me, thanking us graciously for coming to her party. An impromptu photo shoot followed. Ruby designated me photographer, insisting that I provide her with copies so that she could remember the night. She and the other women gathered together, striking a series of dramatic poses. Then Ruby put down her flowers and returned to her customers, taking turns talking with and attending to each, until she finally sat down with the one who had brought her the roses, drawing her body close to his as he draped his arm gently around her back.

For Ruby, Sampagita was a place where she could be a glamorous host. She liked being in charge and running her own business, and she enjoyed the prestige and status that went along with being the boss. She described the role of a mama-san as being "the leader of the bar," and "like the owner of the shop." According to Ruby, the primary difference between working as a mama-san and working as a hostess was that as a mama-san she was responsible for looking after all customers, even if they were not her own. She had to circulate through the bar, making sure that all customers were satisfied, and assist her hostesses in increasing customers' tabs. When I asked her why she had become a mama-san, she complained about working in bars run by Japanese women, grumbling about the constraints put on her: "When I was a talent it was really terrible. I had to listen to everything the mama said. 'Don't smoke around the customers. You have to sit properly, like this.' They have rules for everything," she said. She also complained about her drink-back quota. "In a week it's up to fifty, and if you don't hit it, you don't get a ¥100 per drink. For example, if you get forty-nine that's not enough, just by one, and then you don't get your bonus." Ruby explained that her frustration with the exploitation of her labor eventually drove her to open her own club: "When I was at Club Fantasy [the bar where she had been working] I really worked hard at my job. I had a lot of customers. I tried as hard as I could, but only the mama made money. I didn't make money, that's how I felt. For example, even if I had a lot of customers come, I went around, right, getting customers to drink. If they ordered a lot the mama of Club Fantasy really made a lot of money . . . but my salary, it wasn't that big. My hard work wasn't reflected in my salary." Ruby also complained that her mama-san had expected her to pay penalties for infractions that Ruby had felt were unjustified. It was at that point that Ruby had started to think about taking customers from that club and opening her own place.

Being a mama-san was one of the few jobs, apart from factory work, piecework, and hostessing, available to Filipina women in Central Kiso, and it was the only one of these that allowed the women some degree of control over their labor. For Ruby and other Filipina women, who often spoke of dreams of starting their own business, being a mama-san was a way to achieve these dreams and to access money and power. However, the knowledge of Japanese business law and the considerable bureaucracy and paperwork entailed in opening a bar in Japan, to say nothing of the capital needed, made it extremely difficult, if not impossible, for most Filipina women to start a business without the assistance of a Japanese partner. The majority of Filipina mama-sans thus attained their position through one of two methods: by marrying a Japanese man who already ran a club (often the owner of the club where she had worked as a talent), or by marrying a Japanese man and opening the bar together with him. In some of these latter cases, a Filipina woman might convince her husband to open the bar for her. Ruby's case was rather unusual among Filipina women but more common among Japanese women working in bars: she had opened her bar with the assistance of not a husband but a wealthy patron.[58] (I introduce Ruby's patron, Suzuki-san, later in the chapter.)

Among some Filipina women in Central Kiso, Ruby was known to be a generous and fun mama-san, especially when her club was doing well financially, and she invited friends to come for drinks or private parties. Her position offered her the latitude to use her bar for personal events. Although Ruby's birthday party was the first time I had gone unaccompanied to her club when it was open for business, it was neither the first nor the last social gathering that I attended at Sampagita. Ruby not infrequently held private birthday, New Year's, and good-bye parties there, including my own video-taped *sayonara* party, when after nearly two years of fieldwork I left Japan. As the economy worsened and customers became fewer and farther between, Sampagita became a setting for friendly get-togethers or just hanging out. The bar was also sometimes a site of social dramas, such as the public (and sometimes alcohol-fueled) arguments between Ruby and her employees, that created scandalous waves of gossip within the Filipina community.[59] Once, when other spaces were unavailable, I even attended a Catholic Mass there. Father Art, a Filipino priest and activist living Nagoya, led services from behind the bar, his white sacerdotal robes set off against a backdrop of highball glasses and Suntory whisky. Depending on the time of day and the occasion, my Filipina friends would sometimes bring their children, and occasionally their husbands. The children would sing karaoke and run around playing hide-and-seek behind the booths; it was always a fight to get them home to bed. There was usually food, sometimes beer, and always music and dancing.

Her recognized hospitality and generosity not withstanding, Ruby was controversial among other Filipina women in the region for the ways she managed her interpersonal relationships, her business, and her life. Ruby was ambitious. She played by her own rules, sometimes to her advantage and sometimes to her peril. Many Filipina women disapproved of the way that she lived her life, from the choices she made regarding her business, her child, and her marriage to the clothing she wore and the amount she drank. Ruby enjoyed drinking and flirting, and she frequently

Figure 4. Once, when other spaces were unavailable, Mass was held at Ruby's bar, April, 1999.

got herself into trouble on account of both. She also enjoyed shopping at discount stores in the nearest cities and wearing bright red lipstick, long painted fingernails, and tight and revealing outfits with large designer logos (which few women in Central Kiso wore at the time). She was known for making insensitive comments to other Filipina women, usually when she was drunk, and to her distress and sometimes indignation (for she rarely saw herself as in any way responsible for her interpersonal problems), she frequently found herself at the center of fights or gossip. Rumors spread that when business was slow Ruby employed unethical and "immoral" business practices, such as overcharging customers, shortchanging her staff, and engaging in prostitution. A number of Filipina women in Central Kiso told me that they thought she took things too far. They worried especially that her actions would reflect poorly upon all Filipina women in the area. These women were embarrassed by Ruby's irreverent and promiscuous behavior, bawdy comments, and flashy appearance.

Ruby was not the only controversial Filipina mama-san in town. Many Filipina women complained about other Filipina mama-sans in the region as well, asserting that these women forgot that they were "Filipina" and acted like they were above others. For example, another mama-san was notorious for being "haughty" (*mayabang*, Tg.), abusing her power, and acting like she was superior to other Filipina women simply because she was in a position of authority. One Filipina friend in Central Kiso described how she had been spited and bullied by this mama-san on numerous occasions when she was working in her bar. The mama-san had singled this woman out for not properly saying "good morning" in Japanese and had embarrassed her in front of the group by forcing her to apologize. She had also refused to let this woman sit with a certain customer, pulling and tearing her costume to get her to move and then fining her for the damaged article. The woman recounted how she had finally stood up to the mama-san, saying in Japanese, "You and I, we're the same. You think about where you came from!" She angrily explained that in her opinion some Filipina mama-sans "just want to be boss so that they can look important."

Filipina mama-sans were frequently subjects of gossip and scrutiny within the Filipina community in Central Kiso. Often rumors spread that these women were abused by their husbands, squandered their money at pachinko, were alcoholics, or had philandering husbands. (Some of these rumors were true.) In regard to this gossip, one Filipina woman told me with regret that Filipina women in Japan have a "*talangka* mentality" (crab mentality, Tg. with Eng.): Like crabs, they try to pull down those who climb to the top of the fisherman's basket. However, while some Filipina women in the region may have been jealous of the status and authority Filipina mama-sans had, others did not envy the stress and difficulty of their lives—to them, being a mama-san was in no way worth the abuse and troubles many of these women faced.

MANLY DESIRES

Suzuki-san was Ruby's business partner. A *sararīman* (literally, salary man; white-collar worker, Jpn.) at a construction company based in the area, he had sold off his retirement plan to bankroll Sampagita and make Ruby a mama-san. Suzuki-san was also rumored to be Ruby's boyfriend and the cause of her separation from her husband. A short, stocky man with thick and wavy cropped hair, he was wearing a navy blue suit and a boldly patterned red and yellow silk tie when I met him during Ruby's birthday party. That evening, Ruby asked me to keep Suzuki-san company while she tended to her customers. So I asked if he was open to an interview, a prospect that he welcomed.

"Well, I'm interested in how and why so many Filipina women have come to Central Kiso," I prompted in Japanese, poising my pen for his response.

"Business," he brusquely responded, "There aren't any jobs in the Philippines. Filipinas will do anything to work in Japan."

"But why is there a demand for Filipina workers in the region?" I pressed.

"During the bubble," Suzuki-san replied matter-of-factly, "new jobs opened up for Japanese women in Japan. They left hostessing, leaving a gap that Filipinas inevitably filled. Naturally, Japanese women are better. But Japanese women have become very scarce." Suzuki-san's explanation flowed seamlessly into a commentary on the exodus of Japanese women from rural areas and local men's interests in Filipina clubs. "In the countryside there is the problem of the bride shortage. This is why Japanese men have turned toward Filipinas. It is a common point all over the world that people want a partner. Now there are many Filipinas married to Japanese men in the area." This, he rationalized, was because of the large number of women who had come to work in bars.

"But how did Filipina women first come to this area?" I asked. At the time, I was still trying to piece together a history of Filipina bars in the region.

"There haven't been Filipinas in Kiso for very long. It's just recently that a large number have been coming," he explained.

"Why?" I pressed.

Suzuki-san restated his point: "Kiso is *inaka* [the countryside]. A time ago there were many Japanese hostesses here, but they went away. Economic times are hard now, so many people are unemployed, but a little while ago, during the bubble, there were jobs everywhere, so Japanese women opted for those instead of hostessing. There are hardly any Japanese hostesses left. A while back brokers came and introduced Filipinas to places throughout Nagano. There wasn't any other choice but to have them come."

As I discussed earlier, Allison has suggested that in hostess bars Japanese men are not paying for sex but to be made to feel like powerful and desirable men. She demonstrates that hostess bars play an important role in constructing a certain kind of masculine subjectivity in Japan: that of a powerful male who can buy a woman to serve him. Allison's conclusions are based on her fieldwork in an elite hostess bar in Tokyo. She describes how, for urban Japanese white-collar men who are emasculated in their work environments, hostess bars are important sites for rearticulating masculine and class-based identities. However, Allison also cites a union organizer who explains that cheap cabarets and other forms of *mizu shōbai* entertainment are popular among blue-collar workers in part because "they see the big dignitaries on the nights of important union meetings indulging" in the pleasures provided at these places.[60] She explains that as hostess bars catering to lower paid workers have become widespread throughout Japan, they have become places where "everyman" can come to be made to feel like an important, powerful man.

I would add that the ways Japanese men in Central Kiso experienced hostess bars were shaped not only by class but also race, nationality, and geography. Beginning in the 1960s and through at least the early 1990s, the figure of the sararīman—the middle-class and usually urban white-collar worker—came to define modern Japanese masculinity. A few men who dated or married Filipina women in Central Kiso had white-collar jobs or owned businesses (a green grocery, a soba restaurant, a construction company). However, as I mentioned, most of them worked in construction or at pachinko parlors or bars. All of these men lived in a politically and economically marginalized region of rural Japan. Moreover, many Filipina women's husbands were ten to twenty-five years older than them and past the *tekireiki* (the "suitable age for marriage," Jpn.), when they met the women they married. These men hardly fit privileged images of masculinity in Japan.

Filipina hostess bars offered these men opportunities to articulate an elite, class-based form of Japanese masculinity, regardless of the fact that they lived in a peripheral region of Japan and, in many cases, did low-status work. Moreover, these bars enabled the men to feel worldly and important by exposing them to a foreign culture that they viewed as inferior to their own. Consider how Suzuki-san positioned himself as an authority on both Filipina and Japanese women—a competent judge of their class and quality. In doing so, he also suggested that he was an expert on Filipino and Japanese cultures. Moreover, by describing Filipina women as inferior to Japanese women ("Naturally, Japanese women are better") and thus less desirable, he asserted Japan's superiority to the Philippines and presented himself as cultivated, wealthy, and powerful on account of his self-identification as a "Japanese man." In these bars, these men could feel superior on account of both their masculinity *and* their Japaneseness. They could identify as Japanese men who possessed the knowledge and the standards by which national cultures could be evaluated, the wealth and power to pay for Filipina women's services, and the global vision to enjoy them.

The ways that Filipina hostess bars made Central Kiso men feel like worldly, wealthy, superior, modern, and elite Japanese men, may have in fact contributed to why some men found Filipina women working in bars appealing girlfriends and wives. Recall Tanaka-san's comments (discussed in the introduction to part 1) regarding why he decided to marry his Filipina wife. Like Tanaka-san, a number of Filipina women's husbands in Central Kiso said that they were attracted to Filipina women because these women "came from a poor country," and thus were "submissive" and had "the good qualities that Japanese women have lost." Moreover, as I suggested, in these bars Filipina women learned to please and accommodate their Japanese customers, serving them drinks and food, encouraging them in their jobs, flattering them, and being affectionate with them. These qualities may have also made the women appealing as potential spouses. Of course, not all husbands of Filipina women expressed such sentiments. One man spoke of the deep respect and affection he felt for his wife, explaining that, unlike other couples, they were not simply physically but also spiritually bonded.[61] Another told me he was looking for someone who he felt would be "a good partner." However, like Tanaka-san, a number of these men were looking for marriages with women whom they believed (not necessarily accurately) they could control or would be dependent on them.

However, while these articulations of Japanese masculinity seemed to add to a man's stature, they also revealed local men's self-consciousness of their marginality relative to white-collar men in urban regions of Japan. Like Suzuki-san, many men in Central Kiso described Filipina women who worked at local bars as less desirable than Japanese women and even less attractive than Filipina women in Tokyo. When I asked one local man, who boasted that he both frequented local Filipina bars and made annual trips to the Philippines to play golf and patronize bars there, why men in the area liked Filipina women, he responded abruptly, "They don't." He explained that there weren't any bars with Japanese women in town; Filipina hostess bars were the only option. The men did not have a choice. This man asserted that he regularly went to the Philippines and had been exposed to many Filipina women. In fact, he explained, on account of the fact that Kiso was in the countryside, the Filipina women at local bars were ugly when compared with those he had met at bars in Tokyo. I asked this man why, then, were there so many successful Filipina clubs in town? The man explained that Kisofukushima was just a small town, implying that there was little else to do but visit bars. Then he added that the Filipina women employed at these bars come and go every six months, and therefore the women were always "fresh" *(furesshu).* When prodded, he also told me that Filipina women had a reputation among Japanese men for being cute and sexy; they were known for having attractive figures and long legs, in particular. Moreover, he added, these days, their dark skin was considered fashionable and sexy. He mentioned a trend in urban areas in Japan in which different groups of young (often high school–aged) women frequented tanning salons or used creams to darken their skin.[62]

Similarly, Suzuki-san told me that hostess bars began hiring Filipina women in Kiso because "there wasn't any other choice but to have them come." He explained that during Japan's economic bubble, Japanese women had opted to leave jobs at hostess bars in the area to find better jobs in cities. Suzuki-san also connected this trend to the "bride shortage," the absence of Japanese women interested in marrying local men. He suggested that in both of these cases, modernization had made men in Central Kiso undesirable patrons and husbands for Japanese women and forced these men to turn to Filipina women.

In saying that Filipina women had inevitably replaced Japanese women in local bars, these men could not separate their assertions of cosmopolitan masculinity tied to Japanese modernity and affluence from their sensitivity to the region's marginality vis-à-vis places like Tokyo. Just as Filipina bars were places where rural and blue-collar men could be made to feel like worldly, desirable, and affluent Japanese men, these men's experiences in these bars rested upon the fact that rural and working-class men were in fact considered undesirable partners by urban (and sometimes local) Japanese woman in part because of their occupations and geographic location. Most patrons of the Tokyo bar that Allison describes were married, and few of the elite men who patronized such establishments would have considered marrying a Japanese woman who had worked in a hostess bar. In contrast, I was told that many Japanese men in rural areas had few marriage prospects outside the bars. Japanese residents in Central Kiso viewed Filipina women as available to men from a "wealthy" and "modern" country like Japan. Thus local men's assertions of their masculinity in these bars were also shaped by their self-consciousness regarding the region's positioning within Japan, and specifically the ways that the very political-economic processes that contributed to the establishment of hostess bars in Central Kiso have marginalized people there. I return to this point in chapter 3. Here, however,

I want to suggest that, for both Japanese customers and Filipina migrants, the contradictions and ambivalences through which these bars developed prompted unexpected outcomes.

ON BARS AND MARRIAGE

Although attitudes among young people in Japan have recently been changing, for many years social adulthood was believed to begin with marriage.[63] Men in Central Kiso faced considerable social pressure to marry before hitting an age ceiling (which at one time was thirty but has been gradually inching upward). Some local residents told me that an unmarried man over the age of thirty-five seemed irresponsible, as if he were unwilling to take on the responsibility of a wife and children. Others said that if a man was still unmarried in his late thirties, people began to suspect that "something was wrong with him." One young woman told me that men in the region felt pressure to marry so that others would not think they were "gay" *(gei),* suggesting prevalent homophobic attitudes in the area. My friend Tessie's husband's cousin maintained one evening during a casual dinner at his home that marriage was an obligation, not a choice.

Although I was told that in the past local men had rarely married Japanese women who worked in local hostess clubs, in the 1980s and 1990s Filipina hostess bars became places where a number of men in Central Kiso came to find companionship, potential girlfriends and wives, and in some cases romance and love. For example, one Filipina friend told me that her husband's brother had spent a lot of time at a local bar because, seeing how well his brother's marriage to her had turned out, he too had been "looking for a Filipina" to marry. In fact, a number of men in the region attended Filipina clubs expressly in search of a spouse.

Although Filipina women in Central Kiso told me that they had not planned to marry a Japanese man when they first came to Japan as an entertainer, these women soon learned that some of their Japanese customers might be looking for serious relationships. Moreover, as I have suggested, courtship, romance, and love became important frameworks through which many of these women learned to make sense of their relationships with men they met in hostess bars.[64] Many Filipina women described how their husbands had courted them while they worked in bars, and how their feelings of affection for these men had grown, in part because of the men's persistence. As I later discuss, for many of these women, marrying a Japanese man offered new opportunities for both fulfilling dreams of romance and family, and crafting socially legitimate lives and selves in Japan.

As sites of encounter, then, these bars were more than capitalist spaces of labor and consumption. Rather, they were spaces where differently situated agendas and forms of desire came together through the intimacies of everyday practice, creating new possibilities and constraints for Filipina migrants and Japanese men in Central Kiso. These bars became such spaces on account of the overlaps and gaps that formed as histories of cultural dance performance and sex tourism in the Philippines converged with those through which hostess bars have developed, rural areas have been marginalized, and rural women's desires for their lives have changed in Japan. The coming together of these histories shaped Filipina women's and their Japanese customers' ambivalent and unequal experiences in these bars. For Filipina women, hostess bars offered worlds both of shame and anxiety and of glamour and possibility. These women felt vulnerable and exploited in these bars; however, they also sometimes felt clever, glamorous, and desirable. Similarly, just as these bars reminded local Japanese men of their exclusions from dominant discourses of modern Japanese masculinity that centered on participation in urban, white-collar, and middle-class worlds, they offered these men new opportunities to feel like worldly, affluent, modern, and powerful Japanese men. In this sense, these bars offered important spaces in which different historically shaped experiences and forms of desire came into unequal and productive relation. Marriages between Filipina migrants and Central Kiso men were one form these relations took.

CHAPTER 2

America and Other Stories of Filipina Migration to Japan

What kind of journey is desire that its direction is so deceptive?

Judith Butler, Subjects of Desire

Cora, Ana, and I were sipping tea at a small coffee shop beside the high-way when Cora suddenly sighed. Glancing around the restaurant's tired interior and out the window at the nearby mountains, she explained, "I never thought that I would marry a, what do you call it, a *probinsyado*" (a hick, Tg.). Then she and Ana began chuckling. "You too?" Cora asked Ana in Tagalog. Ana nodded knowingly. I had heard Cora and Ana make similar comments before. During an interview at my home a few months earlier, I had asked them about their expectations for their lives when they came to Japan as entertainers in the 1980s. "I didn't think I would wind up living in a place like this that's really in the boonies, where there is nothing but mountains," Ana had explained. Cora had agreed, "I never thought that I'd wind up living in the countryside. It never really crossed my mind. I couldn't even picture it. But I also never thought that I would marry a Japanese man."

During another interview toward the end of my stay in Central Kiso, Cora told me about her life in the Philippines and why she had decided to go to Japan as a migrant laborer. She explained that at the time, her father was unemployed and her family could afford to eat only a few days a week. Cora's uncle had worked as a performer at resorts in Japan during the 1970s, and he had recruited and trained her to go as an entertainer. Cora had met her husband a week after coming to Central Kiso on her second six-month contract. (She had been assigned to work at a bar in the region by her promotion agency; her first six-month assignment had been in Tokyo). She explained that although she had not been romantically interested in her husband at first, she had grown to love him after he courted her for more than five months, frequently requesting her at the bar where she worked and taking her out on her two free Sundays a month to church and dinner in Matsumoto, a nearby regional city. (Cora's husband was not Catholic; he waited in the car while she attended Mass.) When Cora's husband proposed marriage, Cora told him that she was committed to financially helping her family in the Philippines. She explained that although she loved him, she would marry him only if he would support this commitment. Cora's husband agreed to this condition, and they married soon after her contract ended.

Ana had also met her husband when she was assigned by her promotion agency to work at a bar in Central Kiso. She told me that she first started dating him in an effort to get over another man who had jilted her during her previous contract in Nagoya. Her husband had gotten her pregnant, and a few years later, after she had returned to the Philippines and had the baby, they had a *"dekichatta kekkon"* (shotgun wedding, Jpn.). Ana told me that she had initially come to Japan after failing her licensing exam at a technical school in the Philippines. A friend had suggested going as an entertainer, but Ana had not expected that she would be working in bars. "I knew we had dance and singing rehearsals, but I didn't think it would be a place like that," she explained. She told me that before she had left for Japan, she had not thought carefully about what she would be doing there. She had only thought of her excitement about finally traveling abroad. "I was like a child," she reflected. "Am I really going?! Am I really going?! That's all I could think about."

I asked Ana how she had imagined Japan before she first came. "I thought Japan would be different from the Philippines," she replied in Japanese. She then switched to English, "I thought that, like America, it would be . . . what is the word? Very 'modern.'"

"You mean like New York or Los Angeles?" I asked for clarification. I knew that she had never been to the United States, and I was trying to get a sense of how she had imagined it.

"Exactly!" she replied. "I thought that it would be like that. I pictured Japan modern-style. I thought it was like America. When I came to Central Kiso, I was like 'What?! What's this?!' There was nothing but mountains. There was nowhere to go out. I've been to the Philippine countryside. It's like this. But I didn't think there were places like that still in Japan."

If Filipina hostess bars in Central Kiso offered sites of encounter that enabled marriages between Filipina migrants and local Japanese men,

Filipina women's experiences in these bars, and in the region more generally, were also informed by the desires and expectations that had
brought them to Japan. Transnational labor migration is not just a
means of managing political-economic marginality. It is also about the
imaginative dreams and pleasures that can be found abroad.[1] Yet how
do people make sense of migration experiences that bring them to places
they never imagined—much less dreamed—they would find themselves?

Because of the temporariness of their job contracts and visas, every Filipina woman in Central Kiso with whom I spoke said that she had not expected to remain in Japan for long when she first came as a labor migrant.
Moreover, every one of those women who had met her husband while
working at a hostess bar in Central Kiso insisted that she had not
planned to marry a Japanese man when she went abroad. Most of these
women told me that they had boyfriends in the Philippines at the time and
plans to return home. They offered reasons ranging from love to pregnancy.
to political-economic considerations (and usually some combination of the
three) to explain why they had decided to marry their Japanese husbands.[2]
However, even those women who told me that they loved their husbands
and had developed good relationships with their in-laws expressed at least
some degree of ambivalence, reservation, or frustration with their lives in
rural Nagano. Many of these women described Central Kiso as an unplanned destination. They expressed surprise, and even wonder, to find
themselves living in rural Nagano married to Japanese men.

In this chapter, I focus on the narratives these women told about the
migration paths that brought them to their lives in Central Kiso. Specifically, I consider how their commentaries about their past lives in the
Philippines and their dreams of traveling to "America" shaped the ways
these women understood their experiences in the region and their place
in the world. My aims are twofold. First, in focusing on the ways these
women described the dreams that prompted them to go abroad, I mean
to evoke how migration involved at once experiential and narrative practices of self-making for them. I take inspiration here from Mary Steedly
who uses the expression "narrative experience" to evoke the ways that
stories and experience are coproduced in everyday life.[3] Steedly tells us
that stories do not simply express life experience; they are themselves lived
out, structuring imaginations and assuming flesh and quotidian form.
Steedly focuses on narratives as part of the ongoing, dialogic, and
constrained ways that people selectively make and remake the past as they
craft lives and selves in the present. Here I extend Steedly's notion to consider not only how Filipina migrants in Central Kiso narrated personal

histories as they crafted lives and selves, but also how the dreams they imagined for their futures shaped their everyday lives.

Second, by focusing on how discourses of America figured in the ways Filipina women described their migration to rural Japan, I suggest that their migration experiences cannot be understood simply in terms of binaries of home and abroad, or travel and dwelling, that scholars have previously used to understand migrants' lives.[4] Such models have been useful for identifying the ways that migrants live in worlds shaped by forms of both movement and stasis. They have also helped us understand the ambivalent ways that they craft lives between nation-states. However, such approaches overlook the multiple and relational geographic imaginings that inform migrants' understandings of movement and place. As I argued in the previous chapter, Filipina women's decisions to go to Japan as entertainers were forged against the backdrop of (simultaneously) cultural and political-economic relations involving people in Japan, the Philippines, and the United States. Correspondingly, these three countries did not exist independently in these women's imaginations. They occupied shifting and relative positions in the itineraries of these women's dreams. By paying attention to how these relational geographies informed the women's understandings of their lives in rural Nagano, I mean to explore migration not as means to an end or as a directed (or back-and-forth) movement, but as part of a broader process of continuing on—a segment along the routes some people travel as they endeavor to realize their dreams.

As I discuss the ways that relational imaginings of Japan, the Philippines, and the United States shaped these women's migration experiences, I also gesture toward how their narratives reflected larger sets of relations through which our lives (theirs and mine) were imbricated. Much debate has surrounded the question of how ethnographers should position themselves in their texts. As I have suggested, my strategy is to draw attention to the ways that my ethnographic relationships were themselves part of the zone of encounters—that translocal web of relations among people in Japan, the Philippines, and the United States—that I map in this book.

In what follows, I first explore the stories that Filipina women in Central Kiso, and one woman named Tessie in particular, told about their decisions to leave the Philippines and go to Japan as entertainers. Then, I look to the ways that Filipina women in Central Kiso spoke of America as a figure of desires shaping their decisions not only to go to but also to remain in Japan. I conclude that when situated in relation to these two sets of desires, Central Kiso appeared to many of these women as a way station along the road to a better future—somewhere they found themselves stuck as they made their way from a place they were trying to leave behind to one they dreamed of reaching.

THE PHILIPPINES (STORIES TO LEAVE BEHIND)

I'll begin, then, with Tessie and what she called her "story" as she relayed it to me one night. Many Filipina women in Central Kiso referred to accounts of why they or other women came to Japan—narratives of their former lives in the Philippines and their reasons for leaving—as their "stories." Even when speaking Japanese or Tagalog, they used the English word with me to mean a woman's autobiography, or "the story of one's life" (*kwento/istorya ng buhay,* Tg.). These stories were most frequently associated with disappointment, tragedy, or despair. They were narratives of a difficult or sorrowful life in the Philippines that had forced women to leave. Yet just as stories suggested pasts full of hardship and suffering, they also gestured toward these women's dreams of transforming their lives and leaving those pasts behind.

I had known Tessie for nearly fourteen months when she first told me her story. I found that although Filipina women in Central Kiso seemed to assume that every Filipina woman in the region had a story, most women did not readily share their personal histories, even among themselves. One woman declined my request for an interview, explaining that it was too painful to talk about her life in the Philippines. She said that doing so brought back memories she preferred to forget. Even Tessie, who was frequently the confidante of other Filipina women in the region, told me that she knew the backgrounds of few Filipina women in Central Kiso, only of her closest friends, and then sometimes only select details. Just as many Filipina women in the region were reluctant to reveal details of their current lives, they were concerned that they might be judged critically or disparaged by others if their pasts were known. They were averse to becoming the subject of *tsismis* (rumors or gossip, Tg.), and they felt that personal information could be dangerous if it traveled into the wrong hands. For many of these women, coming to Japan was a means to reinvent themselves and find a new beginning, in part by distancing themselves from the life they had left behind.

Like Tessie, some of the Filipina women I knew best in the region did eventually share their stories with me. Other women offered selected details about their lives in the Philippines and why they had come to Japan. These details sometimes changed. I often learned about the personal histories of Filipina women in the region in the same way as I learned about current happenings from them: by matching up details and fitting sound bites together like puzzle pieces. Some of these women immediately or unexpectedly shared information with me because I was not Filipina and therefore understood to be in some sense outside the group and thus not viewed to be a threat as a *"tsismosa"* (a gossip, Tg.). Others said that they did not mind telling me things because I would be writing about people anonymously and my work would be published in English, in the United States, and several years in the future. However, as I will discuss later in this chapter, some of these women were embarrassed to speak with me about their pasts precisely because I was from the United States.

To some degree, Tessie's story fits a familiar mode of storytelling in the Philippines about the tragedies and familial commitments that lead people to seek a better life abroad.[5] It also resonates with reasons for Filipina migration to Japan that have been discussed by other researchers.[6] However, in relaying Tessie's story, I do not intend for it to stand as an explanation for why all Filipina women in Central Kiso went to Japan as entertainers or as emblematic of all of these women's lives in the Philippines. If anything, Tessie stressed in her story how personal circumstance was an important factor motivating her decision to work abroad. Or in Cora's words, "Everyone's story is different."

Rather, in suggesting that Tessie's story conformed to broader narrative genres, I mean to situate it within the intertwined ethnographic, social, and political-economic contexts that shaped both these women's lives and their narrative strategies. As I discuss later, working in hostess bars in Japan was highly stigmatized. This stigma shaped not only the migration decisions these women made but also the stories they told about them. Moreover, when these women interacted with me, they were very sensitive to the relative privilege of my life in the United States and my status as a researcher. More than straightforward explanations of these women's migration routes, their stories reflected how these women had learned to see their lives in the Philippines and who they wanted to be in Japan, in the world, and in their relationships with me.

A DREAM OF ESCAPE, OR TESSIE'S STORY

I first met Tessie through Cora, who brought me to Tessie's house one afternoon soon after I had moved to the region. I immediately liked her. Like Cora, she was a leader who had a restless energy and a strong sense of self. Over the course of the first year I knew Tessie, she shared something of how she had come to meet and marry her husband. She told me, for example, that her husband had been a customer at a local bar where she had been assigned for her third six-month contract as an entertainer (as a "third-timer," as Filipina women I knew would say). Tessie also told me that she had not planned to marry a Japanese man when she first came to Japan in 1984 and that she had dated her husband for nearly three years, thinking long and hard before she accepted his marriage proposal. His parents had objected to his marrying a Filipina, she explained, and she had refused to marry him unless he promised her a separate residence from theirs. She told him that she was not going to live with his parents "if they don't want me." However, it was not until a night more than a year after I had begun fieldwork in Central Kiso that Tessie shared the details of her story with me.

It was a crisp evening in mid-autumn, after the rice had been harvested and the leaves had started to change, but before the apple trees were divested of their prized fruit. Tessie and I were sitting in the living room of her house, chatting while she ironed and folded the laundry. I watched as she carefully pressed her children's underwear, folding them into neat squares. Tessie was meticulous and methodical in everything she did. Scrupulous about her appearance, she favored neatly pressed slacks and polo shirts, and she wore her fashionably cut hair short and sometimes dyed a deep red or golden brown. She didn't like to be idle and would think up projects for herself when nothing else was at hand. Before her husband bought her a car, when she spent long days alone in her home in the countryside, she would occupy herself by redecorating the living room, moving around furniture, rehanging wedding portraits, and sewing new curtains and pillows modeled after pictures in a worn copy of *Better Homes and Gardens* her sister had sent her from the Philippines. I used to tease Tessie that every time I came over (which was often several times a week) I entered a different house. Soon after she learned to drive, Tessie took on a part-time job at a local ballpoint pen factory to fill her days, working late into the night to clean her house and do the laundry. "I want to keep busy," she would tell me in Japanese. "I hate being cooped up in the house all day."

That evening, Tessie's husband had taken their children up to bed, leaving us to discuss her ongoing project: together with Cora and the assistance of Sister Ruth, a Filipina missionary and (self-described) Marxist-feminist activist who ran a shelter for Filipina migrants in Nagano City (the prefectural capital about three hours away), Tessie was trying to organize Filipina women in the region into a group. Both Cora and Tessie were devout

Catholics and grassroots activists. Their faith in God and their commitment to serving him by helping others had motivated them to organize prayer meetings aimed at bringing Filipina women in the area together in worship and mutual support. Through their connections with Sister Ruth, the two women had developed reputations for coming to the assistance of Filipina women in the area who were having problems. They were trying to build on their experience assisting others to develop a local organization that could work for the rights of Filipina women in the region.

Tessie and I talked about the challenges of Filipina women's lives in Central Kiso and of organizing them. We began discussing many of these women's desires to work in bars so that they could support their families in the Philippines. Some Filipina women in Central Kiso, I knew, had come from poor families in rural areas, often from provinces near Metro Manila: Laguna, Cavite, Pangasinan, Bulacan, Bicol, and Rizal. Recently, another Filipina woman Tessie and I knew had estimated that at the very least half of the Filipina women in Central Kiso had grown up in what women called "squatter areas," communities of urban poor who did not own the land on which they lived.[7]

I asked Tessie if what this woman had told me was true. She suddenly grew silent. "To tell you the truth," she said with hesitation and, I sensed, some embarrassment, "we were a kind of squatter." I knew that Tessie had grown up in San Juan on the other side of Smokey Mountain. I had heard her speak in the past with a mixture of grief and disgust about the notorious garbage dump where people survived on the refuse. Going home from work every day, she would recall, the stench alone was insufferable. However, she had never said much else about her life in the Philippines and why she had come to Japan. Based on Tessie's middle-class sensibilities and her allusions to the then stable finances of her family in the Philippines, I had assumed that she was from a relatively secure economic background. I had imagined that, like the few middle-class Filipina women I had met in Tokyo who had worked as entertainers, she had come to Japan to find independence or adventure or to escape problems at home.[8] That night, however, I learned that my assumptions about Tessie's socioeconomic background had been wrong. Her voice inflected with both pain and pride, prodded by my questions and pausing toward the end to allow me to record notes, Tessie told me her story in a mix of English, Tagalog, and Japanese. It went something like this:

Tessie was the second eldest of five girls. When she was a child, her family lived in a house in San Juan. It was just a small concrete structure with a corrugated tin roof, and her family had not owned the land on which it was built. But it was their own home, she stressed. San Juan was OK then. But as she grew up, she told me with a pained expression, all around her house, shacks and ramshackle dwellings began to appear, sometimes overnight. She just could not figure out where all the people had come from. Now, she lamented, San Juan was a mess, full of drugs and gangs. What was more, "Erap" Estrada, who was then president of the Philippines, had been mayor of San Juan when she was growing up, but he had done nothing to help her community. He had reneged on his promise to give the land to those who had long made it their home, and who had nowhere else to go. That was why, Tessie explained, she and everyone she knew from San Juan disliked Erap.

Tessie's father had been a seaman. He had met her mother in Manila, where both had moved from their home provinces to find work. One evening before her father was scheduled to go aboard ship, he went out drinking with some friends. Before he went to sleep that night, he took some sleeping medicine, as he commonly did, perhaps misjudging the dosage because he had been drinking. Tessie was only ten years old at the time, and she did not remember the details well. What she did remember is that her father went to sleep but did not wake up. She explained that he remained comatose for two days before finally, in a panic, her mother took him to a hospital. At the hospital, the doctors told her mother he needed brain surgery. Her mother refused to allow them to perform it, suspecting they were only after money. At a second hospital, doctors electrically stimulated her father's heart and he awoke, but he was not quite the same. Tessie suggested that he had suffered some brain damage. He could still talk and communicate, but he could no longer really work, at least not on a ship.

At that point, Tessie's father took up tailoring, setting up a small shop in front of their home. However, his income was no longer sufficient to support their family. Soon they had to sell their belongings—first their stereo, then their television, and later even their furniture—just to have money to eat. Tessie's mother started working at a nearby convent, cleaning and helping with the cooking. Tessie's father passed away a few years later, leaving her mother alone to care for Tessie and her four sisters. At that time, Tessie also cleaned at the convent, receiving a small work scholarship so that she and her sisters could finish high school. It was very, very difficult, she stressed. She did not have any friends during high school because she was so busy working.

After she finished high school, Tessie hoped to attend college. For several years she took classes part-time while working three days a week as a salesperson at Greenhills Mall, a popular mall in Metro Manila.[9] (She spoke with longing, and some bitterness, of the women from the wealthy nearby subdivisions who would come in to shop.) Midway through Tessie's studies, her elder sister, who was supposed to work and help support Tessie's schooling, eloped with her boyfriend, sabotaging Tessie's plans to finish college. At that time, Tessie's younger sisters were taking dance classes so that they could go to Japan, and Tessie's mother pushed Tessie to accompany them. She argued that Tessie was older and stronger than her sisters and should go to look after them. Believing that they had little chance of finding living-wage jobs in the Philippines without college degrees, Tessie and her sisters had devised a plan: they would work in Japan and save their money, staying just long enough to build a small house in another part of Manila.

Tessie and her sisters were conservative with their earnings, and they accomplished their goals. They pooled their money and bought a small duplex in Manila, where two of her sisters and their families lived, and a mini-mart with an apartment on top that her mother and youngest sister managed. "It's just a small business," Tessie explained, but it was enough to provide her mother and sisters with a modest living and enough extra money to help out those in their community who were in greater need. (At the time of my primary research, Tessie was the only one of her sisters living in Japan. However, a few years later, her youngest sister also married a Japanese man living in Osaka, and her mother began managing the store alone.) Tessie was proud of her family's accomplishments. She spoke again about San Juan and the sorrowful lives of those who live there. Then she shook her head in dismay, "In the squatters so many get married so early." "Because they get pregnant?" I asked for clarification. "There are so many," she said, this time shaking her head and adding with vigorous affirmation, "You have to be so careful. You really have to watch yourself." And then after a thoughtful pause, "But if you have just a little dream or ambition, maybe [you] will not do that. . . . Not a big dream . . . just to escape from that lifestyle."

Tessie's story was a narrative of labor migration to Japan as a route to a better future for herself and her family in the Philippines. In her story, she highlighted the ways that going abroad as an entertainer enabled her to help her family find financial stability and new opportunities for their lives. Tessie also presented herself as a certain kind of person in her story. First, in relaying her reasons for going to Japan, Tessie presented herself as a woman with a dream and the determination to realize it. She spoke

critically of both the Philippine government, which reneged on its promises
to grant land to her community, and her elder sister, who foiled her educational aspirations by eloping with her boyfriend. Despite these disappointments, Tessie and her younger sisters devised a successful plan to help her
family move out of San Juan. Through hard work in Japan and disciplined
saving, they had purchased homes and a business in the Philippines.

Second, in narrating her story, Tessie not only identified herself as an
ambitious, determined, and disciplined woman who fulfilled her goals, but
also as a dutiful and responsible daughter and sister. She described her ini-
tial decision to go to Japan as a matter of following her mother's request.
She explained that she had not planned to work to Japan, but that she decided to go only after her mother asked her to accompany her younger sisters and watch over them. Going to Japan was a means of fulfilling certain kinship obligations, obeying her mother, and fulfilling her role as an
elder sister. Tessie also told me that she went to Japan because she suspected that her mother was tired of cleaning for a living, and she wanted
her to be able to retire. At the time of our interview, Tessie still supported
her mother and sisters by working in a factory and doing piecework at
home, sending money to the Philippines every month to help tide them
over. (When I visited her in 2005, 2006, and 2007, she was still sending
money home.) She also sent and brought home enormous boxes of household and personal products—nylons, chocolates, towels, electronic equipment, coffee, clothing, and toys—which allowed her family in the Philippines to live with some of the material comforts that she enjoyed in Japan.

JAPAYUKISAN

I do not want to imply that Tessie misrepresented herself, or that her commitment to her family was insincere. However, I want to draw attention
to the ways that by framing her migration decision as a means of following a dream of helping her family, Tessie's story offered a self-conscious
counternarrative to negative images of Filipina women in Japan. At the
time of my primary fieldwork, Filipina women who went to Japan to
work in hostess bars were pejoratively called (in both Japan and the
Philippines) *japayuki* or *japayukisan*.[10] Literally in Japanese "one who
has traveled to Japan," the expression was first popularized in Japan by
Tetsuo Yamatani, a Japanese freelance writer and documentary film-
maker, who used it in his 1983 film *Japayukisan: Tōnan Ajia kara no
dekasegi shōfutachi* (Japayukisan: Migrant Prostitutes from Southeast
Asia). Yamatani later published two widely read books on the subject:

Japayukisan (1985) and the later revised edition *Japayukisan: onnatachi no Ajia* (Japayukisan: Women's Asia) (1992), both of which have gone through multiple printings, including one of the latter text in 2005.[11]

Yamatani's work, as indicated by the title of his film, focused sensationally on one group of migrant women from Southeast Asia who worked in the sex industry in Japan. However, he suggested their experiences represented those of all Southeast Asian women there. Yamatani meant to draw attention to the exploitation of these women on account of unequal relations between Japan and their countries of origin. However, he made this point in part by arguing that the large number of migrant women coming to Japan from the Philippines stood as testimony to the Philippines' lagging modernity. His very use of the term *japayukisan* reflects this claim. The expression recalls the *karayukisan* (literally "one who has traveled to China"), those Japanese women who from the late nineteenth to early twentieth century were sent abroad as prostitutes to financially assist their natal families and further the nascent Japanese state's development efforts.[12] Yamatani's use of the term *japayukisan* thus rested on the idea that, because Filipina migrants in Japan were helping support the Philippine economy, and because the Philippine government endorsed their work in sex industries abroad, the state of the Philippines in the 1980s paralleled that of Japan in the late nineteenth and early twentieth centuries: the Philippines (and correspondingly its citizens) was stuck in a stage of development that Japan had long advanced beyond.

During the 1980s and 1990s, the term *japayukisan* widely came to be associated in Japan with foreign women, and especially Filipina women, who traveled through both licit and illicit channels to work in hostess bars and perform other forms of sexualized labor. Despite laws in Japan prohibiting entertainer visa holders from engaging in commercial sexual relations (and the fact that many did not), popular media often suggested that all Filipina women in Japan were prostitutes and thus immoral, opportunistic, backwards, greedy, desperate, and criminal.

In the Philippines, too, women who went to Japan to work as entertainers were widely viewed as immoral and desperate: willing to do anything for money. As one Filipina woman from an upper-middle-class background whom I met in Tokyo explained, "Nice Catholic school-bred girls don't go to Japan." Another Filipina woman I met in Central Kiso told me that she could not return to her hometown in Mindanao because she had worked in bars in Japan. She was branded in her community. This woman told me that if she returned to the Philippines, she planned to live in Manila, far from her family and community. A different Filipina friend explained that there was a social stigma attached to working at a bar in Japan that marked the entire family and affected a woman's future chances for marriage. When I visited the Philippines with Ligaya—one of the few women I knew in Central Kiso who had met her husband through a marriage broker and who claimed that she would never set foot in a hostess bar—her niece Mely summed things up things succinctly: "The reputation of *japayukis* here is not very good; they are thought of as prostitutes." Ligaya's other relatives qualified their similar remarks, explaining that not all women who go are "like that," that it "depended on the woman." However, Mely, whose father had worked for years in Saudi Arabia to send his daughters through college, dismissively added, "Most *japayukis* go to Japan because they want to marry a rich Japanese." She explained that these women think that they will be able to help their families in the Philippines by doing so. Gesturing to a small *sari-sari* store in the neighborhood, Mely told me that some women who went to Japan to work as entertainers were successful: they were able to save money and could open their own businesses when they came home. But when I asked if she, her sisters, or her cousins, who then worked in offices or as nurses and physical therapists, had ever thought of going, they all shook their heads in horror. They said that they didn't even have friends who had gone.[13]

All Filipina women I knew in Central Kiso were aware of the stigmas associated with bar work, and these stigmas undoubtedly shaped the stories they told about their past and present lives. I noticed, for example, that when Filipina women in Central Kiso relayed elements of their personal histories, they usually stressed that going to Japan as an entertainer was a choice of last resort or that they were only partially informed about the work they would be doing there. Many of these women also described tragic and unexpected events that had forced them to go abroad to find a better future, sometimes drawing attention to their decisions in dramatic ways. Cora, for instance, requested that we have "background music"—a mixed tape of ballads and love songs—playing as she recounted her story to me. The tragic and dramatic tone of these stories undoubtedly reflected significant elements of the women's experiences. They certainly reflected the fact that these women found aspects of their jobs in hostess bars oppressive and demeaning. In the previous chapter, I explained that they often complained about lecherous customers who sometimes sexually accosted and even raped them. They also described exploitative or unsupportive bosses. Yet even when these women suggested that they found enjoyment and satisfaction in their work in bars, or simply enjoyed the possibilities of independence, freedom, romance, beauty, and modernity it promised, they found it difficult to speak of these pleasures without qualification. These women instead focused on the dreams of helping their families that, they explained, had inspired them to take these jobs, the disappointments they found in them, and the determination that had inspired them to leave the Philippines and look for something better abroad.

AMERICA (THE POSSIBILITIES OF TRAVEL)

The stories Filipina women told about their migration decisions thus suggest that they viewed going to Japan as an entertainer in two conflicting ways. On one hand, it was a compromised move when viewed in the context of the stigma attached to bar work, and the difficulties of it when compared to other forms of work for which women in the Philippines went abroad, such as nursing. These other labor migration routes were generally not available to women from their socioeconomic and educational backgrounds. On the other hand, going to Japan offered an appealing, and even glamorous and exciting possibility for trying to realize dreams of a better life for themselves and their families in the Philippines.

Yet if Filipina women in Central Kiso regularly discussed desires to help their families back home, and most of them spoke of missing aspects of their lives there (and even had hopes of returning), their dreams for their futures did not necessarily focus on the Philippines per se. As Tessie's story suggests, many Filipina women in Central Kiso also spoke critically about the situations they had left there. Like Tessie, they complained about the lack of employment and educational opportunities, the failures of the political system, and problems with crime, drugs, and violence in their communities. If these women were committed to their families and longed for aspects of life back "home," they also said that they would return only under certain conditions. As Ana explained, she wanted to move back to the Philippines only if she "could trust the police there, the crime rate was lower, and jobs could be found." In short: she said that only if things changed in the Philippines and it became more like Japan and the United States would she want to return. Similarly, most Filipina women I met in Central Kiso did not want to go back to the Philippines they had left nor, having worked as entertainers in Japan, could they easily expect to return to their former lives there. Instead, these women characterized the Philippines as a place that one had to travel from—and in some sense leave behind—to find a better future. They distanced themselves from their pasts there and suggested desires for an elsewhere.

In the remainder of this chapter, I explore how women's imaginings of both travel and a place they called America informed their understandings of this elsewhere in relation to their lives in rural Nagano. I consider how and why their dreams took the shapes they did. I'll begin with a conversation I had with a woman I call Angela.

Angela was tall and thin with serious eyes and a disarming smile. She lived in the government-subsidized apartment complex on the Kiso River. Busy caring for her mother-in-law and children during the day and working in a club at night, she usually kept to herself, attending only sporadically the gatherings other Filipina women in the region organized. Although I had seen her at some of these, we had never exchanged more than friendly greetings, not even when I stayed with a mutual Filipina friend in the apartment complex during the last weeks of my fieldwork. I was therefore surprised when she came to my going-away party, and especially when she approached me with a wide grin as we walked to Sampagita where the *nijikai* (after-party, Jpn.) was being held. She asked in Japanese how long I had been in Central Kiso. "Nearly two years," I responded. I then asked her the same question. Twisting her long brown hair behind her ears, she told me that in April of the coming year it would be five years since she'd been married. Was she a permanent resident yet? I asked. Not yet, she told me; she had just gotten her first three-year visa. She wanted to get permanent residency as soon as possible, though, she said. It was a hassle to have to go back and forth to the embassy to get her passport renewed. She hesitated for a moment and then explained in Japanese, "I want to become a Japanese . . . because I want a Japanese passport. If you have a Japanese passport, you can go anywhere, right? You can go all over, right?" I remembered that earlier in the evening she had briefly commented that she had relatives in the United States, and that she had long dreamed of visiting. She had also given me a going-away gift, which surprised me because I hadn't known her very well; but a lot of people, both Japanese and Filipino, seemed to be doing that, telling me that they wanted to come visit the United States and to please remember them. Angela added mindfully that now that her husband was being nice, he was being good about getting her visa, but if that changed, she would have no choice but to return to the Philippines or to overstay her spousal visa. "I don't know why I came here. I don't understand the language. . . . I really want to go to Canada. Because I have a lot of relatives there," she said in Japanese. Then she started speaking again about her relatives who lived in North America.

Among the Filipina women I knew in Japan, visas and passports—my own, theirs, and other Filipina women's—were a frequent topic of conversation. Consistently, the first thing a Filipina woman in Central Kiso asked me when we met was what kind of visa did I have and how did I get it? If my U.S. passport (and renewable year-long student visa) was a magical bridge that facilitated my mobility and enabled my passage toward a destination, their Philippine passports served a contrary purpose: they evoked immigration gates tightly shut; they were barriers to an outside world and obstacles standing in the way of where these women wanted to go. A Filipina woman named Susie whom I met at one of Cora's parties asked me straightaway if it were easy to get a visa as an "American." She had just arrived in Japan on a spousal visa, her recent marriage arranged through a cousin also wedded to a Japanese man. "Only rich people in the Philippines can get tourist visas," she told me in Tagalog as she turned her eyes away from mine.

Women sometimes asked me to help out with visa paperwork or applications, necessarily submitted in Japanese or English, for relatives who hoped to visit Japan. I gladly obliged, and we giggled as they listed the reasons that other Filipina friends had advised them Japanese immigration officials would find most convincing: I want my sister (cousin, aunt, mother) to learn about Japan's beautiful culture and rich heritage; she has always dreamed of seeing Mount Fuji and of experiencing an authentic tea ceremony; I want her to learn about my wonderful life here. Filipina women who did not have documents but were getting married and applying for legal residence also occasionally asked me to assist them. For example, I once helped a Filipina friend rehearse in Japanese what some married friends she knew had suggested she say in her interview with an immigration officer: I want to be a good Japanese wife and to raise my children to be good Japanese citizens. I sensed these women's hopes that my involvement in their application processes might have magical efficacy, that an application I had assisted with would not be denied, and I felt their disappointment and frustration when their applications came back refused. Filipina women I met in Central Kiso planned future trips to visit me in the United States, asking how women from backgrounds like theirs might obtain visas that would enable them to travel there. They asked how they, too, could stay in Japan for a year without obligation.

Holding a U.S. passport and receiving a steady income in the form of research fellowships that mysteriously provided for my travel and living expenses with no apparent responsibilities, I was a perplexing incarnation of desire for these women. Although none of them wanted to get a PhD in anthropology, and most of them suggested that I needed to get married and have children as soon as possible, they were both envious of and awed by my mobility, by the freedom and funds I had to go and do what I wanted. When, midway through my research, I told Tessie and some others that I had received a second fellowship that would allow me to make three trips to the Philippines and that I was hoping to accompany them home, they were both thrilled and deeply jealous. On the one hand, they relished the thought of introducing their "American friend" to family and neighbors back home. My presence would raise their cultural capital in their communities and verify their successes in Japan. On the other hand, however, there was something unjust about the fact that they scrimped and saved to secure the money—to say nothing of the luxury of time and the permission from their Japanese families—necessary to travel home every few years, while I, without family or ties to speak of in the Philippines, could come and go so easily. I saw the injury in their eyes when I first told them about the fellowship, in the extended pause they took, standing tight-lipped and self-composed before they responded to my declaration, and I felt it in the pointed questions they asked about how such a thing could be possible. I was immediately embarrassed by my thoughtless and naked glee. Later, before I left each time for the Philippines, Filipina friends in Central Kiso reminded me— masked by good humor but in so many words—how jealous they were and how lucky I was.

My presence provided an opportunity for Filipina women in Central Kiso to share stories about relatives or friends in the United States and about their own dreams of moving or vacationing there. Like Angela, these women excitedly told me about neighbors, sisters, cousins, aunts, and uncles who lived in New Jersey, Oregon, Arkansas, and even Canada. When I asked Marivic about her life in the Philippines, she initially responded in a mix of Japanese and English that she was embarrassed to tell me: "Lieba-san's lifestyle . . . in America . . . it's really good, right. I'm jealous." "New York?" she queried knowingly. "Los Angeles," I responded. Her gaze floated into the distance as she continued: "My grandfather's older brother went into the U.S. Navy and so now they're in the U.S., in Los Angeles. They're doing nursing. Is it easy to go now if you're a nurse in the Philippines? If you pass a test?" Pilar, a short, round woman with an unfailingly cheerful disposition, told me (brightly) that I looked "haggard" one day when I visited her house. I had my date book out, and she was comparing the photo on my international driver's license with my current state, explaining that I now had dark circles under my eyes and was too thin. She paused to look over the license. "Do you know what my dream was?" she asked in confident English, supplying the answer without pause, "to become an American. Green card. Maybe someday I'll still go."

GETTING TO "AMERICA"

Like Angela, Marivic, and Pilar, almost every Filipina woman I met in Central Kiso told me at one time or another that she dreamed of visiting or living in a place they called "America." These women relayed a range of dreams about the pleasures and comforts of professional lives in cities like New York and Los Angeles; of purchasing fashionable commodities—Levis and Guess jeans, Gucci watches, and Coach and Louis Vuitton purses (which, regardless of these items' actual geographical origin, they associated with life in the United States)—and of the possibilities for mobility attached to holding a U.S. passport. The things and people that these women associated with "America" were prized symbols of status and figures of desires.

Of course, it is not surprising that the United States became a point of orientation around which these women organized their dreams of a better life. Stories about the successes of Filipina/o immigrants in the United States widely circulate in popular culture in the Philippines and are also reinforced when such Filipinas/os return to the Philippines as wealthy benefactors and tourists. These *balikbayan* (Filipinas/os living abroad who return home, Tg.) are viewed in the Philippines at once with envy and as shameless on account of their extravagant spending and for regularly drawing attention to what the Philippines lacks when compared to their lives abroad.[14] The United States is also an important place where Filipina/o elites go for higher education and where Filipina/o celebrities often visit and sometimes live. The desires to go to the United States that Filipina women in Central Kiso shared with me were not simply desires to go to "America-the-place." They were also desires to inhabit these worlds.

These desires have historical roots in the U.S. presence in the Philippines over the past century. Americanization was an integral part of U.S. colonial policy in the Philippines. In the early twentieth century, the U.S. government imposed English as the language of instruction in Philippine schools and modeled the Philippine educational system and curricula after those in the United States. Over the past century, U.S.-based corporations have also viewed the Philippines as a key market for selling commodities and mass media—food, books, clothing, movies, and music. Today, U.S. American expats are among the wealthiest and most privileged residents in the country. Despite the sometimes brutal and often exploitative ways that people in the United States have treated those in and from the Philippines, these dynamics have produced what some in the Philippines self-consciously refer to as a "colonial mentality," "the unflinching belief that everything made in the United States—movies, music, fashion, food—is automatically better than anything made in the Philippines."[15] It has also fostered dreams of the United States as, in Fenella Cannell's words, "a place of power, wealth, cleanliness, beauty, glamour, and enjoyment." As a result, Cannell tells us that in the Philippines, going to the United States as a migrant laborer has come to be viewed as a means for becoming "wealthy, prosperous and freed from the burden of subjection which poverty brings."[16]

In some sense, too, the dreams of America expressed by Filipina women in Central Kiso were dreams of the very privileges and pleasures these women associated with labor migration, which centered on the United States but were not necessarily exclusive to it. Catherine Choy tells us that with the large-scale migration of Filipina nurses to the United States in the 1960s, labor migration came to be viewed in the Philippines as means for middle-class women to gain upward career and class mobility.[17] During this time, travel agencies in the Philippines served as recruitment and placement agencies for exchange nurses to the United States, and they emphasized the opportunities that working abroad would offer to see the world and transform an ordinary woman into a cosmopolitan, independent, and modern woman.

Building on Choy's study, one could say that the dreams of America that had led Filipina women to Japan were more than dreams of going to the United States. They were also dreams of the very possibilities of labor migration as a form of travel, with all its resonances of success and racial and class privilege.[18] That is, the desires Filipina women in Central Kiso expressed about going to Japan as entertainers centered on labor migration as a marker of middle-class success that was multiply, but not exclusively, tied to the United States. For these women, labor migration suggested access to colonial and capitalist power, financial security, independence, and the very possibilities of living a "modern life." Viewed as a form of travel, labor migration was at once a metaphor for, and a route to, privilege, choice, and self-actualization—not only a form of mobility, but also an end to itself.

JAPAN (STUCK ALONG THE WAY)

This dream of America was one that many Filipina women in Central Kiso were looking for when they decided to go to Japan as entertainers. Recall how Ana was excited to go to Japan because she was finally traveling abroad to a "modern place" that she imagined was "like America." In the Philippines, Japan came to be widely seen as a desirable destination for labor migration during the 1980s as it came to have an increasing economic presence in the country. After the oil shock of the 1970s and the increased value of the yen and rapid inflation that followed, Japan began to export manufacturing to other parts of Asia.[19] During this time, Japanese tourism in Asia also began to increase. In *Underground in Japan,* an autobiographical novel about undocumented Filipino/a migrant laborers in Yokohama, Rey Ventura explains of the Philippines during the late 1980s and early 1990s:

> There is no Japanese Dream, and yet Japan, for the Filipino *[sic]*, has become a second America. . . . [M]ore and more, we see Japan as part of our future. The Japanese are now the largest investors and aid donors to the Philippines. They are our wealthiest tourists. More and more Filipinos are studying Nihonggo [*sic: Nihongo,* Japanese], in new language schools and on television. Even the beggars and street-vendors of Manila have developed a Japanese patter.[20]

Yet if going to Japan as an entertainer (and staying as the wife of a rural Japanese man) promised Filipina women possibilities of travel to a "second America," it was not quite the same thing. While the American Dream clearly has a hold on a popular imagination in the Philippines, as Ventura bluntly tells us, "there is no *Japanese* Dream."[21] That is, Japan does not hold the longstanding and privileged place in the Philippines that the United States does. Indeed, the Japanese occupation of the Philippines— although spanning fewer than four years (1941–1945)—is often remembered as the most brutal period of the country's more than four hundred years of colonization. In contrast, the U.S. colonial era (although certainly not without its share of brutality) is popularly associated with the transformation of the country's educational system and the pleasures of consumption and Hollywood. Reflecting on these differences, Sister Ruth once

observed that while Filipina/o immigrants to the United States were quick
to consider themselves "American," most in Japan remained "Filipino."
When I began my fieldwork, not one Filipina woman in Central Kiso had
yet (as they put it) "become a Japanese [citizen]." However, like Angela,
several women I knew were contemplating changing their nationality.
(When I returned several years later, a few women had.) While all women
I knew wanted permanent residency in Japan, giving up their Philippine
citizenship to take Japanese nationality was something that most of these
women did not take lightly. Like Angela, Filipina women in Central Kiso
who told me that they were considering naturalization said they were doing
so for pragmatic reasons, such as the hassle of trips to Tokyo and Nagano
City necessary to renew passports and residency permits and the promise
of mobility that Japanese nationals enjoyed (such as the ability to travel to
the United States without a special visa).

Moreover, if Filipina women like Ana had expected to find "America"
in Japan, many of them were disappointed with the version of it they
found in Central Kiso (as in fact are some Filipina/o migrants who come
to the United States expecting to find "America" there).[22] Although one
Filipina woman who had grown up in an urban part of the Philippines
told me that she had come to enjoy living in the Japanese countryside,
most Filipina women in Central Kiso with whom I spoke complained
that their lives in the Philippines had been, in at least some ways, more
modern, cosmopolitan, or exciting than their lives in rural Japan. Ana
once compared the two this way: "Even where my family lives in the
provinces in the Philippines, there are shops and things to do. It's not as
empty and lonely as this."

In addition, many of these women's dreams for their marriages had not
panned out. Many expressed restlessness with their lives in Central Kiso
and dissatisfaction with their relationships with their husbands and in-
laws, a point to which I will also return in chapters 5 and 6. They were
frustrated with their inability to fully express themselves in Japanese, angry
at the discrimination they experienced, and bored with their daily routines
("my *wanpatān*" [one-pattern], they would joke, using a Japanese-English
phrase that was popular). One afternoon while we prepared dinner,
Tessie's cousin Tisya, with whom I was living at the time, confided that a
number of Filipina women she knew in the region wanted to leave their
Japanese husbands. When I asked why, she responded in a mixture of
Japanese and Tagalog: "Their husbands aren't good." For example, she
explained, the men spent all their money in bars or didn't come home at
night.

Even a woman like Tessie, who considered herself happily married and "lucky" because her husband was supportive of her activism and her desire to send money to her family in the Philippines, told me that she had considered leaving her husband at one time or another. One day when I was helping Tessie with her Japanese, she started to complain that her skills weren't very good because she didn't like studying and because her husband never taught her anything. She confessed that she didn't really care about learning the language because she didn't want (or plan) to stay in Japan forever. "I never had a dream to come to Japan and marry a Japanese," she explained, "That's why I don't care about learning Japanese culture and traditions." "Why did you do it?" I asked. "Why did you marry a Japanese man?" Just a few weeks earlier I had heard her encourage another pregnant cousin to marry her Japanese boyfriend because "there's nothing to go back to in the Philippines. There are no jobs there." But that day she simply repeated my question to herself slowly and then shook her head back and forth in wonder. "I myself don't know," she said in Japanese. "I myself don't know."

ON ESCAPING, TRAVELING, AND GETTING STUCK

Lisa Rofel tells us that desire is a "historically, socially, and culturally produced field of practices."[23] By this she means that people are not born as desiring subjects but come to understand themselves as such through historical, social, and political-economic processes. Rofel's work opens up the question of how and why people configure and claim desires in certain ways. It encourages us to consider how people's senses of themselves as desiring subjects shape their experiences of their worlds.

Here I have suggested that Filipina women articulated desires for their lives and futures through the stories they told about their migration decisions. These narratives were central to how they crafted senses of self. They gave form to these women's experiences, just as they reflected the possibilities and constraints of their everyday lives in rural Nagano. In this sense, these women's understandings of their migration decisions cannot be understood apart from not only the conditions of their lives in Japan and the Philippines but also the "tropes and conventions . . . the borrowed plots, moods, rhythms, and images," such as that of the American Dream, that shaped these women's stories about them.[24]

I have also suggested that both these narratives and the desires they registered were configured through relational imaginings of mobility and place. According to such imaginings, Japan, the Philippines, and the

United States were relatively organized place-worlds in the landscapes of these women's dreams. As Filipina women in Central Kiso made sense of their desires relative to these relational geographies, they came to understand their dreams as partially—but not wholly—fulfilled in their everyday lives in rural Nagano. When viewed in relation to these women's lives in the Philippines, Japan appeared a better place to be; however, when viewed in relation to women's dreams of America, it was a disappointment.

Caught between desires to "escape" from a difficult life in the Philippines and dreams of getting to the place they called "America," Filipina women like Tessie felt stuck in rural Nagano. Although Tessie did not want to stay in Japan, she also did not want to go back to the Philippines. Her family still depended on her financial support and, as Tessie told her cousin, "There's nothing to go back to in the Philippines. There are no jobs there." Feeling stuck is an uncomfortable kind of dwelling. It's a restless, frustrating kind of being. It is different, I think, from the forms of dwelling that scholars have contrasted with modes of travel and mobility.[25] It is also a kind of dwelling that is not easily understood through terms of home and abroad often stressed in literature on migration and diaspora. Memories of Tessie constantly and frantically redecorating her home come to mind here, of her dwelling *on* her dissatisfaction with her dwelling and her inability to dwell *in* it. For Tessie and many other Filipina women in Central Kiso, dwelling and traveling were not counterposed. They were two sides of the same golden coin: finding a place where one could comfortably dwell meant finding a place in the world from which one could travel freely.

However, instead of being able to both travel and dwell, many Filipina women in Central Kiso suggested that they felt stuck: with jobs that they were ashamed of doing and that stigmatized them, in marriages that they sometimes (and in some cases often) wanted to leave, and in an "empty and lonely" rural mountain town somewhere along the road to their dreams. These women saw themselves as not yet having arrived in the place they wanted to be—a place that perhaps did not even yet exist. In the meantime, they lived with the pleasures their lives in the rural region afforded them, with the knowledge that even if they wanted to they could not easily go back to the Philippines they had left, and perhaps above all with the dream that someday they might find themselves both dwelling and traveling somewhere better.

CHAPTER 3

Japan in the Kiso Valley, the Kiso Valley in Japan

Prosperous middle-classness is the postwar Japanese national
identity. The hard years after surrender have congealed as
fable, and even the malaise now setting in after the bursting
of the bubble economy only confirms the degree to which
prosperity has become the norm.

Norma Field, *From My Grandmother's Bedside*

Matsubara, my landlady Emiko's shoe and clothing boutique, was
housed in a striking new building that was poised along the narrow two-
lane highway that ran the length of the valley. The structure had been a
gift to Emiko from her late husband Toshiharu when he had learned that
he was dying from liver disease. Toshiharu had decided that the new
building would stand as testimony to Emiko's ability to rebuild and carry
on, and he had spared little expense in its construction. The storefront
was built in exquisite contemporary style, with a gentle sloping roof
trimmed with wood stained deep sienna. Inside, the building boasted
pale hardwood floors and smooth walls and beams of prized local *hinoki*
(Japanese cypress). The shop floor was filled with racks of new shoes,
including fashions from Europe and the United States, and a small wing
off to the right of the entrance showcased contemporary yet practical
Western-style clothing and accessories.

Toshiharu had not been mistaken about his wife's abilities. Emiko was
a smart and capable businessperson, and despite the downturn in the local
economy, her boutique was turning a profit. She provided her clientele
with reasonably priced and desirable, as well as necessary, items. The bulk
of her business was in footwear required for public school uniforms. She
also had one of the few shoe-fitter licenses in the county, which enabled
her to reshape shoes to fit calloused and arthritic feet; elderly folk from

miles around depended upon this service. However, the store attracted customers from near and far not only because of necessity. Matsubara was Emiko's maiden name, and she had built her business on the legacy of her father, a well-respected local geta-maker. Yet perhaps even more important than this connection to the past was Emiko's forward-looking eye: she took regular trips to Tokyo and Nagoya to ensure that Matsubara—like Emiko herself, with her shiny, jet-black, Cleopatra-style (her description) hair and her chic, but practical and never ostentatious, fashion sense—brought an element of understated elegance and cosmopolitan style to the rural valley.

I not infrequently stopped by Matsubara to chat with Emiko and her parents, who lived nearby and regularly came in to visit. When the store was busy, Emiko would graciously introduce me to customers, explaining that I was a student from Tokyo University who was living in her family's extra house and researching the area; on slow days, we slipped into the back to drink tea and eat snacks. One winter afternoon, I brought in a roll of photographs from a recent trip to the Philippines to share with Emiko. I had just gone "home" to Bulacan Province with Ligaya, a Filipina friend to whom Emiko had introduced me when I arrived in the area, and Ligaya and I had attended her niece's wedding while there. The groom's father was an official in a new housing development outside Cavite, and the wedding had been an impressive affair held in a famous local cathedral with a picture-perfect bridal party in matching lavender satin gowns and elegant *barong Tagalog* (formal Filipino menswear, Tg.). As Emiko thumbed through my photos of the ceremony and reception (a catered party held at a local community center), she gasped in disbelief. From the representations of the Philippines she had seen on Japanese television, Emiko stammered, she had thought everyone was desperately poor and lived in slums! My photographs contradicted this impression, and Emiko was flabbergasted.

Looking up from the photos, Emiko divulged that she had recently heard that two Chinese women had come as brides to a nearby village, both through arranged marriages, like Ligaya. Emiko knew only one of the men involved, she said, but he, like Ligaya's husband, was an employee of the village hall. And he was older, she added (in his forties she guessed) but a "very respectable person."

"Few Japanese women are willing to come as brides to the countryside and live with their mothers-in-law," Emiko explained, "especially if the man is over the *tekireiki*. Because they come from poorer backgrounds, Chinese and Filipino women are less self-centered and harder working than young Japanese women. That's why they're willing to come. They're like traditional Japanese women. They're patient."

Then she added, without missing a beat, "Kiso is really becoming *kokusaiteki* [cosmopolitan]."

"Kokusaiteki, you said?" I wanted to make sure that I had heard Emiko correctly as I jotted down her comments in my notebook.

"It really is! It's shocking!" Emiko affirmed.

Emiko's casual characterization of Filipina women as both "like traditional Japanese women" and part of an emergent and desired cosmopolitanism in the region posed an interesting contradiction. The cosmopolitan is usually figured in contradistinction to the traditional. This is particularly the case in Japan, where the development of a unique and timeless "Japanese tradition" is frequently associated with both geographic isolation and national policies of seclusion. How, then, can we understand the relationship between Emiko's two claims? How did Filipina women simultaneously figure in local imaginings of both the traditional and the cosmopolitan? What can this tell us about the desires that local residents brought to their relationships with these women?

In this chapter, I explore how Emiko's seemingly contradictory claims were similarly tied to the ways that local Japanese residents imagined their place within Japan and Filipina women's place in the region. I argue that for Central Kiso residents, both Filipina women and the cosmopolitan figured as "spectres of comparisons" through which they came to see themselves as Japanese in relation to popularly circulating discourses of Japan's affluence and modernity. I take the notion of the "spectre of comparisons" from Benedict Anderson, who borrows it from late nineteenth-century Filipino nationalist and writer José Rizal to illustrate the ways that nationalism "lives by making comparisons."[1] As Anderson explains, the spectre of comparisons is that ghostly apparatus that reflects one's "home" as it might appear through an inverted telescope. It is a kind of phantom sleight of hand that evokes "a new, restless double-consciousness" by enabling a person to simultaneously see something up close and as it might appear from a point far, far away.[2] According to Anderson, this dizzying optical inversion, which reveals the immediate topography as it levels it into a landscape of manageable comparison, enables a shifting perspective through which one comes to view one's own history analogously to that of another's.

By considering how Filipina migrants and the cosmopolitan figured as spectres of comparison for local residents, this chapter explores incarnations of Japan at its rural margins. In recent years, scholars have worked to historicize and thereby denaturalize essentialist and racialized notions of Japanese national and cultural identity by considering how such discourses gained currency both in Japan and around the world. Some have considered how particular ideologies or discourses of race, ethnicity, culture, and nationality become hegemonic in Japan, while others have tracked the effects of these discourses on ethnic minority or colonized populations.[3] Still others have linked discourses of Japaneseness to those notions of race, ethnicity, and nationalism that circulate on a global scale.[4] Here, I build on these arguments to suggest that in addition to attending to the ways hegemonic discourses of racial and national difference circulate on national and global scales, we need also to explore how regional, local, and personal contingencies shape these discourses in historically and geographically specific ways. How did rural residents' marginal positioning within dominant understandings of Japaneseness shape the ways they negotiated these discourses in terms of the cosmopolitan and of the increasing numbers of Filipina women in the region? Not all Kiso residents linked the increasing presence of Filipina women with an emergent cosmopolitanism in the region, as Emiko did. In what follows, I explore the language of everyday desires through which people living in Central Kiso framed their hopes, dreams, and longings in terms of the promises and threats of incorporation into a modern, affluent, and cosmopolitan nation. While in no way do I mean to be an apologist for racist attitudes, I have tried to situate local residents' claims within interpersonal engagements and translocal political-economic relationships. I aim to contribute to our understandings of how regional and personal struggles and identities inflect the production of meanings of Japaneseness and, thus, the particular local configurations through which certain notions of difference and sameness are sustained and transformed in contemporary Japan. In doing so, I also consider how the cosmopolitan figured as an axis of difference in these processes, offering Central Kiso residents a global reference point in relation to which they constructed local and regional senses of national identity.

ENGLISH LESSONS

The hot and humid days of *zansho,* the lingering summer heat, marked the end of the otherwise clement Kiso summer and foreboded the arrival of typhoon season. I tried to focus on the whirr of the cicadas and the cool green of the surrounding rice fields as I trudged through the sticky afternoon air on my way to Sachiko's coffee shop, Coffee Shop Kaori, where I knew the air conditioning would be on. Kaori was not on the main road. It was hidden behind the boxy form of Asuku, one of the two large supermarkets in town. Built beside Sachiko's family home about ten years earlier, the café had been designed in a much-coveted log cabin style, complete with a wood-burning stove that warmed the small building during the long, cold winter. The shop was tastefully decorated throughout the year to reflect each season, and its six tables sat gracefully along a wall of windows facing the river.

Despite its somewhat obscured location, Kaori had a following. It was a popular haunt for a select group of locals: housewives whose husbands were at work, nurses and doctors from the nearby hospital, and others who enjoyed the ambiance and wanted to be part of the scene. It also attracted a smattering of tourists and owners of vacation homes in the area who were sufficiently in the know. Regular customers acknowledged each other with a bow and a greeting as they entered, joining friends at the short counter that Sachiko single-handedly manned, while less familiar patrons peeked up from cups of "American coffee" and conversations to see who had come in. Sachiko herself not infrequently stepped onto the floor to welcome old friends or introduce people to one another, that is, when she wasn't hidden in the kitchen by a stylish set of hand-dyed curtains, busy preparing pizza toast, pilaf, or *yakisoba* (pan-fried noodles).

Outgoing and charismatic, Sachiko was one of the first people I met in town. She wore her hair cropped short and dyed a stylish auburn, and she rarely stepped out of the house without lipstick. I soon came to appreciate Sachiko's company (and her tasty cooking). Thoughtful, witty, and intelligent, Sachiko had well-formulated opinions and a knack for telling stories about the past. Shortly after we met, Sachiko informed me that she would be my "Japanese mom." She explained that her own twenty-six-year-old daughter was studying photography in New York City. Sachiko's aegis proved fortunate for my research. Her family was well established in the area, and she maintained a sizeable field of social contacts as adeptly as she did her small, elegantly manicured garden. Many of her childhood friends were now running the local government and other key businesses and associations, and she was an active member of the women's chamber of commerce.

Kaori was a great place to meet people, particularly local elites, and to hear town gossip. I often took refuge there from the extremes of heat and cold and loneliness that came and went with the seasons. That day I found myself, once again, seated at Sachiko's counter between Yoshida-san, the owner of the local tofu shop, and Murai-san, the plumber's wife. Sachiko and Yoshida-san had been elementary school classmates, and both were enthusiastic members of the beginning English class sponsored by the town hall. Yoshida-san's shop was just down the block from my house, and I often ran into him wearing the Kodiak Island sweatshirt he had bought on an annual fishing trip to Alaska. Whenever he saw me, he approached with a coy smile, anxious and excited to practice a new English phrase. "How old do I look?" he would enunciate in well-rehearsed tones. Then, quickly switching to Japanese, he would ask with a bashful glance if the phrase were correct and could he try out some more.

That day, however, Yoshida-san was too focused on a story that Sachiko was telling to bother practicing his English. Since I'd entered the shop, he and Murai-san had sat transfixed as Sachiko relayed the recent adventures of a childhood friend, now the editor of a fashionable women's magazine and living in Tokyo, who had unexpectedly visited the area. When Sachiko finished, there was a lull in the conversation, and I decided to take the opportunity to change the subject and ask about the region. I began to ask Sachiko questions about living in Central Kiso, hoping that she would expand on her family's history in the area and her attachment to the local landscape; both were topics I had heard her mention with pleasure in the past.

"What kind of place do you think Kiso is?" I asked, pulling out my notepad. Perhaps because she had her friend's life in Tokyo on her mind, Sachiko's response was unexpectedly sour. She paused and looked up from the cup of coffee she was preparing, her usual smile pulling into a thin, rigid line. "Many locals have a complex about being *inakamono*" (hicks), she reprimanded. "Not only are they self-conscious that outsiders—and specifically urban folk—see them this way," she explained, "but also they feel like there's nothing in Kiso. There aren't any subways and there's nothing to do for entertainment." This perception was not aided by television, Sachiko maintained, which almost exclusively focuses on life in the big cities. ("Just once, couldn't they do a program about *our* lives?!" she had complained in an uncharacteristic outburst a few weeks earlier, surmising that many residents in Kiso shared her frustration.)

Agreeing with Sachiko, Yoshida-san added that language use was another factor: Because Tokyo dialect is standard, most people think that it is the most beautiful way to speak and look down upon those who use local dialects. In Kisofukushima, I heard Kiso-ben (Kiso dialect) spoken only on occasion, usually when talking with elderly folks and sometimes in conversations among town hall officials, most of whom were men who had grown up together in the area. More often, people self-consciously joked with me about the dialect, objectifying it as a cultural remnant or local idiosyncrasy and asking playfully whether I could understand some of its characteristic word usages. To some degree, people around me were trying to be polite by avoiding local ways of speaking, which were more difficult for me to understand. However, some also liked to tell me that most people in the area spoke *hyōjungo*, standard Japanese, a dialect based on upper-class speech patterns of the Yamanote district of Tokyo.[5] Reminding me of Kisofukushima's history as a post town and of the valley's role as an important travel route during the Edo period, residents would expound that locals spoke *hyōjungo* on account of their regular dealings with lords and high-level officials who used to pass through the area. The names of these officials, they would advise, were extensively catalogued and on display at the nearby Fukushima Sekisho Shiryōkan (Fukushima Checkpoint Museum). People would maintain that during the Edo period, residents of the valley were culturally ahead of even Tokyo, as travelers on their way from Kyoto brought the latest arts and fashions through Kiso first. Sachiko didn't bother making these familiar points that afternoon, however. She simply concurred with Yoshida-san: language use was another reason that people in urban areas dismissed country folk as unrefined.

Embarrassed to have prompted such a prickly response, I tried to redirect the conversation onto gentler ground by asking Sachiko whether she identified more as a "Japanese person" (Nihonjin) or a "Kisoite" (Kiso no hito; literally, a Kiso person). Her expression softening, Sachiko responded that because everyone around her in Central Kiso was Japanese, she had never, until recently, really thought "I am a Japanese person." In her childhood when students made fun of a classmate who was a resident Korean *(zainichi kankokujin)* she felt bad as children do, but she did not consider her Japaneseness to be a marker of her difference from him.[6] In her eyes, he too was "Japanese" but (sadly, she added) teased because he was different in other ways.[7] She began to strongly feel that she was Japanese, she explained, only about ten years ago, when the Japanese government began sending JET English teachers to the area on a *kokusai kōryū* (international exchange) program.[8] She had also felt it strongly a few years back while on a vacation in Switzerland. Everyone there was so tall that she really felt that she was Japanese, she said dramatically, straightening her back to draw attention to her petite five-foot frame and playfully rolling her eyes upward to look at a much taller invisible neighbor.

She then began to speak enthusiastically about the JET kokusai kōryū program sponsored by the national and local governments, which she believed had had a very positive effect on the area. As a result, she explained, those in Kiso have had to rethink what is around them. More than wanting to learn English, Sachiko maintained, she wanted to learn about other countries. Now, she said, there were several *"gaikokujin"* (foreigners; literally, people from foreign countries) living in the area: three JET assistant (English) language teachers (ALTs) from the United States, Britain, and Canada, who worked at local junior high and high schools, and one coordinator for international relations, employed at the county offices.[9] Sachiko explained that everyone in the town wanted to get to know these people, but that they felt that they could not because they didn't speak English. In general, she said, people wanted to speak to foreigners, but they were hesitant to approach them because they were self-conscious that their English was inadequate. "That's why," she explained, "all Japanese want to study English: because it is the 'international language' and can be understood everywhere." She continued, "Before, we could just think about 'Japan,' but now we have to think about 'Japan in the world.' Everyone is expanding her vision." She maintained that now when foreigners came to the area, she wanted to introduce them to Kiso and to show them, "This is Japan." "In Tokyo," she added, "many people can speak English, but not in the countryside, in Kiso."

Sachiko's remarks about life in Tokyo, her trip to Switzerland, and the recent regional presence of JET English teachers evoke how an urban, middle-class, cosmopolitan way of being in the world figured as part of a language of everyday desires for many local residents and highlight how this mode of being was framed in terms of Japaneseness. In Central Kiso, access to the cosmopolitan was often related in terms of *kokusaika* (internationalization) in the region and the opportunities for international exchange it enabled.

Kokusaika was first popularized as a national project in the early 1980s by Prime Minister Yasuhiro Nakasone.[10] Officially, the term stressed the need for a shift in popular attitudes because of increasing economic interdependence between Japan and other countries, especially the United States and Western Europe, or what is often in Japan called "the West" *(seiyō)*. It referred both to processes of change already underway and to a desired direction or course for the future. During the 1980s the national government initiated a number of projects under the kokusaika rubric. Many of these focused on education, and most initially and almost exclusively focused on the West, which has long been viewed as a model and standard for gauging Japan's achievements of culture, modernization, and progress.[11] The JET program, which brought English teachers to rural (and urban) areas throughout Japan, was a representative kokusaika project. The program encouraged international exchange with foreigners—primarily, although not exclusively, those from the United States, Canada, and western Europe—as a means of fulfilling Japan's role as a wealthy, modern, and developed member of the "international community." The program was initiated to forward kokusaika's broader official goal of enabling Japan to play a more active role in the world. It aimed to do this by helping create a nation of Japanese people who were fluent in "global" languages and standards of culture—"cosmopolitans" *(kokusaijin)* of sorts.

Many scholars have argued that rather than looking outward and encouraging tolerance of foreign cultures, kokusaika emerged as part of a nationalist discourse. It did not figure the cosmopolitan as antithetical to Japanese culture but was both part and product of the ongoing production of a discourse of Japaneseness that posits Japan as a racially and culturally homogeneous country of middle-class people.[12] Central to this discourse was, what William Kelly has called, a "New Middle Class ideology" that emerged in the postwar period.[13] According to Kelly, by the 1970s and 1980s, this ideology redefined standards of achievement, desirability, and possibility in Japan in gendered terms of a nuclear family in which the husband worked for a large corporation, the wife was a full-time homemaker, and the two children were hardworking students. I would add that the middle-class ideals that developed in Japan during this time not only idealized certain organizations of education, labor, and domestic relations, but also defined new and shifting standards of consumption—the desirable and feasible ways through which success might be evidenced. In Japan of the 1960s, the standards of consumption were the "three sacred treasures" *(sanshu no jingi)*—a refrigerator, a washing machine, and a black-and-white television. By the 1980s, these standards were transformed so that they were defined on an individual (as opposed to a household) level in terms of international travel, English conversation lessons, and consumption of U.S. American and western European products. Through kokusaika, a *kokusaijin*, literally an "international person," came to popularly refer in Japan to "a well-traveled, English-speaking socialite."[14]

For Sachiko, participating in kokusai kōryū (by, for example, speaking English with JET English teachers and vacationing in Switzerland) was a means for charting a path in the internationalizing world. This participation offered a marker of distinction, a form of pleasure, and a means of accumulating cultural capital that was crucial for the future.[15] However,

Sachiko's participation in kokusai kōryū enabled her to do more than
view herself as part of an exciting global future—one already taken hold
in cosmopolitan centers such as Tokyo. She also suggested that she came
to know herself as Japanese through it. As Sachiko explained, it was not
until she came into contact with Anglophone JET teachers that she came
to think "I am a Japanese person" as opposed to identifying as a
"Kisoite." For Sachiko, nationality was one geographically based identity
she assumed among others, such as Kisoite and resident of Kisofukushima.
In this way, being Japanese was a relational identity: it had taken on significance for her only in contrast to these other identities and particularly
when difference was manifest on a national scale. When she encountered
Japanese people from another region of Japan or town in Kiso County,
her regional and local identities took precedence.

If for some Central Kiso residents participating in kokusai kōryū
meant identifying a place for themselves as a Japanese person in the
world, it also meant reflecting on their place in Japan. Thus, insofar as
kokusaika is a discourse of Japaneseness, it is also one inflected by the
ways that an individual is positioned, both personally and geographically.[16] For Sachiko and other Central Kiso residents—people who lived
in what is often considered a backwater—kokusaika not only represented
the possibility of a cosmopolitan future but also brought into relief one's
exclusions from it. Yoshida-san, for example, described the linguistic marginality of the region on account of the standardization of a (Yamanote)
Tokyo dialect as hyōjungo. The presence of local dialects (Kiso-ben,
Kaida-ben, Kurokawa-ben) identified the region as parochial and
unrefined—decidedly not cosmopolitan. And not only local language use
stigmatized the region in such terms. Additionally, local residents viewed
their lack of skill or confidence in their English proficiency as sympto-
matic of the slow progress of kokusaika in the region, especially when
compared to urban centers in Japan (and particularly Tokyo, Japan's paradigmatic "global city") where "many people can speak English."[17] Because, according to Sachiko, many Central Kiso residents were scared or
embarrassed to speak with foreigners, they were also stymied in their ability to engage in kokusai kōryū, which would make them both more cosmopolitan and more aware of themselves as Japanese.

In Central Kiso, as elsewhere in Japan, then, speaking English was a
key marker of cosmopolitanism. Importantly, comparisons between the
region (where, local people told me, few had competency in English) and
Tokyo (where, they asserted, many people spoke it) reveal not only the in-
adequacies local residents felt in relation to those in Tokyo but also the

ways that for these residents the cosmopolitan and the urban were linked. People in Central Kiso often figured the cosmopolitan in comparative degrees based not only on language proficiency (or the density of English speakers in the area) but also on the presence of certain amenities, such as movie theaters, *raibu hausu* ("live houses"; nightclubs that play live music), dance and theater performances, and fashionable shops and restaurants. These were establishments that both symbolized and enabled participation in an affluent, modern lifestyle and that were sorely lacking in Central Kiso (but found throughout Tokyo and in other cities in Japan). I noticed that many Central Kiso residents made little distinction between urban centers in Japan and the world beyond insofar as the latter was seen as an extension of the former. Both were viewed as points on a cosmopolitan continuum to which some Central Kiso locals had occasional privileged access, but that was, by and large, beyond the reach of most.

The way many residents conflated the cosmopolitan and the metropolitan became clear to me in discussions about "the Jazz Concert," a *machi zukuri* (town-making) event held in the town in November 1998 and fondly recalled by local residents long after it had passed. A local man who had moved to New York City to become a jazz musician had performed a small homecoming concert as part of a Japanese tour he was making with his two U.S. American band members. In preparation, the town hall staff had spent an entire afternoon transforming the old community center lecture hall into a jazz club, constructing a small stage and low cocktail tables out of salvaged wood and decorating them with remnant fabrics, lights, and candles. Nearly two years later, one town hall official invoked the evening as an occasion when *"tokai no bunka"* (city culture) had come to Kiso. He didn't bother specifying whether the city to which he was referring was Tokyo, where clubs with live music were found throughout hip districts like Kichijoji and jazz shows could be found all during the week, or New York City, where the musicians lived and played. "Even here in the middle of the mountains, we can experience a taste of urban culture," he said to me with both pride and longing.

According to many residents, one problem with the region—a problem taken as both a symptom and the cause of other socioeconomic problems—was that there was not enough of the cosmopolitan in it. People were self-conscious about what was and was not kokusaiteki about Kiso, and the cosmopolitan was by definition that which was not local, that which had prestigious links to the West or to urban places within Japan, such as Tokyo or Nagoya. These were places imagined to be closer than Central Kiso to the world at large. While some long-time

residents, like Sachiko and Yoshida-san, had toured through other parts
of Japan and abroad, most were not well traveled. A trip to Tokyo was
for many extravagant. People were self-conscious about being parochial.
The kind old woman with the lazy eye who worked down the road at the
stationery shop cited a proverb when I asked her how to take the train
to Matsumoto, a regional city about an hour and a half away. "A frog
in a well knows nothing of the great seas," she responded, explaining
that she had never been there. I met more than a few elderly women who
had never left the county, and most people who had traveled either do-
mestically or abroad had done so only a few times in their lives. At her
boutique, Emiko rented suitcases to those who planned to go on a trip,
but who would likely not need luggage again.

Sachiko and others spoke with excitement about volunteering at the
Nagano Olympics in Nagano City (about three hours away) or going to
see plays in Tokyo or Matsumoto. These were exciting, cosmopolitan
things that one needed to do once in a while to keep one's life from getting too dull. However, they were also painful reminders of what was
lacking in the everyday life of the town, and of how small and parochial
urban folk imagined it to be. Unlike Filipina women I met, who spoke
of their dreams of living in the United States, Japanese residents were
more focused on incorporating parts of the cosmopolitan West—
including me—into the town. One local government employee suggested
creating a long-term job for me doing internationalization machi zukuri
at the town hall. Others suggested I marry a local man. And I received
endless requests to teach English. Locals regularly approached me at
public functions to practice their language skills, explaining that English
was their "hobby" and expressing interest in learning more; others recounted stories about vacations in Europe and Australia. I was an appealing opportunity for local residents looking for a cosmopolitan encounter.
The desire to relate to me on such a level no doubt shaped the stories
people told me about the region.

For Central Kiso residents, participating in kokusaika through machi
zukuri, travel abroad, or interactions with local English teachers or U.S.
American researchers meant more than the pleasures of belonging in the
contemporary world. It also meant building a better life for oneself in
Japan. It meant taking control of one's future at a time when the local
economy was becoming increasingly unstable. In this regard, machi zukuri
events such as the jazz concert were attempts at making Central Kiso,
and by association its residents, into a place that mattered in the world.
It meant becoming part of a cosmopolitan world by incorporating those

elements that would accomplish this goal: urban cultural events, U.S. American researchers affiliated with prestigious universities, a classical music festival.

However, if participating in certain internationalization activities offered local residents a means for crafting a sense of cosmopolitanism, then it also marked their marginality to such discourses. Jennifer Robertson has argued that internationalization and rural nostalgia have existed in a dialectical relationship in Japan, that is, in a relationship "characterized by articulated homologies" in which internationalization figured Japan's relationship vis-à-vis the world in the same way that rural nostalgia figured rural areas vis-à-vis Japan (read: contemporary urban affluent Japan as metonymized by Tokyo).[18] Whereas for urban folk this may have meant that rural nostalgia and internationalization were "two mutually constitutive modalities of modernity," for people in rural areas, rural nostalgia and internationalization meant a double displacement from what it meant to be Japanese in any modern, urban, and cosmopolitan sense.[19]

In popular discourses of modern Japan, the Kiso Valley is valued primarily in terms of its historical contribution to the nation. It figures as part of such narratives primarily insofar as it is viewed as a repository for a traditional and vanishing Japanese past.[20] The region is usually remembered as the site of the eleven post towns of the Kisoji, an official highway controlled by the Tokugawa Shogunate (1603–1867) along which travelers made their way as they traveled between Kyoto and Edo (now Tokyo).[21] For urban folks, this history marks legacies of rural Japanese tradition. However, when Central Kiso residents spoke with me about how the region was during the Tokugawa period, they focused on how cosmopolitan it was at the time. As I have explained, they would maintain that during the Tokugawa, Kisofukushima was culturally ahead of even Tokyo (Edo) as travelers on their way from Kyoto brought the latest news and fashions through the town when passing through the barrier station. These residents also often spoke with nostalgia about the Kisoji Boom, a domestic tourism campaign during the 1970s and early 1980s that brought national attention and money to the Kiso region by reconstructing and marketing its role during the Edo period.[22] When local residents discussed this campaign, they did not just stress the attention the region garnered for its historical status. They also focused on the ways that during this moment the Kiso Valley was incorporated into progressive narratives of national development and widening reaches of domestic economic growth and the prosperity. For these residents, the Kisoji Boom was not only a period in recent history when the local tourism economy was booming. It was also a time when people felt like the Kiso region mattered in Japan and the world.[23]

However, if Central Kiso residents stressed the ways the Kiso Valley was a historically interconnected place on account of its location on historical travel and transportation routes, they also viewed this cosmopolitanism (and recognition of it) as having been somehow lost over the past twenty or so years as domestic tourism declined and the local economy stagnated. Unlike the southernmost region of the Kiso Valley (and especially the villages of Magome and Tsumago) where many historical buildings remained, and even to some degree Narai, which was a bit to the north, most efforts to attract tourism to the central region of the Kiso Valley were faltering. Although local residents had pinned their hopes on historical and environmental tourism to revitalize the local economy, they sometimes spoke with bitterness about the ways that the Kisoji Boom had simply been a "fad" for fickle urbanites who viewed rural areas as part of a disappearing past.[24]

Cosmopolitanism was a key trope through which many Central Kiso residents made sense of their positioning within a modern Japanese nation. Sensitive to how they appeared in an urban imagination, they expressed feelings of inclusion and exclusion in Japan and the world at large in terms of their access to the cosmopolitan and its incorporation in the region. In this sense, the cosmopolitan was a figure of everyday desires, both essential and elusive, through which local residents articulated themselves as certain kinds of modern and urbane Japanese subjects. It was something to which they aspired, and something which, living in a rural valley, they could never completely get their hands around. One could grab hold of it for a moment, long enough to manage a taste, but one's grasp was always tenuous. The cosmopolitan was the province of those who lived elsewhere, in urban centers or the West. For Sachiko and many other residents, then, kokusaika was at once that through which one accessed a modern, cultured, and cosmopolitan sense of Japaneseness and that to which Central Kiso residents had limited claims. In this light, we might reread Sachiko's comment that she came to know herself as a Japanese—to really think "I am a Japanese person"—when she met JET English teachers and visited Switzerland to mean that it was only when she was engaging in certain activities she associated with an urban, affluent, and cosmopolitan lifestyle that she could recognize herself as Japanese, that is, as a person from modern, prosperous, middle-class Japan.

However, Sachiko's comments were significant not only for what she included in the cosmopolitan but also for what she elided. When Sachiko spoke of gaikokujin in Central Kiso, she mentioned JET English teachers who had come from the United States, Australia, Great Britain, and Canada. Yet the numbers of Filipina women living in the region *far* outnumbered those from these other countries. When I began my fieldwork in 1998, there were 156 Filipina women registered in Central Kiso on both entertainer and spousal visas. In contrast, there were a total of 7 people registered from the United States, Australia, Great Britain, and Canada *combined*. There were even more than double the number of Filipina women in the region than resident Koreans (the next largest group of foreign residents), who at the time numbered 74. Moreover, most Filipina women had at least some (and some women had a high level of) proficiency in English—described by Sachiko as the international language and a key measure of kokusaika. However, Sachiko never mentioned their presence as contributing to cosmopolitanism in the region. In fact, throughout my fieldwork I noticed that Filipina women did not even appear on most people's radars as gaikokujin, at least not as people worth mentioning (or, perhaps people thought, worth mentioning to someone like me). On my first day visiting the area, when I asked at both the tourist information booth and the inn if there were any gaikokujin in the area, I was told that there were very few, only a small number of English teachers employed at local schools.[25] I received the same responses consistently during the first few months of my stay. Only much later that first evening, when I finally asked the owner of the inn specifically about "Ajiajin" (Asians) did he tell me there were a number of Filipina women employed at local bars. I learned how significant the presence of Filipina women in the region was from the JET coordinator for international relations in the town, a Pakistani-British man holding a diplomatic visa who, during the first weeks of his residence in the region, was repeatedly stopped by local police assuming he was an undocumented migrant laborer. This man told me that he regularly noticed large groups of Filipina women congregating outside the supermarket and that the county had sponsored the Mothers' Class to help those married to Japanese men adjust to life in the region.

To understand how local residents articulated Japaneseness in locally inflected ways, then, we also need to consider how they made sense of the increasing presence of Filipina women in the region.

THE BRIDE SHORTAGE

Usually a paragon of tact, Sachiko inhaled audibly and rolled her eyes whenever I mentioned Kato-san's name. She had known Kato-san for decades, since they were elementary school classmates. And although she didn't dislike him ("He's a good person," she would insist), I suspected that Kato-san got on her nerves. I also suspected that Sachiko was not alone in finding Kato-san something of a bother. At best, Kato-san might be described as self-promoting; at worst, he was a serious braggart. Of late, Kato-san had been seizing every available opportunity to discuss his current "independent research" on a local mountain plant—research, he boasted, that was leading to "new and important discoveries" about the region and that "would soon be published" (by another childhood friend who ran a local print shop). Kato-san liked to showcase his knowledge not only of local flora but also on a range of topics regarding the region. He would assert that his expertise was cultivated during his nearly twenty years of employment at the now closed local forestry management office. It was no surprise to Sachiko that Kato-san searched me out as an audience. He regularly approached me at Furusato Kōza (Hometown Lectures) and other machi zukuri events, eager to share with me information that "few others knew."[26] He did little to disguise his self-satisfaction when, at first out of a feeling of obligation but later in genuine interest, I requested several private interviews with him. During one such audio-recorded interview, I asked Kato-san about the increasing number of Filipina brides in the region:

L: Well, I'm also interested in why foreign brides have been coming to this town. I'm also researching that . . .

K: Foreign brides, right? Well, there are many from Southeast Asia, and especially the Philippines. But that's true not only for this town but throughout Nagano Prefecture. There are many throughout the prefecture.

L: But why are there so many in this town [which is often described as] "in the middle of the mountains" [yama no naka; read also: remote]? Is that related to the regional economy? And what kind of effect is the presence of these women having in the region?

K: Well, those are very interesting questions. I too have thought about them quite a bit. To put it simply, compared to Japan, the Philippines is poor. China too. So if people from those countries come to Japan, they can earn money, right? Besides they don't come on real work visas, they come on entertainer visas, to sing, to dance; these are the visas that those people enter on. There are a lot of them. Because Japan, Japanese people, they're all rich right? At any rate, local men go to karaoke, to bars and snacks, and they meet many Filipinas there. But that's not only true of Kiso. It's true of Nagano Prefecture as a whole, especially places in the middle of the mountains like this. Kiso is inaka, right? Therefore, city folk just won't come as brides. Men are leaving and going to the cities because there aren't women who will come as brides. That's why in nearby villages like Ōtaki and Kaida, those areas, it's even worse than in the town of Kisofukushima.[27] Because they're even *more inaka*. That's why. For as many men as there are who don't leave, there are brides who won't come. . . . That's why at places like those [snacks, cabarets, bars], local men get to know the women, and there are many cases of kokusai kekkon.

L: Well, what kind of influence do you think that will have on the town?

K: What? International marriage?

L: Yes, international marriage.

K: Well it really has no bearing. Because nobody pays attention anymore. For example, the American military occupied Japan after the war. They came here and we looked at them wide-eyed. But now I don't even notice people like you. Because there are so many foreigners [gaikokujin] here already. So you don't see them. They don't stand out. . . . It's a sign that we're internationalizing, you see?

L: Is the fact that many Filipinas are coming as brides also evidence that kokusaika is progressing?

K: Can you can say that, that the presence of Filipinas is part of kokusaika? [Kato-san paused.] Well, for example, when people like you come, people who come to study, who come because they *want* to work regardless, that's kokusaika, right? But Filipinos are poor. Because they're poor they come to rich Japan to earn money. Based on that point, it's not kokusaika, you see?

L: What kind of thing is kokusaika?

K: Well isn't kokusaika about people from Japan, people from America, people from the Philippines, people who are working and studying, etc., *at the same level?* That's what I really think. The ways that *these* Filipinos come here, settle down, get married, that [spoken with hesitation and doubt] could be internationalization. But, it's on account of poverty that Filipinos and Chinese are coming. Because of poverty, they come to Japan to work. Or else they stow away on boats from China, without visas. They are part of that trend. To put it bluntly, they're a form of cheap labor. Aren't we just importing laborers from foreign countries? For example, in Tokyo an overwhelming number of the people who work on things like road repair are foreigners. However, few Japanese people will do those kinds of jobs. Japan has a lot of money, to some extent too much money. It's become too rich, rich, *rich* [He said "rich" the third time in English]. So fewer and fewer people will do those jobs. But in the Philippines, China, those areas, they are still rural people. They are still undeveloped. Those are developing countries, right. That's why a lot of them come to work. The situation is extreme. It might be strange to put it this way, but isn't Japan just importing cheap labor? And this importation of cheap labor sometimes turns into international marriage because brides aren't coming. Aren't these Filipinas getting married because they are poor?

L: Could you explain that again in regard to Kiso?

K: Well the women enter as cheap labor, because the Philippines, where they were born, is poor. So they come up around Ōtaki, here in Japan. They come here to work and to save money. But they like it here. They get together with someone. Japanese men may not really want to marry Filipinas, but the Filipinas come here and Japanese brides won't. Because it's in the middle of the mountains, because it's a cold place. Japanese women won't come to the *inaka.* Therefore, isn't it the case that we're importing these *people,* these brides, as laborers, as people for work? We're importing them. The men don't go to a foreign country and fall in love. It's not like you, coming here to study. It's not like the men meet someone like that. It's just that life in the Kiso countryside is easier than life in the Philippine countryside. That's the way many of these kokusai kekkon happen. They're really not cosmopolitan kokusai kekkon that are part of kokusaika. In the cities it might be different, but in Kiso, in Nagano Prefecture, I think it's different than in places like Tokyo, Osaka, Nagoya.

L: If I came to like a local person and married him, that would be kokusaika?

K: Yes.

L: Do all kokusai kekkon occurring in cities have a connection with kokusaika?

K: But some Filipinos there are working in bars and snacks too, right? That's how they get together with Japanese men and maybe even marry them. . . . The men can't meet anyone else.

L: [hesitantly] So [in those cases too] it's a desperate measure?

K: Exactly!

Later in our interview, Kato-san offered an example based on his years at the forestry management office in a neighboring village before it closed. He explained that in the office there had been two categories of employees: those who worked inside at white-collar jobs and those who worked outside doing forest maintenance. Most of the white-collar jobs were reserved for men from outside the region. These men were transferred from urban areas and moved around regularly. According to Kato-san, these men became appealing marriage prospects for local women who wanted to leave the region. He relayed how on numerous occasions he had witnessed local women going after these office workers. "They tried their best to ignite passions and get the men from the cities to like them. Because they figured that if they married these men they could go somewhere." Kato-san explained that the men from the village who were out doing forest maintenance were left behind. He advised that I check the marriage age for men in local villages. He assured me that an overwhelming number of men marrying Filipina women were over thirty years old. He explained, "Women from the villages are looking for ways to go to the cities. Men who must stay in the villages can't find brides. Filipinas figure that they'll live in the countryside even if they return to the Philippines, but life is more difficult in the countryside there. Compared to the Philippines, they figure that life in prosperous and [rural] Kiso is better. It's not that these people purely fall in love. The men get brides; the women escape poverty. That's the cause of most so-called kokusai kekkon in Kiso. It's different from the kokusai kekkon in the cities, I think."

According to Kato-san, marriages between Filipina women and Japanese men in Central Kiso stemmed from desperation, not "love," and thus were not cosmopolitan international marriages, like those occurring in urban areas. Prompted by labor conditions, poverty, and desperation, these marriages stood in contrast with the cosmopolitan, which was figured in terms of desire, individual free choice, class status, and egalitarian exchange. Cities were where international marriages that were truly about kokusaika—about meeting people from other countries, most notably educated and elite workers from the West (and possibly other places)— took place. Cities were where cosmopolitan Japanese people, freed from the burden of necessity, were able to stand on the same level with other modern folk.

Most men in Central Kiso with whom I spoke who were not married to Filipina women were reluctant to say that there was anything appealing about these women when compared with Japanese women. In fact, most Japanese residents in Central Kiso whom I asked (including some Filipina women's husbands) agreed that it was only because Japanese women had become scarce in the countryside that men in the region had turned to Filipina women as brides. For these residents, the increasing number of Filipina brides painfully reflected the geographic and economic marginality of the region vis-à-vis cosmopolitan centers such as Tokyo. Kato-san also acknowledged this marginality. He explained that marriage for local women offered a potential ticket to urban centers, to "somewhere," as opposed to remaining in Central Kiso, the obscure countryside, a *nowhere*.

However, Kato-san also mediated the exclusions suggested by the increasing presence of Filipina women by stressing how Central Kiso was part of "affluent Japan."[28] First, Kato-san cited the presence of Filipina brides not only in the region, but also throughout rural Japan. He both situated what was happening in the region within the larger phenomenon of international marriage and stressed that the area was part of larger geographic entities such as Nagano Prefecture. In this way, Filipina women's presence in the region provided a vehicle through which he imagined Central Kiso's relationship to other rural regions of the country and linked it to a pan-Japanese trend.

Second, in situating Central Kiso within Japan, Kato-san stressed Japan's wealth in relation to other countries in Asia such as China and the Philippines. In making a sweeping comparison between "wealthy" Japanese people and "poor" people in the Philippines, he stressed that Central Kiso, and its residents, was part of a modern, prosperous, middleclass country. Kato-san asserted that compared to life in the Philippines, life in rural Kiso was easy because of its location in a now developed and wealthy Japan. Overlooking class differences within Japan and the Philippines, he articulated a hierarchy in which life in the Philippines was at the bottom, life in urban areas was at the pinnacle, and life in rural Japan, in Central Kiso, lay somewhere in between (life in the town of Kiso-fukushima ranking higher than life in outlying villages).

According to Kato-san, Filipina women in Central Kiso had come to Japan to look for work because life in rural Japan was better than life in the rural Philippines. Kato-san might have been surprised to learn that more than half of the Filipina women living in the region did not come from the rural Philippines but from poor urban communities in and around Metro Manila, long a very cosmopolitan city. I doubt, however, that this piece of information would have made much difference in his views. Kato-san's point was that *all* Filipina/o people were poor in relation to *all* Japanese people. Distinctions between rural and urban regions of the Philippines were immaterial because, for him, cosmopolitanism indexed not only spatial relationships but also those of national modernity and development. He believed that both urban and rural areas of the Philippines were underdeveloped when compared with Japan. Kato-san's assertion resonated with comments I often heard many people in Central Kiso make about life in the Philippines, and other parts of Asia in general. For example, when I mentioned to middle-aged Japanese women friends in Central Kiso that I had studied in the Philippines and visited many times, they were invariably nonplussed. "What was it like?" they asked before quickly responding themselves, "Very poor, right?" These women then mentioned images of slums that they had seen on the news in other popular media. Based on such images, they imagined all life in the Philippines as antithetical to the modern and cosmopolitan and, certainly, as less advanced and developed than even rural Japan.

AFFLUENT JAPAN

Kato-san's comments struck me as particularly ironic in light of the ways that the very nationalist projects that had enabled Japan's spectacular postwar economic growth—the basis of its status as a "wealthy" nation— had also consistently marginalized the region, including destroying the local forestry industry that had once provided his livelihood.[29] Over the past few decades, national economic growth projects in Japan had proven bittersweet in places like Central Kiso. The regional economy had been tied to the whims of the central government and urban desires, and the economic recession that had affected Japan since the early 1990s had hit Central Kiso harder and faster than urban areas. In the postwar period, the national government had launched a massive campaign to reforest mountainsides denuded from war mobilization and earlier industrialization efforts. These campaigns promised to use modern, scientific forestry techniques to bring mountainous regions a prosperous future, and they had initially provided jobs and brought workers to the Kiso region. However, in the 1960s, as the Japanese national economy grew and the country experienced shortages of wood products, Japan began to import large quantities of wood from Southeast Asia, Siberia, and North America. This cheaper wood soon replaced domestic timber and by the 1990s accounted for more than 80 percent of the wood consumed in Japan.[30]

By the late 1990s, when I first came to the region, the steady decline of the local forestry, tourism, and construction industries and the paucity of viable possibilities for an economically independent regional future had inspired a sense of instability to many living in the area. It was as if the legs on which they had been standing had been steadily withering and might at any moment give way. And while people in Central Kiso had to some degree benefited from, and identified with, postwar national affluence, as I have suggested the prosperous middle-class national subject who emerged through it was by definition an urban subject. That is, although urban economic growth in Japan was enabled by labor and natural resources from Central Kiso, it was tied to discourses of modernity that situated places like Central Kiso as part of a vanishing rural past and an Other against which a modern Japanese self might be constructed.[31]

Not surprisingly, many in Central Kiso had ambivalent relationships to national economic growth projects and the ways the region was positioned within them. Throughout my fieldwork, residents expressed ambivalence about the ways that such projects simultaneously offered advantages and pleasures and made the area vulnerable. Longtime residents I asked widely

agreed that the standard of living in the area had dramatically improved
since the 1950s. Sachiko repeatedly shared stories about the poverty of her
childhood during the immediate postwar years. These years stood in stark
relief to the relative comfort and affluence of the present day. Emiko
maintained that everybody in Central Kiso had a roof over their head and
food to eat, and most lived with some comforts and luxuries. However,
local residents were also aware of the exclusions and losses—in population, regional stature, and economic possibilities—they sustained on this
account. And many with whom I spoke were understandably dismayed by,
if not bitter about, the Janus-faced treatment they (like all of rural Japan)
have received in the urban public eye the simultaneous celebration of regional landscapes as nationally, spiritually, and historically valuable and
the dismissal of rural areas as backwards. Central Kiso residents were
aware that they lived these contradictions in everyday, material, and
political-economic ways. For people in the region, being part of a "modern, wealthy Japanese nation" was at once a goal, an accomplishment, and
a threat.

FACILITATING COSMOPOLITANS

My landlady Emiko was one of a small number of people whom I met
that were hopeful about the region. An unflagging optimist, she once told
me that she wanted locals to believe that they could make Central Kiso
a cosmopolitan and exciting place to live. She wanted to convince people
"we can do it." Emiko's optimism was reflected in her claim—which, as
I have indicated, was not a popular one at the time—that the region was
becoming more cosmopolitan on account of marriages between Filipina
and Chinese women and local men. Admittedly, Emiko had personal
stakes in championing the region and in constructing the women's presence in such terms. First, her family was among the (relative) elite who
had remained in the area. She once told me that her family had been "gō-
zoku" (landed farmers), and as I mentioned in an earlier chapter, she
prided herself on coming from, marrying into, and maintaining connections with "good" local families. She was one of those who stood to
gain the most from regional growth. Second, Emiko was known throughout the town as a cosmopolitan. She cultivated this identity, and it also
contributed to her boutique's success. For example, when I rented
Emiko's parents' extra home, she had to propose our agreement to the
family who owned the land on which the house (that her family owned)
had been built. Emiko strategy was to explain to the landowners that

I would be helping her with her business because it was "becoming very international." Third, Emiko traveled more than most people in the area. At least once a month she went to Nagoya or Tokyo for her business, and she had also traveled widely abroad. She had recently done a homestay in Sacramento (California), had visited western Europe on several occasions, and during the course of my fieldwork went on tours of both Sweden and Israel. Fourth, Emiko maintained friendships with several people who lived in the Tokyo metropolitan area. She regularly visited these urbanites, and they occasionally visited her. Emiko's daughter was at the time studying at a fashion school in Tokyo, and hoped to spend a few months in New York. She had agreed to then return and take over Emiko's clothing business. And Emiko's son, who had also gone to Tokyo to study music, had recently mentioned getting a shoe-fitter license, just in case his jazz band did not take off.

Emiko had also taken to befriending JET English teachers and other foreign researchers and tourists who came to the town. As I have mentioned, fluency in English was an important marker of prestige and cosmopolitanism in the area, and Emiko was recognized and admired as one the most proficient English speakers in Central Kiso. She actively cultivated this identity by speaking English with Anglophones in public spaces, and she also attended the weekly advanced English class sponsored by the local government. When I met townsfolk and told them I was living in Emiko's house, they often nodded knowingly, "Oh yes, she can speak English very well."

Moreover, Emiko was Christian. She belonged to a small church in the area. While being Christian placed Emiko in something of a marginal position in the town—she once explained that Christians had a long history of persecution in Japan, and the church in town had fewer than fifty members—it also cemented her identification with a Western, if not international, world. In fact, Emiko's English proficiency and her Christian faith were closely tied. She had initially learned English from a Canadian missionary, Barbara, who had spent nine months in the region several years back as part of a program through the local church. Barbara had invited Emiko and her friend Sumiko to walk along the river at seven o'clock each morning to discuss the Bible. Barbara spoke only English, and Emiko and Sumiko had used the opportunity to improve their language skills. While Sumiko decided to forgo any connection to the church after Barbara returned to Toronto, Emiko found Christianity useful for coping with her husband's illness and the new life she faced after his death. She decided to convert.

Emiko was actively interested in new ideas and experiences, and she
prided herself on being open-minded: it was integral to how she constructed her sense of self. She maintained that she did not have a problem with the large numbers of Filipina and the gradually increasing number of Chinese women coming as brides—trends that were to some
degree controversial among some Japanese residents. "My nature isn't to
see people in terms of *what* they are but for *who* they are," she often told
me. Toward the end of my stay, a middle-aged Filipina woman named
Mariann came to the area through an arranged marriage to a widowed
veterinarian. For Mariann's first few months in the region, Emiko was
her lifeline, going out of her way to help her get settled and adjust to life
in the area. Of course, Emiko's intentions may not have been entirely
selfless—Mariann spoke English well, and Emiko was intent on practicing hers—but her commitment to this woman, whom she perceived as
similarly Christian, was sincere.

However, if Emiko was personally invested in claiming that Filipina
women's presence contributed to the region's cosmopolitanism (as a
means, in part, of articulating her own cosmopolitan outlook), she also
was selective about the Filipina women whom she mentioned in casual
conversation and with whom she associated. As I mentioned, she respected and befriended women like Ligaya and Mariann. However, both
of these women were married to men with white-collar or professional
jobs. And perhaps more important, both Ligaya and Mariann had *omiai
kekkon* (mediated marriages), as had many older Japanese women in the
region, including Emiko's mother. While a small but growing number of
Chinese women in the area met their husbands through some form of
marriage mediation, at the time of my primary fieldwork Ligaya and
Mariann were two of only four Filipina women I knew of in the region
who had met their husbands that way. In other words, the Filipina
women whom Emiko described as contributing to Central Kiso's emergent cosmopolitanism were not those who had met their husbands while
working in bars. As I mentioned in chapter 1, Emiko had told me that Filipina women employed at bars were working as prostitutes and must be
poor and desperate to do such work. Even those residents who sympa-
thetically believed that Filipina entertainers simply wanted to help their
families and respected these motivations still questioned the women's
morality or positioned them as part of a past that most Japanese women,
on account of Japan's wealth and modernity, had progressed beyond.

Moreover, if Emiko claimed that the region was becoming more cosmopolitan on account of Filipina women's increasing presence, she did not

necessarily view the women as cosmopolitans themselves. Note that
Emiko said that *Kiso* was becoming more cosmopolitan because of the increasing number of foreign brides, not that the women themselves were
cosmopolitan. Emiko was a strong, independent woman who financially
supported herself and her children. Ultimately, she looked favorably upon
changing ideas about gender and family in the region that she associated
with cosmopolitanism. She believed that in a modern, cosmopolitan society women might be able to think of themselves as individuals and have
access to choices and mobility previously reserved for men. She told me she
objected to the way that in the past women were viewed as a financial burden to their families, which she identified as an old-fashioned way of thinking in Japan. Her enthusiasm about the increasing cosmopolitanism of the
region was in part enthusiasm for the increasing opportunities she believed
that it brought to Japanese women. However, she took for granted that
these new economic opportunities were facilitated at the expense of Filipina women.[32] If Emiko viewed Filipina women as contributing to making
Central Kiso kokusaiteki, she imagined that the women did so indirectly
or with qualification, in part by enabling Japanese women's independence.
Emiko's comments rested on subtle but significant distinctions between *facilitating* regional cosmopolitanism and *being* cosmopolitan.

Like Emiko, some Japanese residents in Central Kiso did express
interest in and concern about the lives of Filipina women in the region.
Emiko was one of a small but growing number of Japanese residents who
befriended these women (some less selectively than she did), and who
went out of their way to support them. While I was conducting my fieldwork, one nursery school aide, Miyoshi-san, started a grassroots cooking
group at the community center for Filipina and Japanese mothers. She explained that she was responding to concerns expressed by some Filipina
mothers that they did not know how to prepare enough Japanese dishes.
Sensitive to the politics of such an endeavor, Miyoshi-san did not want
the exchange to be one-sided. She suggested that the Filipina mothers also
teach Filipino cooking to Japanese mothers as a form of "international exchange." For the duration of the group's meetings, seven young Japanese
housewives regularly attended, interested and excited to learn about the
Filipina mothers' lives and culture and happy to contribute to helping
them feel more comfortable in the area. And Filipina women I knew also
participated in local festivals or machi zukuri efforts by performing Filipino dances, sponsoring booths with Filipino foods, and teaching Filipino cooking classes. This participation was always well received and appreciated as contributing to kokusaika in the area.

Notwithstanding such efforts to make these women feel at home, cultural citizenship was for them conditional. As Kato-san suggested, kokusaika was believed to involve egalitarian exchange. Thus to be viewed as contributing to kokusaika in the region, these women had to present themselves in particular venues and in particular ways, eliding aspects of their lives in the Philippines or their work histories in Japan. Women were self-conscious, and sometimes expressed frustration, about these unspoken expectations. Father Art once expressed concern that Filipina women had to present themselves and their culture as objects to be consumed—to offer themselves "in a fishbowl," as he put it—to receive any cultural recognition. Moreover, most residents did not view Tagalog (or other Filipino dialects) as an important language to know in an international arena; many Japanese residents (and sometimes Filipina women too) viewed Japanese as a more useful language to speak. As a result, most Filipina women were not encouraged to teach their children Tagalog or other Philippine dialects. A few women were even discouraged from speaking them at home. Instead, some women were encouraged to speak English with their children, something that gave them a measure of cosmopolitan status (although most Japanese residents in the region with whom I spoke were in fact surprised to learn that Filipina women could speak it at all).

For most Japanese residents, Filipina women figured as foil for what was cosmopolitan and cultured in Kiso, and in Japan in general. As Emiko explained, the numbers of foreign brides had increased in the area not simply because young Japanese women were unwilling to marry local men, but because some local Japanese men preferred women who came from humbler backgrounds and were less self-centered and more willing. "They're like traditional Japanese women. They're patient," as she put it. For many in the region, including some of their own husbands, Filipina women figured as part of a vanishing Japanese past, one that had been lost on account of Japan's economic growth and Japanese women's shifting attitudes toward marriage and family. Later in our conversation Emiko explained that "Westernization" and increasing political-economic opportunity had led young Japanese women to move away from a gender-kinship system that centered on women's domestic roles and specifically their obligations to their husband's household. Emiko explained that while such changes had created opportunities for young Japanese women, many of these women were stuck in a transition. Although these shifts had enabled young Japanese women to become financially independent, the changes had been so swift that they were still emotionally immature. Swept up in their newfound independence and individuality, they had not cultivated the emotional skills—such as patience and perseverance—that were important for maintaining social relationships, if not the fabric of a society. In her view, Filipina women, who still retained these qualities, could patch things over in the meantime. In this process, they might, in sometimes indirect and qualified ways, contribute to Central Kiso's cosmopolitan future.

THE SPECTRE OF COSMOPOLITANISM

Like Sachiko, Kato-san, and Emiko, almost every Japanese person in Central Kiso with whom I discussed the presence of Filipina women in the area either directly or indirectly spoke of the Japanese economic miracle, Japanese wealth, and Japanese cultivation. With numbing regularity, they articulated a hierarchy of affluence and development in which a poor and undeveloped Philippines stood in the shadow of Japan, a powerful and advanced nation. One Filipina friend's husband told me that the Philippines reminded him of the Kiso of his childhood, of Japan before the war and the "economic miracle" that followed. In other words, for him the Philippines represented a past that Japan had long progressed beyond. A few people explicitly, if self-consciously, told me that they "know it's not a good thing, but in Japan there is a 'ranking' *[ranku]* where Japanese people think that people from the West are above them, but that people from Asia, like Filipinas, are below them." Many explained that because I was from "the West," I was seen as special. Some even spoke of an "inferiority complex" *(konpurekkusu)* that Japanese people felt toward "Westerners" *(seiyōjin)*. In contrast, they explained with regret, many Japanese people viewed people from the Philippines as inferior to those from Japan. In other words, articulations of Japan as a wealthy and developed nation did not stand alone but were always marked and positioned according to Japan's relative status vis-à-vis the Philippines or the West or both. That is, they rested on a hierarchy of development in which the West was articulated as the standard of that which was modern, advanced, cultured, and cosmopolitan and the Philippines was defined as a poor and backwards place.

The circulation of these discourses of Japanese affluence was not unique to Central Kiso. Similar discourses have long circulated throughout popular media in Japan. For example, John Lie writes of a dominant discourse of Japaneseness that claims Japan as a racially and culturally homogeneous nation of middle-class people.[33] He explains that this discourse of Japaneseness is predicated on two complementary notions. The first is a notion of Western superiority and wealth, where the West stands in for high culture even when claims are made of Japanese cultural superiority. The second is the comparison of Japanese affluence with "Third World poverty" in which people from other parts of Asia are viewed as lower class and culturally inferior. Such a discourse can be widely found in Japanese popular media, for example, in representations of the Philippines in television news reports. Central Kiso residents echoed these discourses in their discussions of Filipina women in the region and their desires for a form of cosmopolitanism that they associated with the West. For instance, Cora once complained about watching national news clips with her mother-in-law that discussed life in slums in the Philippines. She relayed with annoyance how her mother-in-law, had presumptively commented, "You're lucky that you're here and no longer in a place like that."

At the same time, however, in a place like Central Kiso, a place where longtime residents have come to feel in some ways excluded from Japanese modernity, these discourses also took on somewhat different inflections. As I have suggested, local residents expressed mixed feelings toward popular discourses of modern, cosmopolitan Japaneseness. Japan was an ambivalent figure of desires in Central Kiso, and many residents' contradictory positioning within dominant discourses of Japaneseness created conflicting feelings about the increasing presence of Filipina women in the region. We might say that Japanese residents engaged in a kind of *doubled-talk* when speaking of Filipina women's presence in Central Kiso. In one sense, the growing presence of Filipina women in the region marked a legacy of Japan's successes in the world (and by national association their own) in contrast to what was commonly viewed as a poor and underdeveloped Asia. They understood these women's presence as evidence of the region's shared achievement of preeminence in the world by virtue of its Japaneseness. This status was primarily distinguished in terms of wealth and class, but it was also believed to be derivative of cultural, social, and for some biological superiority. For many Central Kiso residents, the growing presence of Filipina women in the region became an opportunity to assert that Japan was an advanced country and a global economic power—a country in which everyone was middle class, modern, successful, and cosmopolitan—and to situate Central Kiso squarely within this vision. In another sense, however, the increasing presence of these women also marked the marginality of the regional economy and of rural life in the face of the national government's reinvention of Japan since the Second World War. Local residents were sensitive to the fact that the decline of the local timber industry, and later the tourism economy, had contributed to a downward spiral of depopulation and underemployment in the region, and that this situation was increasingly exacerbated by the ongoing recession in Japan and the national government's recent policies regarding rural areas. The presence of Filipina women in the region thus also pointed to its undesirability, both to the "bride shortage" from which it suffered and the social and economic marginalization to which this was tied.

By making it impossible for Central Kiso residents to view the Kiso Valley (and by extension themselves) apart from how the region might appear to the world outside, both kokusaika projects and Filipina women's presence offered essential yet double-edged spectres of comparison that enabled local residents to imagine themselves as part of an affluent and modern Japanese nation, and by extension a cosmopolitan world, while making them painfully aware of their exclusions from them. And just as kokusaika projects provided access to both a "modern" Japanese world and the world at large, they also reminded local residents that the only gaikokujin, if one could call them that, coming into the region in any significant numbers were "Asians." As spectres of comparison, the increasing numbers of Filipina women and the emergent cosmopolitanism in the region offered Central Kiso residents opposing mirror visions of what the region might be, each optical effect both reflecting and destabilizing the other as they together offered "Japan" as an ambivalent figure of desires.

PART TWO

Terms of Relations

ONE AFTERNOON MY FILIPINA FRIEND Ande and I were making lunch for her Japanese husband and son. I volunteered to prepare *tamagoyaki*, a Japanese-style omelet, to go with some cold noodles we were serving. Having consulted a Japanese cookbook, I had thought that I knew how to make the egg dish, but after observing me for a moment, Ande quickly intervened. She corrected the way I was beating the eggs, explaining that I should only mix them lightly, leaving the white and yellow slightly intact. She then told me that I had the fire under the pan on too high. "My mother-in-law taught me," she explained of her husband's then deceased mother. "I was the yome," she added, self-consciously stressing the final word. "Did she teach you other things as well?" I asked. "Oh Lieba," Ande replied, "it was like she expected me to forget the first twenty-five years of my life."

What must a Filipina woman do to be a good oyomesan, that is, a good bride and daughter-in-law? And how do Filipina women feel about and respond to these expectations? How do their desires and agendas for their lives relate to those of their Japanese families and communities?

In the first half of the book, I explored how and why Filipina hostess bars became sites of encounter for Filipina migrants and Japanese men in Central Kiso, and I considered the discrepant forms of desire that Filipina women and Japanese residents brought to their interactions. In this half of the book, I turn to the ways that marriage offered a node of intersection through which these desires came into productive relation.

As I will show, for both Filipina migrants and Central Kiso residents, marriage offered both possibilities and frustrations for transforming one's life and realizing one's dreams. Through marriages to Filipina women, local Japanese men gained wives who bore them children, offered partnership, contributed domestic and sometimes waged labor, and cared for elderly parents. Through marriages to Japanese men, Filipina women found ways not only to financially support their families in the Philippines and craft selves as "good" wives and mothers in Japan, but also to challenge and transform their Japanese communities' expectations of them and assert identities as Filipina.

I suggest that in these marriages, oyomesan figured as a term of relations—part of both a language and a set of conditions—through which

Filipina migrants and Japanese residents linked everyday practices to broader categories of gender, kinship, ethnicity, national identity, and cultural belonging. I also suggest that while defining what it meant to be oyomesan was an unequal process in which Japanese residents often had the upper hand, it was not entirely a one-sided one. Meaning making is always dialogic. People borrow from, anticipate, and relate to the discourses of others as they craft meanings, lives, and selves. As Central Kiso residents and Filipina migrants unequally negotiated their stakes and desires for their marriages in relation to what it meant to be oyomesan, resonances, misunderstandings, and gaps developed among them. When Central Kiso residents referred to Filipina women as oyomesan, they expressed a set of expectations regarding these women's daily practice, and they referenced standards by which these practices might be evaluated. When Filipina women identified themselves or other women as oyomesan, they maintained relationships with people not only in Japan but also in the Philippines, and they defined themselves in relation to other Japanese and other Filipina women. Oyomesan became a term of mutual yet discrepant engagement as members of these groups drew on sometimes resonant and sometimes conflicting understandings of their shared everyday lives. What forms of desire, discipline, and coercion shaped the everyday dynamics of these processes? What cultural meanings, identities, and practices did they bear?

CHAPTER 4

Kindred Subjects

Kinship is a technology for producing the material and semi-
otic effect of natural relationship, of shared kind.

Donna Haraway, Modest Witness

Kinship is not simply a situation she is in but a set of practices
that she also performs, relations that are reinstituted in time
precisely through the practice of their repetition . . . not a
form of being but a form of doing.

Judith Butler, Antigone's Claim

On my way home from Tessie's one afternoon, I stopped by Emiko's shop to share some photographs of Tessie, her family, and me at work in Tessie's in-laws' rice fields. Over the course of the summer, I had assisted in the three-step process of producing rice: planting seedlings, binding and drying mature rice stalks, and feeding the stalks into a machine to separate out the grain. Emiko was curious about the lives of Filipina women in the region. She fingered through glossy shots of Tessie planting rice seedlings with her mother-in-law, both women wearing old floral cotton aprons, matching sunbonnets, and tall rubber boots—outfits commonly seen on women doing farm labor in the area. "Wow, she really is being *shikkari*" (Ehhh, hontō ni shikkari shite iru ne), Emiko gasped. She explained that many young Japanese women would not be willing, as Tessie had been, to work in the fields with their in-laws. Emiko was surprised, and impressed. "She's like a traditional Japanese woman" (Mukashi no Nihon no josei mitai), she explained. She later remarked that Tessie was an "ii oyomesan."

The Japanese term *oyomesan* is an honorific or polite form of the word for "bride" or "daughter-in-law," *yome,* made by adding the honorific prefix

Figure 5. Some Filipina women in Central Kiso help their in-laws, drying rice in their rice fields, September, 1999.

"o-" and the polite suffix "-san." An ii oyomesan is literally a "good bride and daughter-in-law." The yome/oyomesan has widely been regarded as a position for a woman within the *ie*, or corporate household, a kinship formation that is generally associated in Japan with a traditional, rural, and essentially Japanese way of life. Correspondingly, the yome/oyomesan is frequently understood as a traditional and distinctively Japanese kinship role for women.

Central Kiso residents' characterization of Filipina wives in the region as ii oyomesan thus poses something of a paradox. Since at least the 1950s, and some would argue earlier, dominant discourses of national identity in Japan have maintained that the country is racially homogeneous, and Japaneseness has widely been imagined as a biogenetically based identity.[1] Some have even attributed features of Japanese culture to Japanese racial purity. Moreover, rural Japan, in particular, has been viewed as a last bastion of a vanishing traditional Japanese past.[2] As I have explained, most Filipina women married to Japanese men in Central Kiso came to the region to work in hostess bars and were initially disparaged as prostitutes and foreigners. Why, then, have local Japanese residents come to describe some of these women as ideal, traditional

Japanese brides? What does it mean that international marriages with Filipina migrants have come to be viewed in Central Kiso as a means of maintaining nostalgic ideas about traditional Japaneseness?

In this chapter, I explore when, why, and to what ends Japanese residents in Central Kiso identified Filipina women as ii oyomesan, and I consider how they reworked meanings of Japaneseness as they did so. Since at least the 1960s, the refusal of many young Japanese women to marry and live in rural areas has challenged not only gender-based social hierarchies but also the sustainability of everyday social life in these regions.[3] Households in Central Kiso needed people to care for elderly, bear and raise children, and work in local businesses and fields. Some households needed the financial contribution of another working adult to get by. At the time of my fieldwork, a number of local men were lonely and wanted companions, caretakers, and families. Kokusai kekkon, and particularly marriages with Filipina migrant laborers, has become one means through which some Central Kiso residents manage this political-economic and social shift. In practical, everyday ways, Filipina women help keep life in rural places like Central Kiso on its feet. Yet, as I have explained, many Japanese residents in Central Kiso viewed the Philippines as a less advanced and developed country than Japan, and thus as inferior to it. Just as local residents like Emiko recognized and appreciated the contributions some Filipina women were making in the community, they viewed the increasing presence of these women as a reflection of the region's marginality vis-à-vis places like Tokyo. They were also committed to maintaining distinctive senses of Japanese and regional identities.

In this chapter, I argue that when Central Kiso residents identified Filipina women as ideal oyomesan they were attempting to negotiate their marginality within Japan. They were recognizing the central role Filipina women were playing in the region, and they were shifting the terms of Japaneseness to manage their ambivalence to these changing realities of their everyday lives. Doing so, however, was not a process of multicultural inclusion. Nor was it a process that can be understood apart from relations of power. Rather, as I will show, by selectively identifying only some Filipina women as ii oyomesan, Central Kiso residents established standards of behavior for judging (and thereby disciplining) all Filipina wives in the region. They also engaged a notion of Japaneseness that was based on an affective and everyday practice that residents could selectively identify with people (whether Japanese or Filipina) who behaved in ways that they found most amenable.

TERMS OF KINSHIP AND JAPANESENESS

At the heart of this chapter lie questions about the ways that Central Kiso residents both maintained a sense of traditional Japaneseness through their relationships with Filipina migrants and reworked the basis for reckoning Japanese identity in the region through this process. Kinship, Donna Haraway tells us, is a powerful framework for establishing boundaries of sameness and difference.[4] It is at once a language and a set of practices for identifying (and naturalizing) if, and on what basis, a person is recognized as kin and kind. In such a capacity, kinship has been central to the production of nation-states and national identities, usually in ways that prescribe unequal gender roles for men and women.[5] Yet what provides a basis for reckoning national belonging in terms of kinship is historically contingent and malleable—shaped and reshaped in relation to cultural, political-economic, and technological shifts.[6] People self-consciously negotiate the terms of kinship and belonging as they relate changes in the present to their understandings of the past and desires for the future. In doing so, they create new systems of meaning. People also self-consciously negotiate meanings of kinship to resist, challenge, and rework the foundations of national belonging.[7]

Here I consider how recent relationships with Filipina migrants are reshaping understandings of kinship and national identity in rural Nagano. My approach both draws upon and differs from two bodies of literature that have explored configurations of relatedness and belonging in Japan. First, it engages previous anthropological and sociological studies that have focused on the yome as a particular permanent position (the spouse of the *atotori*, or successor) within an ie. These studies have demonstrated that within an ie, people stress the continuity of the household over personal ties and that, unlike a nuclear family, the ie is a corporate group that holds property in perpetuity.[8] This literature has helped us understand formations of relatedness and belonging in Japan that contrast with those found in other parts of the world. However, it tends to take for granted precisely what I want to call into question. That is, it assumes that there is something essentially and definitively Japanese about the ie and the role of the yome within it.

Second, in more recent years, historians of modern Japan have challenged the notion that configurations of kinship and family in Japan, including those tied to the ie, are timeless and essential feature of Japanese culture. Some have argued that what has today popularly come to be known as the ie is a reinvention of Meiji government leaders intent on creating a modern Japanese state.[9] Others have traced the ways popular newspapers and women's journals during the late nineteenth and early twentieth century defined ideal womanhood in relation to women's roles in the household.[10] Takashi Fujitani illustrates how the imperial household became a site for reimagining and disseminating domestic ideals during the early Meiji period.[11] Jordan Sand shows us how understandings of family and domesticity were tied to shifting spatial configurations of the home.[12] However, these historical studies have tended to focus on state policies or popular culture in Japan to demonstrate the ways that kinship was deployed to define modes of national identity and to discipline Japanese women. My approach differs from this body of work by focusing on how the role of an ideal yome/oyomesan is being reworked today through intimate relationships involving not only Japanese people but also Filipina women.

My aim in this chapter is to draw attention to everyday cultural encounters between rural Japanese residents and Filipina migrants as key sites in which notions of Japanese kinship and identity are reinscribed and transformed. In particular, I am interested in the productive ways that power worked through Central Kiso residents' use of this category both to define what Japaneseness meant in locally relevant ways and to discipline Filipina women to behave accordingly. What stakes did Central Kiso residents have in identifying some Filipina women as ii oyomesan? How, why, and to what ends did oyomesan become a convenient and compelling term for some Central Kiso residents to make sense of their relationships with these women? How did they rework Japaneseness in this process?

In what follows, I focus on oyomesan as a term (at once part of a language and a set of conditions) through which discourses of Japaneseness were renegotiated in Central Kiso. I first consider how local residents defined what it meant to be an ii oyomesan in terms of a set of gendered affective and everyday practices. I then explore how identifying some Filipina women in such terms provided a practical basis for disciplining these women to adopt certain stances and behaviors—managing the home, interacting with neighbors, deferring to one's husband, preparing meals, caring for in-laws, and raising children—in a manner that local residents identified as "the Japanese way." Finally, I consider how local Japanese residents' identification of Filipina women as ii oyomesan privileged a notion of traditional Japaneseness that implicitly challenged biogenetically based conceptions of national belonging that have dominated in Japan over the past half century.

A GOOD BRIDE IS SHIKKARI

Let me, then, return to Emiko's comments about Tessie. Emiko had likened Tessie to a "traditional Japanese woman" when she saw photos of Tessie working alongside her in-laws in their rice field, a job that, according to Emiko, Japanese brides once compliantly performed but that most young Japanese women were now unwilling to do. Remember, Emiko had said that Tessie really was "being shikkari." Often used with verbs for tying, fastening, or grasping, shikkari is a mimetic word that can function as an adverb meaning "tightly," "securely," or "fast." *Shikkari shite iru*—that is, *shikkari* conjugated with the present progressive verb *shite iru* ("to be doing" or "to be in a state of") from *suru* ("to do" or "to make into")—can be used as an adjective to describe objects, such as steps, building foundations, or bodies that have a solidity or firmness of base. The expression is also used in regard to people to describe a temperament, attitude, or disposition that is reliable and certain. A person who is shikkari can be counted on. She is committed to making the utmost effort to be responsible, thorough, careful, and complete.

In Central Kiso, I often heard the expression "shikkari shite iru" used to describe young married women (both Filipina and Japanese) who were working hard and fulfilling social and familial expectations of them in their households. I heard the expression used most frequently in discussions of these women by middle-aged and elderly folk (who were disproportionately represented in the rural region). However, I sometimes heard local people in their twenties and thirties describe these women in this way as well. I soon realized that regardless of who used this term, it assumed a somewhat different inflection when used to describe Filipina women.

What it meant for Japanese women to be shikkari was most clearly explained to me by Morimura-san, a farmer from a village north of Kisofukushima who had recently gotten engaged. Morimura-san had met his Japanese fiancée through a local government–sponsored *omiai* (introduction) party in which his village invited ten (Japanese) women from different regions of Japan to visit the area and meet prospective bachelors. Morimura-san was one of only two men in the area who had made a successful match through the event, and his face radiated excitement for his good fortune and upcoming wedding. His fiancée was from a neighboring prefecture, and she was interested in farming. His eyes shone when he explained that they were going to work his cabbage fields together.

"I didn't think there was a woman like her out there in the world," he gushed.

At my request, Morimura-san produced a photograph.

"She's cute," I prodded.

Morimura-san smiled sheepishly and flushed. "Shikkari shite kureru to omou" (She'll manage things well for me, I think), he responded.

"What do you mean by 'shikkari'?" I pressed.

"Um well, being shikkari means managing things like, for example, housecleaning and things around the house, to manage them, to be capable of doing a proper job of them. And well, it also means managing relations with people around the neighborhood. A person who can manage those things properly might be described like that. And as for the opposite, *shikkari shite inai,* she would always be asking for her husband's opinion, be dependent on him, asking 'How do I do this? How do I do that?' She wouldn't be able to decide things based on her own judgment, to manage things herself."

Like Morimura-san, a number of residents in Central Kiso suggested that a yome who was being shikkari maintained a gendered household division of labor, managing domestic responsibilities including housecleaning, cooking, and looking after elderly in-laws. Many also stressed that she maintained cordial and reciprocal relations in the community. I was told that a good yome regularly greeted and assisted neighbors and maintained relations between her household and *tonarigumi* (neighborhood association) by passing on *kairanban* (neighborhood circulating notices) and paying monthly dues.[13] Moreover, she minded local social customs and ways of socializing by maintaining a pleasant disposition. By being shikkari, a yome/oyomesan became a nodal point between a household, the community, and the nation. Through her daily practice, she mediated between the three, maintaining a household's position within the community at large and its status as a unit within the town or village and by extension the state.

I was also told that a good yome was capable—that is, she had (or acquired) the knowledge, skills, strength, and independence—to carry out her responsibilities. As Morimura-san put it, she needed "to be capable of doing a proper job." She also, I learned, was compliant and willing to adjust to new surroundings and care for those around her. A good yome was expected to defer to her in-laws, even if this meant sacrificing her own desires. She also gave up the ways of her natal community and household and assimilated ("*dōka,*" as some put it) to the ways of her affinal family and community, down to adopting her mother-in-law's cooking style.

In many cases, women were instructed in the ways of their new household by their *shūtomesan,* their mothers-in-law, which historically made for difficult and painful relationships between the two women.[14] For example,

Kawaguchi-san, my Filipina friend Ana's mother-in-law, relayed a painful story about her relationship with her own mother-in-law when she first came to Central Kiso from a village in northern Nagano in 1948. It was just after the war, and times were difficult for people throughout the country. A mutual relative had arranged for Kawaguchi-san to marry and for the couple to be adopted by her father's childless elder brother who worked in the firewood and charcoal business in Kisofukushima and was relatively well off. Kawaguchi-san described her life with her adoptive parents as unbearable. Her mother-in-law was painfully strict and conservative-minded, a *"Meiji no hito"* (old-fashioned; literally a "Meiji person"), Kawaguchi-san explained. Nearly fifty years older than Kawaguchi-san, she complained about everything her adopted daughter did, even the way she ate her meals. She bullied her constantly and fed her little more than rice mixed with barley and some pickles. In those days, Kawaguchi-san explained, "Ultimately, being a bride meant being a work hand." When a woman's mother-in-law told her to do something, the yome was not supposed to say no. She was supposed to defer to her mother-in-law in every way, and she always served her in-laws their meals first, offering them and her husband the choicest bits and then eating the leftovers alone afterward.

I found, however, that because being a *shikkarimono no yome*, a capable bride and daughter-in-law, involved competence in local and household styles and conventions, what it meant for a Japanese women to be a good bride—what she might need to learn and the adjustments she might be expected to make—took on different nuances when used in reference to women who were raised in different kinds of households or regions.[15] I found too that these adjustments were expected to be even greater in the case of Filipina wives. That is, whereas Japanese women from outside the region were believed to need guidance to adapt to regional, household, or occupational differences in their affinal households, Filipina women were believed to need more extensive and special instruction on account of their having come from another country. As Kawaguchi-san explained, a Filipina bride was different from a Japanese bride because "a Japanese bride would naturally blend in. Because a foreign bride doesn't know a thing, you have to teach her. Customs are different; ways of socializing are different; country by country, they're different for everyone. And beyond that . . . each household even does things in its own way, right?" Being Filipina added an additional and significant degree of difference that needed to be addressed in a schema in which difference and sameness were reckoned in concentric, scaled spheres that gradually moved outward from household, to community, to region, to country.

Most Filipina women's in-laws, husbands, and even neighbors instructed these women to conduct their everyday lives in particular ways and to adopt specific affective stances. Filipina women were taught to manage behaviors that ranged from preparing and serving Japanese foods in their new household's style, to greeting and interacting with neighbors, to caring for special features of Japanese homes, such as *shōji* (sliding wood and paper doors), futons, and tatami mats. In 1995, the county *hokenfu* (public health nurses), Nagaoka-san and Itoh-san, also began a government-sponsored class, the Mothers' Class (mentioned in the introduction), to help foreign brides adjust to life in Japan.[16] Nagaoka-san and Itoh-san told me that, although they had been working with Filipina mothers in the region for nearly a decade, in 1994 they had noticed a significant jump in the number of Filipina women who were coming in for the health examination provided for infants at the public health center. The nurses had felt overwhelmed. Not only did they find themselves having problems communicating with these women, and therefore unable to provide guidance, they also sensed that many of these women were feeling confused and isolated. They concluded that these women might benefit from insights gleaned from other Filipina women who had been living in the region for longer periods of time. The two nurses came up with the idea for a class intended to help these women feel less isolated and make friends with other Filipina women in the region. They hoped that the class would enable the women to work together to resolve cultural differences and uneasiness with childcare they experienced in Japan.

As Nagaoka-san and Itoh-san organized the class, they consulted Filipina women in the region about what they wanted to learn. During the first year (1995), the class met monthly to focus on food preparation and practical matters such as riding the train. In the second year (1996), the nurses expanded the group's activities to include a *kanji* (Chinese characters) class to teach the women to read and write in Japanese.[17] In 1998, Nagaoka-san and Itoh-san also started a support group for the women to share problems and concerns they faced in their everyday lives. (As I mentioned in the introduction, I attended these classes and support group meetings during my fieldwork.) As part of the support-group program, the nurses sponsored a series of lectures to help the women feel less isolated and to teach them about Japan's health care system and child-drearing in Japan. For example, during one of the meetings I attended, a local elementary school principal dogmatically lectured the women about *shitsuke,* literally "discipline" in Japanese, but what he (in my view, patronizingly and chauvinistically) described as "uniquely Japanese

ways" of rearing children to be respectful and self-confident members of
Japanese society.[18]

The Mothers' Class was formed in part in response to the interest and
requests of Filipina women in the area, many who were committed to ad-
justing to life in Central Kiso. In all of the meetings I attended, the nurses
made considerable effort to listen to the women, support them, and accommodate their needs. Many Filipina women appreciated these efforts
and responded positively to these meetings (including, to my surprise, the
lecture on *shitsuke*). However, it was in no small part local residents' expectations that Filipina women conform to what they defined as "Japanese" ways of doing things, and the difficulties women faced accommo-
dating these pressures, that shaped their desires for such a group. It is to
a discussion of these expectations that I now turn.

NIHON NO YARIKATA (THE JAPANESE WAY)

"Japanese women's personalities and ways of thinking are different from
Filipinas," Suzuki-san, Ruby's patron, told me as we sat at the bar at Sampagita the night of Ruby's birthday party. That evening I asked Suzuki-
san about the recent increase of Filipina women to the region and about
what was expected of a Filipina woman who married a local man.
Suzuki-san took the opportunity not only to respond to my query, but
also to outline the differences he saw between Filipina women and Japanese women and to expound his theory of culture and character.

"Japanese people are detail-oriented and think deeply before making
a decision," he said, "but Filipinas are *iikagen* [irresponsible, careless,
lackadaisical; the opposite of shikkari] and give up halfway. Even if a Filipina were instructed as to how to do things shikkari, she may not be able
to comprehend it."

He then turned to his theory of cultural difference:

"My guess is that the Philippine climate is hot. Generally people from
hot countries are iikagen. That is how Filipinos seem to Japanese. Japanese ways of thinking are detail oriented, but from a Filipino's point of
view doing things iikagen might be commonsense."

"What must a Filipina woman married to a Japanese man do to blend
into Japanese society?" I asked, masking my discomfort with his comments.

Suzuki-san explained that getting Japanese nationality was difficult.
"However," he said, "if a Filipina marries a Japanese man, then she is
to become like a Japanese. She has to become a Japanese. . . . She has to
learn Japanese traditions. She has to learn customs from years back. She

must make an effort to learn them." Suzuki-san expressed frustration with Filipina women who did not make such an effort. He advised me to ask Filipina women what they thought about Japanese culture and if they thought that they could adapt to it.

Like Suzuki-san, many local residents with whom I spoke maintained that, to be shikkari, a Filipina woman had to learn to do things the Japanese way. These comments expressed an often taken-for-granted assumption that because these women lived in Japan, they had to do things in a certain manner. ("This is Japan!" was the tautological response I commonly received when I asked Japanese residents why doing things the Japanese way was necessary.) Yet the Japanese way did not necessarily refer to a fixed, traditional, or essentially cultural practice (or even one found throughout the Japanese archipelago). When local residents described a Filipina woman as doing things shikkari, they meant that she had learned to do things according to the ways that local residents believed they had been done in the region in the past or were—and should be—done in the region at the time. As I discuss in the concluding section of this chapter, the very act of identifying Filipina women as (or as not) being shikkari offered local residents a key opportunity to define "the Japanese way" in a manner they found most amenable, for example, in terms of preparing foods in a local style or respecting and caring for elderly in-laws. Nonetheless, whether or not a Filipina woman could manage these behaviors became a key criterion through which Japanese community members in Central Kiso evaluated her as a capable bride.

Moreover, as many Central Kiso residents believed that all Filipina women married to Japanese men should learn to do things the Japanese way, they also believed that *some* Filipina women could manage to do so more adeptly than others on account of innate features of their character. Thus, shikkari not only offered a standard of discipline by which to evaluate a bride in general terms. It also provided a means by which some Filipina women who were believed to be doing things the Japanese way were set apart from other Filipina women.

For example, one day I stopped by Sachiko's coffee shop on my way to Ligaya's house, which was in a nearby mountain village. Emiko and several other middle-aged women were also there that afternoon, and Sachiko was sitting with them as they enjoyed their coffee. When I finished my lunch and got up to leave, I explained that I was headed to Ligaya's, casually adding that Emiko also knew her, that they too were friends. Emiko immediately interjected: Ligaya was "different than ordinary

Filipinos," she explained. "She's really being shikkari." The other women nodded with interest.

Emiko had likely made this comment to protect her (and my) reputation. As I mentioned in chapter 1, she had cautioned me early on in my research that some in the region might call my character into question if they knew that I associated with Filipina women who had worked in bars (which Ligaya, as I mentioned in the previous chapter, had not). However, Emiko's comment also suggests that local residents described Filipina women as shikkari not only to differentiate between "Japanese ways" and "Filipino ways" but also to differentiate *among* Filipina women in the region.

In this regard, local residents attributed a given Filipina woman's ability to be shikkari to more than her ability to acquire the skills necessary to manage Japanese household practices. They also attributed it to innate and individually rooted features of her character. For instance, during our interview, I asked Kawaguchi-san what she had taught Ana when Ana had entered their household. Kawaguchi-san modestly demurred, "Well, it's not that I've taught her anything particularly great. That child learned naturally *(shizen ni oboeta),* by imitating what she saw me do. Because that child is pretty smart. That's why she came into our household rather smoothly." To explain how Ana had learned, Kawaguchi-san did not use the Japanese word *narau* (to learn or study), for example, with books or in school. Rather she maintained that Ana *"shizen ni oboeta"* (learned naturally); she used the term *oboeta,* an intimate acquisition of skills and knowledge through bodily experience, memorization, and imitation. Kawaguchi-san also maintained that Ana was able to learn in this manner because she was "pretty smart." In other words, Ana learned naturally through an embodied, mimetic practice because of her intelligence, an innate aspect of her character that went beyond whether she was born Filipina or Japanese.

Kawaguchi-san later explained that Ana's performance of her role in her household could also be linked to a common standard of humanity that Ana shared with some "good" Japanese people: "Even though a bride is from another country, she's no different as a person. There's no reason to discriminate on the basis of a person being born Japanese or not Japanese. There are many bad Japanese people, just as there are many good foreigners. So you can't discriminate on that basis. Our bride does everything properly for us, the cleaning, and so on. I always thank her. I'm grateful." In this regard, Kawaguchi-san recognized Ana not only as being smart but also as sharing with some—but not all—Japanese people an intuitive and common sensibility regarding what it means to be a good person, and by extension a good bride and daughter-in-law.

At one point in our interview, I asked Kawaguchi-san if Ana could cook Japanese foods when she first came into their household. This time Kawaguchi-san revealed that she had given Ana instruction, responding, "No. Because she couldn't really, I gave her various kinds of advice."

"Does she sometimes make Filipino food for you?" I asked. Kawaguchi-san told me that Ana never had, although she knew that Ana sometimes prepared Filipino food for herself.

"Have you ever had Filipino food?" I pressed.

"No," she told me. "Not once." She paused for a moment, and then explained, "That one [Ana], she's trying her hardest so that she can become completely Japanese. And well, she probably realizes that Filipino cuisine doesn't suit Japanese people. Moreover, Grandpa is here, and because he doesn't really like things like that, she's restraining herself I think. After we pass away, I don't know what she'll cook, but while we're around . . . [she only cooks Japanese food]."

Japanese national and cultural identity has long been articulated in terms of food culture, so much so that some have argued that Japanese bodies are unique and can only digest certain foods prepared in certain ways.[19] As I detail in the next chapter, Filipina women's families expected these women to prepare Japanese meals on a daily basis, and many refused to eat Filipino food except on occasion, if at all. According to Kawaguchi-san, Ana's efforts at "becoming Japanese" were evidenced by her preparation of Japanese meals. However, the practice of preparing Japanese foods alone was not why Ana was considered a good bride (after all, Kawaguchi-san suggested that after she and her husband passed away she did not know what Ana might cook, and she knew that Ana prepared Filipino foods for herself). More crucial was the fact that Ana was restraining her own desires to accommodate her in-laws and that she recognized that Filipino foods did not "suit" Japanese people and instead cooked Japanese foods that they liked. Doing things the Japanese way was not a matter of never cooking or eating Filipino foods so much as intuiting one's in-laws' wishes regarding the types of foods they wanted to eat and restricting serving Filipino foods to appropriate contexts.[20] It was a matter of character evidenced through an intuitive and affective sensibility that informed an embodied domestic practice.

Ligaya's husband similarly told me with pride that Ligaya had "naturally" *(shizen ni)* learned to do things the Japanese way simply by living in Central Kiso—through daily immersion and exposure to life in the region. He explained that she had managed this because she was intelligent and shared his values about family and household life. These sensibilities extended beyond an acquired knowledge of Japanese culinary techniques to Ligaya's solid character, her skill at learning to speak Japanese, and her commitment to her husband and household. These features of her character had made daily life with her, in the home she created, in his words, "no different" than if he had married a Japanese woman.

However, as Emiko suggested, not all Filipina women were believed to be able to manage things as well as Ligaya. During the course of my interview with Suzuki-san, he began to complain that the problem with many Filipina women was that they did not make enough of an effort to adapt to "Japanese culture." He began to advise me: "You should ask Filipinas why they don't want to blend in. I think that's the most important thing. Please ask them flat out: why don't you try to learn Japanese traditions? If you [Lieba] understand the answers to this question, I think you'll really be able to understand relations between Japanese and Filipinos." Suzuki-san added that there were many Filipina-Japanese couples in Japan, but he speculated that many of these marriages had problems. Then he continued, "Why don't Filipinas try to blend in to Japanese ways? These days, Japanese people don't really trust Filipinas. Please ask a large number of Filipinas what they think of Japanese culture." He offered a sample question for me to ask Filipina women I interviewed: "Do you think that you could incorporate Japanese culture into your way of thinking?" He explained that he was very interested in this question. Then he suggested some additional ones: "Please ask: 'Are you familiar with Japanese culture?' If they say they are, ask them, 'What do you think of Japanese culture?'" He repeated these questions several times, stressing his interest in Filipina women's responses. Then he continued, "If they try to blend into Japanese ways of life, I think Filipina-Japanese marriages would go better. And then there is the issue of older folks not trusting Filipinas. It's all connected, I think. If Filipinas tried to understand Japanese people's way of thinking, if they tried to do things the way Japanese people do them, older folks' ways of thinking about Filipinas would change a little." Suzuki-san then added that part of the problem was that Filipina women worked in bars and therefore were perceived as prostitutes, which gave them a bad reputation among older folks.

Just as Suzuki-san and I were finishing our conversation, Ana arrived at Sampagita to help celebrate Ruby's birthday, and she joined us at the bar. I introduced Ana to Suzuki-san, and she explained that she worked at Satonoya Soba, her household's business. Suzuki-san recognized the name of the soba restaurant immediately. He smiled widely and asked, "That's you?" Relaxing deeply into his chair, Suzuki-san then decided to take advantage of the opportunity and ask Ana some of the questions he had just suggested to me.

"What do you think of Japanese culture and ways of thinking? Are you making an effort to adapt to them?" he began.

Ana smiled politely, resting her hands demurely in lap. She explained that yes, everyone around her was Japanese, so she was trying to adapt to Japanese ways.

"Are you making an effort to do things the Japanese way because you live with a Japanese family?" he continued.

Again, Ana responded affirmatively. She said that she did things the Japanese way because everyone around her was Japanese.

Suzuki-san double-checked to make sure he was being understood: "You do things different in the Philippines, right, family customs and all, the way you eat?"

Ana said yes a third time. She explained that, for example, just once when she had moved in with her family she had tried to eat with her hands as she did in the Philippines, but her mother-in-law had stopped her, saying it was *"kitanai"* (dirty) so Ana never did it again.

This seemed to be sufficient evidence for Suzuki-san. His lips spread into a broad grin. "You're great," he announced, "That's great." He then asked if Ana was planning on staying in Japan for good. Again she said yes. She added that she was deciding now whether or not she would become a naturalized Japanese citizen and that one Filipina she knew, Leeza, had recently decided that she would take Japanese citizenship.

Suzuki-san beamed. All he could do was repeat *"Subarashii!"* (Great!) and nod his head in appreciation.

In short, Filipina women in Central Kiso like Ana who could manage to do things the Japanese way—who were shikkari—were considered *exceptional* Filipina women and accorded recognition as such. Aihwa Ong has intervened in Giorgio Agamben's work on the political role of the exception to argue that it can not only work to exclude subjects but also be a positive mechanism for including selected populations as targets of forms of power.[21] Correspondingly, for Filipina women shikkari was not only a standard for distinguishing between "good brides" and "bad brides." It was also a criterion for evaluating a woman's character and establishing positive exceptions, that is, for determining if a given Filipina woman was the *right kind of Filipina*: an *ii hito* (a good person) and intelligent woman; a woman who respected and cared for elderly, assisted in the family fields,

cooked Japanese foods to please her in-laws, adopted desirable affective
stances, and appropriately comported herself according to prescribed social
convention; a Filipina who could manage to do things the Japanese way; a
kindred spirit. Thus, Central Kiso residents did not simply laud Filipina
women as oyomesan when these women behaved in a shikkari manner. To
various ends, they also evaluated these women as "Filipinas" on this basis.

SOME FILIPINA WOMEN ARE "MORE JAPANESE THAN YOUNG JAPANESE WOMEN TODAY"

Interestingly, local residents used criteria such as "being shikkari" to do
more than evaluate Filipina women in the region in relation to each other.
They also used these criteria to evaluate them in relation to Japanese
women who residents did not feel were Japanese enough. A conversation
I had with my friend Mika's grandmother helps illustrate this point.

One afternoon Mika's grandmother was teaching me how to sugar-
pickle *ume*, Japanese plums. Before putting the fruit in jars with lumps of
rock sugar, she explained that we had to smash them, leaving in the pit
so as not to lose nutrients but puncturing the flesh just enough so that it
wouldn't pucker when the sugar melted. Mika's grandmother used a
cutting board and an empty Asahi beer bottle, skillfully splitting each
firm ume with the bottle's flat bottom. I used a small wooden plum-
sandwiching instrument that Mika's grandmother had devised years back.
As we worked through the large jars packed full of the fruit, Mika's grandmother started to complain. She told me that she had been smashing plums
until midnight the previous night. She had also been doing it all morning—
alone. Neither Mika nor Mika's mother had offered any help.

"My family just ignores me," she complained. "In the old days the
mother-in-law could do whatever she liked. Now being a mother-in-law
is terrible." She grumbled that she arose at six o'clock in the morning and
worked in the fields until ten o'clock every day before preparing tea for
the workers and lunch for her son. Nobody in her family even talked to
her, she said. Then after a pause, she asked: "In America do you take care
of the elderly?"

"Um," I stammered, "to be honest, the situation is often much worse
in the United States. Many elderly live in facilities and are rarely visited
by their families." I was feeling more than a little guilt about neglecting
my grandmother, who was in a nursing home at the time.

Mika's grandmother nodded thoughtfully. "In the Philippines they respect the elderly," she pronounced.

Although Mika's grandmother knew that I was conducting research about the region, I had not yet said anything to her about my interests in the lives of Filipina women. I had not expected it to be relevant because we had primarily spent time together working in her fields and preparing food. "How do you know about the situation of elderly in the Philippines?" I choked, explaining that I was also conducting research about Filipina wives in the region.

Mika's grandmother explained that she had heard a speech at the Kōenkai, a local government–sponsored lecture series that was part of machi zukuri efforts. "A Filipina bride in the village gave a lecture about how people in the Philippines take care of the elderly," she said. "The girl explained that in the Philippines all the siblings work together to take care of elderly parents. She asked why in Japan caring for elderly was left to the eldest son and his wife." Mika's grandmother reiterated that in the Philippines the elderly were very well cared for.

I remembered a conversation with Cora about a speech she had given in town regarding differences in the ways people cared for elderly in Japan and the Philippines. "Are you speaking of Nakamura Cora?" I asked.

"Yes," Mika's grandmother responded, "the oyomesan of the household that runs Nakamura Grocery."

"She takes good care of her in-laws?" I asked.

"Yes," Mika's grandmother replied with a steady nod. She had heard from the Nakamuras and others in the community that Cora worked very hard to help her in-laws. "*Some* people are like that," she said. "Her in-laws sure are lucky."

Then she commented that the oyomesan in her elder sister's household (her elder sister's grandson's wife) was also Filipina.

"Was she also an ii oyomesan?" I asked.

This time Mika's grandmother shook her head no. She complained that both this Filipina woman and her Japanese mother-in-law just kept her elder sister alone in a room all day and rarely spoke to her. "That's why she's going senile," she spat.

Many Japanese residents in Central Kiso described Filipina women as good oyomesan on account of the care and respect they showed to the elderly. This became a key point of comparison between Filipina and Japanese women in which *some* Filipina women came out ahead. Local residents also lauded Filipina wives of local men because of their ability to cook traditional Japanese foods, their willingness to do hard work, their patience, the value they placed on family and community relations, and their deference to their husbands. These practices and affective stances, which were tied to gendered and sexualized forms of domestic labor, were behaviors that local residents found agreeable and that, they claimed, many young Japanese women refused but some Filipina women embraced.

Of course, Central Kiso residents' critiques of contemporary Japanese women resonated with those more widely expressed by the Japanese government and found in popular media throughout Japan. Government officials and media commentaries have repeatedly warned of an impending national crisis caused by the "declining birthrate" and resulting in an "aging society."[22] Much of this discourse centers on the fact that many young Japanese women are postponing or opting against marriage and childbirth. It claims that they are selfish, indulgent, unpatriotic, and irresponsible on this account.[23] Central Kiso residents' favorable comparison of Filipina women with Japanese women resonates with these criticisms, which are often attributed to "Westernization" and the adoption of modern ideals. Their descriptions of Filipina women as traditional, submissive, and obedient also overlap with discourses circulating widely in Japan that present the Philippines as a poor and undeveloped country.

However, if Central Kiso residents engaged these wider discourses, they did so in locally and personally inflected ways. Their estimation of Filipina women as ii oyomesan was based on their concerns for their everyday lives and their interactions with these women. Moreover, in some cases, Filipina women's attitudes and behaviors were *more appealing* than those Central Kiso residents associated with Japanese local ways. Local residents thus also incorporated these attitudes and ideas into what it meant to be shikkari. For example, Mika's grandmother suggested that she found the ways that elderly were cared for in the Philippines, and correspondingly the ways that some Filipina yome in Central Kiso treated their in-laws, more desirable than the ways that her own Japanese daughter-in-law treated her. On this and other accounts, local residents sometimes identified Filipina women as "more Japanese than young Japanese women today." They thus incorporated Filipina women's ideas and practices into what both being an ideal bride and being Japanese meant in the region.

THE STAKES OF JAPANESENESS

Previous studies of Filipina-Japanese marriages in rural areas have suggested that rural Japanese residents' treatment of Filipina women as yome/oyomesan reflects their attachment to a traditional, patriarchal ie system. According to these studies, these marriages reflect rural residents'

backwards ideas about gender and kinship and serve as evidence that
people in rural Japan are stuck in an outdated past.[24] Here, however, I
have suggested that Central Kiso residents had contemporary stakes in
identifying Filipina women as ii oyomesan because doing so worked productively in their day-to-day lives.

First (and perhaps ironically), some local residents were asserting their
modernity and cosmopolitanism when they described Filipina women
in such terms. Recall Kawaguchi-san's claim that her Filipina daughter-
in-law Ana was an adept learner and therefore a good bride. In making
this assertion, Kawaguchi-san recalled her own painful experiences coming as a bride to Central Kiso from elsewhere in Japan. Maintaining that
mothers-in-law today treat their yome with more care, appreciation, and
respect, she differentiated herself from her "old-fashioned" mother-in-law.
She prided herself on treating Ana as a person (as opposed to simply a
household work hand or a foreigner) and thereby presented herself as a
cosmopolitan, open-minded, and modern woman in terms of how she
viewed both people (as individuals) and household relationships (not as
hierarchical corporate organizations but as mutually appreciative and
supportive groups).

Second, when Central Kiso residents identified some Filipina women
as ii oyomesan, they engaged in a disciplinary practice that pressured Filipina women in the region (and some Japanese women as well) to behave
in certain ways. That is, Japanese residents did not simply *describe*
Filipina women as ideal traditional Japanese brides: They *interpellated*
them into gendered discourses of kinship and national belonging.[25] In-
terpellation is a powerful and disciplinary subject-making practice. Recognizing some Filipina women—but not others—as ii oyomesan defined
a standard of behavior for young married women that local residents
found appealing. Consider Emiko's characterization of Tessie as an ideal
bride and daughter-in-law because Tessie was willing to assist her in-
laws in their rice fields, work that Emiko suggested most young Japanese
women were no longer willing to do. When Emiko used the term shikkari
in regard to Tessie, she invoked (and thereby reproduced) a set of be-
havioral criteria for evaluating young married women in the region.

Central Kiso residents' expectations that Filipina women learn to behave in certain ways in some sense recall imperialist discourses in which
colonized populations were expected to assimilate to Japanese ways.[26] Although colonial legacies inform relationships among Filipina women and
Japanese residents in the region, I would caution against reading local residents' attitudes as a direct continuation or modern day incarnation of

these colonial practices. Japan's colonial enterprise in Asia was informed by different discourses of Japaneseness than those circulating in late twentieth-century Japan.[27] In imperial Japan, discourses of assimilation were constructed and mobilized to conceal the problem of citizenship between the colonies and the metropole that contradicted pretenses of a unified Japanese empire and a "Greater East Asia Co-prosperity Sphere."[28] In contrast, Central Kiso residents mobilized discourses of assimilation and Japaneseness to manage their experiences of social and political-economic marginality and to conceal both the inconsistencies and the possibilities of cultural difference within what counts as "Japan."

Third, then, by claiming that some Filipina women were ii oyomesan and thus "more Japanese than young Japanese women today," Central Kiso residents asserted locally based understandings of Japaneseness. As I suggested in the previous chapter, Central Kiso residents were aware that many urban dwellers associated rural areas with a traditional Japanese past. These residents also recognized that this past was at once valorized and forsaken in ways that affected their everyday lives. In likening some Filipina women to "traditional Japanese women," Central Kiso residents negotiated the contradictions of their positioning within dominant discourses of Japaneseness. They asserted their own definitions of Japaneseness and positioned themselves as arbiters of it. In doing so, they maintained their modernity and belonging as part of a Japanese nation. They celebrated "traditional" rural ways as superior to "modern" urban ones. And they expressed a set of desires regarding how a rural place like Central Kiso might fit into contemporary visions of what being Japanese might mean.[29]

Fourth, some Central Kiso residents decided that once Filipina women had married into their families and communities, they had little to gain by refusing to accept these women. Claims that Filipina women were more amenable brides than Japanese women anticipated and challenged an urban imagination where places like Central Kiso are viewed as backwaters where "only Filipina women" would marry local men. Many Japanese residents with whom I spoke were pleased by the prospect that Filipina women married to local men would take Japanese nationality. They took this as evidence of the women's commitment to their families and lives in the region. In a place suffering because few young people were interested in remaining, this commitment counted for a lot. Filipina wives of local men also had children whom they raised as Japanese (and whom many local residents recognized exclusively as Japanese.) These children boosted local school enrollments, bringing in national subsidies and offering hope for a regional future. Thus, if local residents

nostalgically celebrated a traditional Japanese past when they characterized Filipina women as ii oyomesan, they were not referring to the
vanishing past of Japanese modernity for which, some have argued,
urban dwellers long.[30] They were staking a place for themselves within
dominant discourses of Japaneseness while managing their dependence
on Filipina women to sustain day-to-day life in the region.

Significantly, whether or not Central Kiso residents meant to, they also
redefined Japaneseness in this process. All identities (such as Japanese) are
constituted performatively.[31] That is, they are produced, and come to
have social force, as they are repeatedly used to describe people, behaviors, or things. Moreover, insofar as all performatives are historically situated, these citational processes of identification transform identities just
as they reproduce them.[32] Thus, each time Central Kiso residents described
a Filipina woman as an ii oyomesan and "more Japanese than young Japanese women today," they at once reproduced and transformed what these
categories meant. They reinforced the centrality of Japaneseness to life in
the region; however, they also redefined this category in terms of embodied, affective everyday practices (often glossed as "being shikkari") that
had relevance to their contemporary lives. When used to describe Filipina women, these performance-based discourses of Japaneseness overrode
biogenetically based notions of national and racial difference that have
dominated in Japan for the past fifty years. They offered a notion of Japaneseness that, like biogenetically based understandings, was embedded in
the body and rooted in "natural" characteristics. However, the locus of
this natural tie was not blood or genes but in an individual's inherent intelligence and character as evidenced by her performance of gender and
kinship roles.

Yet the narrative I have presented in this chapter is only part of the
story. As I have suggested, kinship positions like oyomesan are made
"real" (that is, to have material consequence in the world) as people identify certain behaviors with them. Thus, to understand how meanings of
Japaneseness in Central Kiso are being reinscribed and transformed
through relationships with Filipina migrants, we also need to consider how
and why Filipina women married to Japanese men in Central Kiso performed their roles in their Japanese families. In the next chapter, I consider
how Filipina women like Cora and Ana felt about their Japanese in-laws'
expectations. I explore when, why, and to what ends they chose to (or not
to) accommodate these expectations and what "being oyomesan" meant
to these women.

CHAPTER 5

The Pressures of Home

The winters in Central Kiso are long and cold. People born and raised in the region will tell you they come from a *"samui tokoro"* (a cold place). They may even recite a line from the Kisobushi (The Kiso Melody), a folk song about the Kiso region that is familiar throughout Japan: *Natsu demo samui.* "Even summer is cold." Some liked to say that the region was colder than even Hokkaido, where at least houses are well heated. Only the newest and most expensive homes in Central Kiso had insulated walls or central heating. Most people I knew warmed their houses the cheapest way, with kerosene stoves. Some, myself included, also taped plastic bubble-wrap to the windows to keep out the chill and stave off pipe damage. Yet despite these efforts, and in large part because of my reluctance to purchase a second kerosene stove, the small house I rented on the Kiso River was almost unbearably cold throughout the winter. For several weeks straight in January and February, the thermometer in my kitchen dropped below −4°C each morning, and I soon found that I had to put fruit and vegetables in the refrigerator to keep them from freezing solid overnight. Like most people in the area, I set up my *kotatsu* (a low covered and heated table) in late October, and I spent the bulk of my day sitting with my legs under it for the next five months.

One Thursday afternoon in late November, after our Japanese class, Cora, Ana, and I huddled in the six-mat tatami room I was heating and using as my bedroom, living room, and office through the winter. The women had agreed to a taped interview, and on the brisk walk to my house from Cora's van we had begun talking about their in-laws. Both Cora and Ana had commented that they felt as though they were "performing" when they were home. Once we had settled under the kotatsu, I asked them to expand on what they had said and how it related to being an ii oyomesan, an expression I had heard Japanese community members use to describe both of these women. We spoke in a mixture of Japanese, Tagalog, and English:

> L: You had said that when you're at home with your family in Japan you felt like you were performing. Why?
>
> C: Because it's like you always need to show your in-laws that you appreciate them, like that. You have to show that they're not doing anything bad toward you, again and again. It's like that, like you have to perform.
>
> L: [To Ana] Do you feel like you're performing?
>
> A: Me, yes, I feel that way.
>
> L: Why are you performing?
>
> A: For me, it's so something bad won't happen. So they think only good things about Filipinos, only good things about Filipina brides.
>
> C: When they see something that one Filipina has done, they think all Filipinas are like that. That's how Japanese people in Central Kiso are.
>
> A: Because, this is the countryside, right? Gossip is terrible.
>
> L: So you want them to think well about Filipinas?
>
> A: Yes.
>
> C: Because they have a bad image.
>
> L: So you have to change their image?
>
> C: Especially because we work in the clubs. They really look down on women who work in clubs. Maybe not all of them, but most. Especially the elderly.
>
> A: They're really old-fashioned.
>
> L: How about when you're at home? Do you feel like you're performing like a Japanese wife?
>
> C and A: At home . . .
>
> C: I'm like that. That's what happens to me.
>
> L: Like you're oyomesan, Japanese?
>
> C: Like that. What is it? It's strange. I change in the kitchen. If I'm there I'm Japanese. When I go up to my room, I'm Filipina. [As Ana says "Filipina," Cora does too.]
>
> L: But in the kitchen you feel like . . .
>
> C and A: Japanese.

L: Why in the kitchen?

C: Because . . .

C and A: You're the oyomesan.

L: In the kitchen you are oyomesan?

C and A: Yeah.

L: But in your own room you are Filipina?

A: Well, you see, of course in my own room I do things my own way.

C: Yes, that's it.

L: But in the kitchen . . . you're . . . [Cora and Ana join in:] oyomesan.

L: When you say oyomesan, you mean, a Japanese oyomesan? [Ana says this last word with me.]

C: Yeah. I know why it's in the kitchen. Because in the kitchen you cook, you cook Japanese foods. You don't cook Filipino foods. They won't eat them. Maybe some people's Japanese husbands and in-laws will eat them, but in our house, they won't eat Filipino foods. If I don't also cook Japanese foods, only my children and I will eat. When you sit day after day at the table. You prepare food for them. You serve them. It's like you're the maid, like you're the maid.

L: Because you're oyomesan . . .

C: They say the oyomesan is like that.

A: That's oyomesan.

C: They treat us like they would treat a child, it's like they're raising us.

L: So . . . who taught you to prepare Japanese food?

C: My mother-in-law.

L: She taught you? [A: Yeah] Do you have to prepare it the Japanese way?

C: Of course! The way you cut . . . [A joins:] the way you eat . . .

A: The way you cook . . .

C: The way you sit . . .

L: For example? How do you sit? How do you cook? How do you cut?

A: Cut? For example, well, if it's *sukiyaki*, scallions for *sukiyaki*, you don't cut them like this [she demonstrates cutting scallions in small rounds]. You have to cut them big and on a diagonal. They say that's how they taste good. And then, if you're cutting burdock for *kinpira [gobō]*, you can't just cut it like this, you have to cut it like that. Because, that's the way to cut them for *kinpira [gobō]*. Of course, in the Philippines, we do it any which way. But in Japan, of course, there's one particular way. If you're making *nabemono*, you do it the *nabemono*-way. If it's *sukiyaki*, the *sukiyaki*-way. If it's *yakiniku*, the *yakiniku*-way.

L: And the way that you sit. How do you sit?

C: Like this. [Cora demonstrates *seiza,* sitting on the floor with her calves neatly tucked under her thighs and her feet together.]

L: You have to sit *seiza?*

C: Yeah. At first.

L: And if you didn't sit *seiza,* they yelled at you?

C: They got mad.

L: And how about the way you served the food?

C: With both hands! But they don't say anything any more. But in the beginning, it was really difficult.

A: Yeah. Now, I've been living there for a long time, they can't say things every day. . . .

C: It's tiring already.

In the previous chapter I considered how some Japanese residents in Central Kiso expanded their notion of Japaneseness to include some Filipina women. I suggested that according to a number of these residents, being oyomesan involved executing a gendered set of everyday practices in a shikkari manner: preparing Japanese meals, maintaining a Japanese home, caring for children and elderly in-laws, maintaining relations with neighbors and community members, sometimes helping with a household business, and adopting certain comportments and affective behaviors. I argued that, as far as some Japanese residents in Central Kiso were concerned, if a Filipina woman could manage these activities, she could be identified as an ii oyomesan.

This chapter asks why some Filipina women in Central Kiso carried out these practices and, thus, behaved in ways that some Japanese community members recognized as consistent with being an "ideal, traditional Japanese bride." It considers how these women's understandings and performances of this role were shaped by their vulnerable positioning in Japan (and more generally a global economy), their senses of themselves as women and as Filipina, their relationships with their families in the Philippines, and their desires for self-actualization both within and outside a domestic realm. I suggest that, in Central Kiso, Filipina women's motivations for performing their roles as oyomesan were mixed, ambivalent, and complicated, and that Japanese community members sometimes identified these women as performing the role of an ii oyomesan when the women self-consciously saw themselves doing something else. Actions, like words, are polysemic. People ascribe multiple and diverse meanings to a given behavior depending on how they are situated and their stakes in it. These ascribed meanings are themselves the products of long histories of encounter and shifting configurations of culture and power.[1] What frameworks of meaning were Filipina women in Central Kiso drawing upon when they performed their roles in their Japanese families? What significance did these women ascribe to their performances? How were these performances tied to other ways these women crafted transnational senses of self?

To "perform" is not only to enact but also to carry out a task. Just as actions can be interpreted in different ways, people can have different motivations for performing a given behavior. To some degree, Filipina women in Central Kiso had little choice but to accommodate their Japanese in-laws' expectations. Their spousal visas were temporary residence visas, issued in graduated periods first for six months, then after a while for one year, and later for three years. Women's visa renewals were dependent on their Japanese families' sponsorship and would not be issued if women separated from their husbands or got a divorce. Most Filipina women in Central Kiso were financially supporting their families in the Philippines; in some cases, they were not only supporting parents and siblings, but also children from previous relationships with Filipino men or Japanese men met during earlier stints working in Japan.[2] Many women with whom I spoke stressed that sending money home was an important objective of their lives in Japan, and their spousal visas enabled them to legally work full-time.[3] Some Filipina women in Central Kiso also received money from their Japanese families to send to the Philippines. Insofar as these women's ability to send money to their families in the Philippines hinged on their Japanese families' financial assistance or, at least, sponsorship of their spousal visas, it also hinged on their performances of their roles as oyomesan.

Yet to assume that Filipina women in Central Kiso performed their roles in their Japanese families solely on account of their political-economic vulnerability would be to overlook the multiple and conflicting forms of desire that shaped their decisions to go abroad in the first place and their feelings about their lives in Japan. As I discussed in chapter 2, many Filipina women married to Japanese men in Central Kiso initially went to Japan to realize dreams of a better life for themselves and their families in the Philippines. Their dreams to support their families in the Philippines were also tied to desires for upward mobility—to purchase homes for oneself and one's parents, put younger relatives through school, and buy brand-name clothing, purses, makeup, jewelry, and home furnishings. In addition, women described their migration decisions in terms of their desires to own their own businesses, be financially self-sufficient, and travel. Filipina women's desires for their lives in Central Kiso were also desires for self-actualization: to be on their own, have an adventure, and find themselves.

These women found some of what they were looking for in their lives as oyomesan. Moreover, as I discuss below, after these women married their Japanese husbands, many of them became committed to their lives as wives and mothers. These roles compensated for their stigmatized employment in bars and resonated with ideals about gender and kinship tied to Catholicism and widely circulating in the Philippines. In other ways, however, women's desires for their lives conflicted with those of their Japanese families. In performing their roles as oyomesan, Filipina women in Central Kiso had to negotiate the tensions that emerged when their visions for their lives did not match those of their Japanese husbands and in-laws. They also had to manage the conflicts that emerged among their commitments to help their families in the Philippines, their desires to become independent, and their senses of responsibility to their families in Japan. These women could successfully perform their roles as oyomesan only insofar as these tensions were managed, whether through self-conscious efforts on the part of the women or through the productive resonances and misunderstandings that emerged between their own and their Japanese families' interpretations of their daily activities. In what follows, I explore how Filipina women in Central Kiso crafted transnational senses of self through their roles in their Japanese families. By paying attention to how these women performed their roles as oyomesan at the microlevel of daily practice, I illustrate some of the ways that the resonances and dissonances in meaning and desire that develop in cultural encounters can work alongside coercive and subjectifying forms of power and pleasure to both sustain and, occasionally, disrupt modes of discipline and domination.

PERFORMING OYOMESAN MEANS
PERFORMING FILIPINANESS

Let me, then, return for a moment to my conversation with Cora and Ana. Like the members of the Japanese community discussed in the previous chapter, Cora and Ana associated being oyomesan with a set of everyday practices that these women identified as distinctively Japanese. In this regard, the women agreed with Japanese community members that Japaneseness was not necessarily linked to a biogenetically based notion of race or ethnicity but to a set of learnable tasks. Japanese residents maintained that a Filipina woman's ability to execute such tasks the Japanese way reflected her innate intelligence or character. However, Cora and Ana described doing things the Japanese way as a frustrating and even forced and self-conscious enactment of a role that involved

both physical and emotional forms of labor similar to those done by domestic helpers (not wives) in the Philippines ("It's like you're the maid.").

Most Filipina women I met in Central Kiso were sensitive to, and
sometimes resentful of, many of the demands and constraints their Japanese families placed upon them. Like Cora and Ana, these women complained that they not only had to manage domestic tasks the Japanese way
but also had to force themselves to interact with their Japanese community members in prescribed manners: to answer the door, greet neighbors
on the street, and interact in social settings in specific ways. They also
complained that they regularly had to reassure their in-laws that they appreciated them. Cora and Ana had learned to cope with their in-laws' expectations by treating their role as a Japanese oyomesan as one they inhabited only in specific situations and locations. They approached being
oyomesan and Japanese as situated identities that they fluidly entered and
exited—for example, only in certain parts of their homes (the kitchen) and
particularly when doing certain forms of labor (such as cooking dinner for
their families). These women understood being Japanese and oyomesan
not as all-defining states, but in terms of particular spatialized practices,
embodiments, and forms of discipline. One might say that they had developed a spatially based form of double-consciousness that shifted as
they moved through different rooms of their homes.[4]

Yet for Cora and Ana, being an ii oyomesan did not simply involve a
strategic, contained performance of Japaneseness. Paradoxically, it also
involved strategic performances of Filipinaness. Martin Manalansan has
argued that performance is an important part of cultural citizenship, one
that does not reflect a monolithic notion of identity and belonging but
that can reflect a diversity of citizen-selves.[5] For many Filipina women in
Central Kiso, performing one's role as oyomesan was a practical strategy not only for maintaining visa status in Japan but also for challenging stereotypes that Japanese residents held toward Filipina women and
redefining what "Filipina" meant. As Cora explained, the women were
"avoiding [their in-laws] being able to say anything bad about Filipinas."

Moreover, being an ii oyomesan was one of the few viable ways that
Filipina women could be recognized as legitimate social subjects in Central Kiso—that is, as what some Japanese residents referred to as "good
people" (ii hito) who were on par with Japanese. The women knew that
the stereotypes Japanese community members held toward Filipina
women affected how they were treated. As I mentioned in the introduction, Cora's in-laws had initially begged the mama-san at the bar where
she had worked to break off Cora and her husband's engagement because

they did not want their son marrying a Filipina woman, and particularly one who had worked in a bar. By demonstrating that she was a responsible and hardworking oyomesan, Cora endeavored to compensate for negative images attached to her past employment in a hostess bar and attempted to transform local understandings of what it mean to be Filipina. She and Ana did not perform their roles as oyomesan solely to maintain smooth relationships with their in-laws. They also did so out of a commitment to improving and challenging dominant perceptions in Central Kiso of women from the Philippines.

THE ACCOMPLISHMENT OF BEING OYOMESAN

As we have seen, through their performances of their roles as oyomesan, Filipina women like Cora and Ana were to some degree successful in transforming their Japanese communities' perceptions of (some) Filipina women. These women sometimes felt a sense of pride and accomplishment that they were able to do so. Foucault has argued that power works productively by making its mechanisms economically advantageous and politically useful and by inducing pleasures.[6] A number of Filipina women with whom I spoke described the pride and pleasures that accompanied successfully performing their roles in their Japanese families in ways that positively affected how Japanese community members viewed and treated them. Moreover, some Filipina women in Central Kiso not only took pride in transforming stereotypes that some Japanese community members held toward them, but also understood the Japanese way as involving a mastery of skills, and they enjoyed the acknowledgement they received for successfully demonstrating competence in them.

For example, one afternoon, Ana and I were sitting in the small apartment where she had lived with her husband when they were first married, which was located above her family's soba restaurant. We were discussing the early years of her marriage and how she had met her husband. Suddenly, Ana announced with excitement, "I got my *eijū!*" (permanent residency). She explained that the documents had come in the mail the previous week. I was surprised. Ana had been married for only six years. I knew Filipina women who had been married for more than ten and who still had not gotten their residency applications approved.[7] "How did you get your residency permit so quickly?" I asked. Ana then summarized her visa history for me: when she had first gotten married, she had been issued a six-month spousal visa. When that expired, she received another six-month visa. Then, she was issued a one-year visa and after that another one-year visa. Then, before the immigration authorities issued her a three-year visa—the next step in a standard progression—an immigration officer had come to investigate her situation. Immigration was suspicious that Ana might simply be an employee in her in-laws' restaurant, her spousal visa a ruse to enable her to work. Ana explained that the shop was closed on the day the officer had come, so he had asked people living in the restaurant's vicinity about her. The shop's neighbors had spoken well of Ana. They had also told the officer how to find her family's house in a nearby hamlet. Ana explained that the officer had visited her home and seen that she was, in Ana's words, "in fact living as oyomesan" and had two children who were Japanese nationals. He had spoken with Ana's in-laws, who praised Ana highly and said that she was trying very hard to adjust to life in Japan. Impressed, the immigration officer had recommended that Ana receive permanent residency.

Ana took pride in her early receipt of permanent residency and the ways it reflected upon her as a person, a woman, and a Filipina. Ana told me that she felt ashamed that she had worked in a bar and that she thought it was understandable that her in-laws initially disliked her on this account and had even questioned whether their son was the father of her children. She explained that if she had been in their situation she would have felt the same way. By successfully performing her role as oyomesan, Ana crafted a sense of self as a legitimate wife, mother, and daughter-in-law in Japan. She also received public (and legal) acknowledgement of this transformation. Moreover, because she received permanent residency and maintained amicable relations with her in-laws, she could present herself as successful in these roles to other Filipina women she knew in Central Kiso (and to family and friends in the Philippines when she called or returned for visits).

Ana also viewed her early receipt of permanent residency as something that set her apart from other Filipina women in the region who could not handle (or perhaps chose not to undertake) such challenges. Ana told me with pride that the immigration official had come to check on her, "because it's a Japanese soba shop and a little famous." She was flattered that her neighbors and in-laws had enthusiastically responded in the affirmative when the officer had asked if she, in her words, "could properly manage the Japanese way of life." She added that two years earlier, when she had brought her children over from the Philippines, the immigration officer at the airport had asked if she had permanent residency yet, commenting that she spoke fluent Japanese. She had told him that she had been in Japan for only four years, and that she thought that

it took at least ten. At that time, the officer told her that getting permanent residency had nothing to do with how many years one had lived in
Japan. She relayed with pride that he had said that it was a matter of
whether "a person could really manage the Japanese way of life, whether
they could manage it well."

In addition to being proud that she had mastered "the Japanese way
of life," Ana told me that learning to do so was valuable. "The Japanese
way of life is a good thing to study," she explained. Moreover, her
"study" was paying off in material ways. Now, she explained, her in-laws
were training her to manage the soba shop after they retired. They listened
patiently to her complaints, and Ana's mother-in-law and husband
stepped in on her behalf when her father-in-law complained that, for example, something Ana had prepared for dinner wasn't tasty. Ana relayed
how they had challenged him, saying, "Why don't you cook something,
then?" She told me that even restaurant customers sometimes whispered
that she was skillful in dealing with her father-in-law, sympathizing that
he was difficult. Lately, Ana's in-laws had been encouraging her to "become a Japanese!" (Nihonjin ni nare!) by taking Japanese citizenship. Ana
was flattered, although she had not yet made up her mind as to whether
or not she would. She had reservations about giving up her Philippine citizenship. However, her children would likely live their lives in Japan, and
she told me (inaccurately, in fact) that she would not be eligible for a national pension in Japan if she did not become a citizen.[8] She added that
she already had selected a Japanese name, Kayo, which she could use on
their *koseki* (family register) if she decided to change her nationality.[9]

For Ana, then, being oyomesan was not only a pragmatic strategy for
appeasing her in-laws, challenging negative stereotypes of Filipina
women in Japan, receiving her permanent residency, and therefore acquiring access to employment and mobility. It also provided her with a
sense of pride and accomplishment, including the pleasures of public
recognition of her mastery of the Japanese way of life, including her ability to speak Japanese. It distinguished her as more than a *japayuki,* evidenced her proficiency in a new set of cultural skills, and marked her as
special when compared with other Filipina women in the region. Moreover, it enabled her to manage what would someday, quite conceivably,
be her own business. Plus, because Ana received a salary for her work in
her family's soba shop, by being oyomesan she was able to send money
to her family in the Philippines and thus occupy a more important position within it.[10] Ironically, then, for Ana, being oyomesan was a route to
a range of achievements not just within a domestic realm but also beyond

it. Through her performance of this role, she was able to present herself as a legitimate wife, mother, and daughter-in-law; demonstrate cosmopolitan competencies; manage a restaurant; and become the breadwinner for her family in the Philippines.

Like Ana, a number of Filipina women in Central Kiso with whom I spoke took pride in the social legitimacy conferred by their performances as oyomesan and the ways it reflected on them not only as Filipina, but also as women and as people. They also took pride in the economic and political advantages that accompanied managing this role—for example, the ability to gain permanent residence in Japan and support their families in the Philippines. These pleasures and senses of accomplishment were part of the ways that power—specifically the unequal political-economic relations that made Filipina women dependent on their Japanese families and the Japanese state for residency permits—worked productively in these women's lives to encourage them to accommodate their Japanese families' expectations.

THE SACRIFICE OF BEING OYOMESAN

If Filipina women in Central Kiso found self-actualization in both Japan and the Philippines by successfully performing their roles as oyomesan, they also crafted senses of self that were based on the difficulties and challenges they faced in performing these roles. For most of the women I met, being oyomesan meant managing two sets of domestic obligations—to both their natal and their affinal households. These women often spoke to me about the toll taken on them by these dual pressures of home. (Their comments were reminders that for many people "home" is not necessarily a safe, comforting, or innocent space; it is a space produced through ambivalence and unequal relations of gender, sexuality, race, and class.)[11] While the difficulties these women faced could be onerous, they also invoked them as evidence of the hardships they were willing to endure to be good family members. For example, many Filipina women in Central Kiso invoked a Catholic rhetoric of self-sacrifice to describe the ways that by fulfilling their roles as oyomesan they both negotiated relationships with their Japanese-in-laws and supported their families in the Philippines. Such discourses of sacrifice and suffering are heavily gendered in the Philippines.[12] When a Filipina woman sacrifices in Japan so that she can support her family in the Philippines, she comes to personify Filipino virtue as a, in Tagalog, babaeng martir, "a long-suffering woman who puts the needs and wishes of others before her own."[13] In the Philippines, the *babaeng martir* is a heroine of both biblical myth and televisual melodrama. To identify one-self as a *babaeng martir* is to craft a noble and dramatic sense of self, to cast oneself as an archetype of legend and screen.

Women in Central Kiso described sacrifices that included having to do things the Japanese way, giving up the hopes and dreams they had for their lives, working long hours doing both waged and domestic labor, and performing emotional labor by remaining affable and keeping their mouths shut in the face of indignities. These women claimed their sacri-fices in the names of their families in the Philippines, their Japanese chil-dren (and sometimes husbands), and their relationships with their in-laws. For example, Cora repeatedly told me that she was in Japan "for [her] family." By this, she at different times meant her children and hus-band in Japan and her family in the Philippines.[14] She sometimes described her relationships with her husband's parents as "my trials"; other times, however, she would ask rhetorically in Tagalog of her Filipino family's persistent requests for money and household items, "Until when?" (Hanggang kailan?). Such a statement might be understood not only as questioning how long Cora's family in the Philippines would expect her financial support but also as a query of broader global political eco-nomics. Today, it is estimated that roughly half of the population of the Philippines is either directly or indirectly dependent on foreign remit-tances from overseas workers.[15] Cora's question thus might also be glossed: until when will the unequal political-economic relationships that force people in the Philippines to depend on remittances from foreign labor migrants for daily subsistence be allowed to persist?

Filipina women in Central Kiso also had to deal with problems and deceptions that developed around their remittances. Father Art some-times complained that Filipina migrants in Japan denied themselves necessities—sometimes eating only instant noodles for weeks on end—so that they could send money to the Philippines. However, he lamented, their Filipino families were sometimes unrealistic about, and wasteful or extravagant with, the money the women sent. He cited cases in which women's families had used their remittances to purchase luxury items such as Rolex watches and then asked their Filipina relatives in Japan for more money to buy necessities like food. Victoria, whom I mentioned in chapter 1 and who worked in Ruby's bar, was once in a bind because she had sent ¥300,000 (about $2,655.00)—many months' savings—to her mother in a rural part of Bulacan province through a remittance account in her brother's name at a bank in Manila. However, Victoria's mother had never received the money. Her brother had spent it on expensive gifts and luxury vacations for himself and his girlfriend.

If some of these women's relatives in the Philippines mismanaged (and stole) the money the women sent, many also acknowledged the sacrifices the women were making on their behalf. The sacrifices made by Filipina migrants in Japan are physically manifest across the Philippine landscape. When I went to the Philippines with Filipina women living in Central Kiso, they and their families there pointed out some of these sacrifices' many forms. They showed me sacrifices shaped as large new houses in gated subdivisions that had multiple air-conditioning units hanging out their windows. I saw sacrifices concretized in small cinder-block *sari-sari* stores and cafés that migrant women's duster-clad mothers managed. I rode in sacrifices shaped as jeepneys that their brothers drove, and that were brightly painted with personal and place names, such as "Sato" or "Tokyo." Members of migrant's families in the Philippines openly expressed gratitude, admiration, and *awa* (pity, Tg.) for their sisters, daughters, and aunties in Japan.[16] Ligaya's sister and niece both told me self-consciously that some people in the Philippines even admired Filipina women who remained in relationships with abusive Japanese men: these women suffered abuse abroad to help their families back home. Ligaya's niece explained that, just as Jesus was a martyr, these women were sacrificing themselves for the sake of their families.

When Filipina women in Central Kiso complained about the sacrifices they made to accommodate their Japanese families' demands, then, their complaints were not only assertions of hardship but also of the lengths to which they were willing to go to fulfill their responsibilities to their families in both Japan and the Philippines. Through their sacrifices, women reminded those in the Philippines of the pains, and possibilities, of their lives abroad. Stressing their commitment to their families and the hardships they faced on their behalf, Filipina women in Central Kiso also compared themselves to other Filipina women in the region with these complaints. Their claims of sacrifice were part of the rhetoric through which they crafted senses of self in relation to, and in relationships with, others in Japan and the Philippines and how they maintained that they deserved respect in both countries.

This discourse of sacrifice reflected some of the ambivalence women felt about their lives as oyomesan—the bittersweet ways it involved both accomplishment and suffering. Women's ambivalence toward this role came out in other ways as well. Sometimes women were reluctant to claim the term *oyomesan* for themselves, even if they took pride in being good wives, mothers, and daughters-in-law and had been described as ii oyomesan by others. For example, as I discuss in the next section, for Tessie, being oyomesan involved sacrifices that she had to some extent prided herself on not having to make.

REFUSING OYOMESAN

Tessie and I ducked under the short curtains framing the rickety sliding wood and glass doors at Satonoya, Ana's family's soba restaurant. Like much of Nagano, Central Kiso is famous for its handmade soba noodles. Ana's in-laws, the Kawaguchis, had been riding the wave of the Kisoji Boom when, in 1976, they left their jobs in the moribund lumber industry and opened the noodle shop. The Kawaguchis also had the restaurant's tourist appeal in mind when a few years later they renovated the old building and restored, what locals identified as, the "Kiso-rashii" (Kiso-esque) style of the structure, with its characteristic white plaster and dark-wood-trimmed facade, tiled roof and eaves, and inside an old-fashioned pressed earth floor and *irori* (traditional sunken hearth). Despite the downturn in local tourism since the mid-1980s, the restaurant was still busy (although not doing nearly as well as it once had), and it was a source of much pride for the Kawaguchis. I was told that until just a few years before I came to Central Kiso, Ana's mother-in-law had overseen the restaurant dressed in elegant kimono, gliding across the shop floor in *geta* (wooden clogs) made from local *nezuko* wood. By the time of my fieldwork, she was almost completely immobilized by rheumatoid arthritis, but she still came in most afternoons to supervise the goings-on. From her perch at a front table she chatted with customers as they entered and exited and, whenever possible, she strained her head to converse with those beside or behind her. Kawaguchi-san also oversaw all the tables in her line of sight, regularly calling out to Ana and Yamashita-san, the other full-time waitress, "Green tea over here!" "Two orders of *morisoba* [chilled soba noodles] over there!" "Check!" And the two scurried about accordingly.

As Tessie and I entered the restaurant, Kawaguchi-san bowed her head and smiled from her usual spot. *"Irasshaimase"* (Welcome), she called out. Tessie and I returned her welcome with smiles and short bows of our heads. We then spotted Ana, who was carrying a tall stack of red and black lacquer trays piled high with noodles. Ana's eyes met ours, and she greeted us with a gentle uplift of her chin and eyebrows. Smiling widely, she instructed us in Tagalog to sit wherever we wanted; she would come by when she had a moment.

It was just after noon and the shop was busy with the lunch crowd. Tessie and I placed our shoes in the *getabako* (shoe cupboard) and took a seat with a good view of the restaurant on the raised tatami platform in the back. We looked at the menu, handwritten on pale cypress blocks hanging above the counter. Agreeing on tempura soba, we turned to watch Ana as she served steaming cups of green tea to newly seated customers.

"Ana is really oyomesan," Tessie suggested. She gestured to Kawaguchi-san with a gentle lift of her chin, "In the future it will be her in the front, wearing kimono . . ."

"What do you mean that Ana is really oyomesan?" I asked. Tessie's comment surprised me. I had assumed that only Japanese people described Filipina women in such terms.

"She *really* sacrificed," Tessie replied. This time she underscored her comment with a dry glance toward Ana.

"Are you also oyomesan?" I asked. I frequently heard Tessie speak of the sacrifices she made to remain in Japan.

"No," Tessie shook her head back and forth in a small, rapid motion, "I just . . ." She shrugged her shoulders and raised her hands loosely into the air, implying that she was free and did what she liked. "I don't live with my mother-in-law," she continued, "but Ana does." And then as an afterthought she added, "Maybe it will change if I move in with my in-laws," a plan about which there had been serious talk.

When Tessie described Ana as "really oyomesan," she was engaging the terms of her Japanese community, indicating that she was knowledgeable about, and had come to recognize in other Filipina women, the practices that Japanese residents associated with being a good bride and daughter-in-law. Every Filipina woman I knew in Central Kiso recognized that whether or not a woman lived with her in-laws, and their temperaments and expectations if she did, was an important factor shaping the possibilities and constraints of her everyday life in Japan; it was a key reference point by which these women compared and evaluated their experiences. Many Filipina women in Central Kiso also knew which other Filipina women in the region lived with their husbands' parents. I realized this when I asked some Filipina friends to help me compile a list of all Filipina women in the area. I had asked these women to name every Filipina woman in Central Kiso that they could and to contribute as much information as possible about each woman: Where was she from in the Philippines? How long had she been married? How many children did she have? Where did she meet her husband? What was her husband's occupation? Did she have a job (and if so where)? Did she live with her husband's parents? I found that my friends knew whether or not a given Filipina woman lived with her husband's parents even if they knew little else about her and had only met her once or twice.[17] I asked these friends how they had acquired this information. Some explained that they had heard stories from other Filipina friends about problems these women were having at home. Others described chance meetings at a local supermarket in which a given Filipina woman had launched into a story about a fight she had with her husband's parents, relieved to finally have someone in whom she could confide, even if only for a moment in the frozen-food section of the local market.

By identifying Ana as oyomesan, Tessie acknowledged the sacrifices that Ana had to make on account of her living situation with her in-laws. These sacrifices invited pity, respect, and even awe. However, Tessie also differentiated her domestic situation from Ana's, explaining that she was "not oyomesan" because, although her husband was the eldest son, she did not live with her in-laws, and thus was under fewer constraints and could make more independent use of her time. She suggested that she had to some degree resisted pressures to conform to the Japanese way. As I also mentioned in chapter 2, Tessie claimed that her Japanese language skills were not especially good because she did not care much about studying or hope to stay in Japan long term. Tessie, as I mentioned in that chapter, had initially refused to live with her in-laws because they had objected to their son marrying a Filipina woman. She suggested that she was not oyomesan because she did not have to be (although, she conceded, her situation might soon change). She had, for the time being, negotiated a living situation that provided her greater independence. This was a point of pride for Tessie. It was evidence of her ability to assert her needs and desires and of her husband's financial ability and willingness to accommodate them.

However, Tessie's claim that she was "not oyomesan" is also somewhat ironic given that many Japanese community members viewed her as an ii oyomesan who was being shikkari. Recall my landlady Emiko's description of Tessie in the previous chapter. And Tessie had on several occasions been approached by neighbors who had asked if she knew of any "nice Filipina women" like herself with whom she might arrange a marriage for their son or brother. How could Tessie be identified as a good oyomesan despite her self-conscious efforts to resist such discipline and her self-identification otherwise? To understand how this was possible, let me say a bit about some of the other motivations women like Tessie had for behaving in ways that apparently made them good oyomesan despite their ambivalence toward the discipline this term implied.

"WE CHOSE THIS PATH"

In 1999, Tessie and I attended the Twenty-Fourth Annual Nagano Prefecture Borantia Kenkyū Shūkai (Volunteers' Research Conference), which was entitled "Hirogeyō kokoro no wa, mitsukeyō jibun no ibasho" (Let's widen the circle of our hearts and find where we belong). Held that year in Kisofukushima, the meeting brought together grassroots volunteers and NGO members from throughout the prefecture to share their experiences. Tessie and I learned about the event from our Japanese-language teachers, Iida-sensei and Okuyama-sensei, both of whom were former elementary school teachers who had devoted their retirement to a variety of charitable activities. Iida-sensei and Okuyama-sensei had asked three Filipina women from the class, including Cora, to speak about their community involvement and their experiences as foreign wives in Japan. They also had encouraged the rest of us to come and support our classmates. So several of us had come to watch the panel.

All of us, both speakers and audience, sat together around a large table. After the talks, the moderators suggested that we go in a circle around the table and everyone ask a question or make a comment. When it came the turn of one smartly dressed, middle-aged woman, she addressed all Filipina women present in Japanese, her eyes solicitous and her voice heavy with concern:

"Are you really happy? That is what I want to know. I am worried about whether or not you are happy that you have come to Japan."

I was sitting across the table from Tessie, and I watched her posture grow rigid. She quickly raised her hand to respond.

"We chose this path, so we have to keep trying," she asserted in Japanese, turning to the woman. Then she addressed the group, "I want Japanese people to broaden their ideas about us."

Japanese residents regularly asked me if Filipina women in Central Kiso were happy in Japan and, despite the sincere concern of the question, it implied that these women may not have had the wherewithal to know what they were doing when they married their husbands and that perhaps they would be happier if they just went home. Tessie responded to this woman's question by asserting her agency in coming to Japan and her commitment to staying, and by inserting Japanese people into the equation of whether or not Filipina women were "happy" that they had come to Japan.

If Ana viewed learning the Japanese way as a skill to master, Tessie sometimes framed her life in Japan in terms of rising to a challenge and maintaining a commitment: "We chose this path, so we have to keep trying." For Tessie, this commitment was manifest in her efforts to organize Filipina wives in the region and make Central Kiso a place in which they could comfortably live. It was also demonstrated by her everyday practice: her meticulous management of her home and her fastidious care of her husband, children, and in-laws. Tessie kept her house spotlessly clean, and her family's clothes were always laundered and neatly pressed. She prepared three homemade meals every day, and she participated in PTA activities at her children's school. She was also appropriately polite to neighbors and deferential with her in-laws. Tessie always assisted her mother-in-law, helping with the rice harvest, holiday preparations, and other things around her in-laws' house. For example, when Tessie was at their home, she always went out of her way to clean up her mother-in-law's kitchen and sitting room when her mother-in-law was busy doing other chores or caring for Tessie's then bedridden father-in-law. Such behaviors resonated with Japanese residents as being shikkari.

However, Tessie told me that she was "not oyomesan." As she explained, she did not try to (or have to) accommodate the demands of her Japanese in-laws in the ways that Ana and Cora, who both lived with their in-laws, did; nor did she see herself as submitting to gendered forms of discipline they imposed. Rather, Tessie framed her treatment of her in-laws in terms of how she was raised in the Philippines to be a respectful, responsible, and caring woman. She believed that she had responsibilities toward her husband's family. ("I eat the rice, so I think I should help out growing it," she once told me in regard to her work in her in-laws' rice fields.) Although Tessie and her mother-in-law's relationship had been tense in the early years of her marriage, by the time I came to Central Kiso it had grown supportive and mutually respectful. One day at Tessie's mother-in-law's house, I watched as Tessie cleaned the kitchen while her mother-in-law went out to feed her cattle. Tessie explained, "My mother in-law is so busy. She doesn't have time to do this, so I just want to help her out."

Tessie crafted a sense of self through these mundane daily practices, taking pleasure and satisfaction in the practices themselves and not necessarily in the rewards associated with doing them the Japanese way.[18] Like many Filipina women I met, she stressed the importance of respecting and caring for the elderly. In much of the Philippines, demonstrating obedience and indebtedness to aging parents is a way of showing gratitude for "the gift of life."[19] Nearly every Filipina woman with whom I spoke emphasized that respecting and caring for elderly people was a commitment that had been instilled in childhood. In Central Kiso, it also became part of how these women defined themselves as Filipina, sometimes in contrast to Japanese people. (Recall, for example, Cora's public lecture, discussed in the previous chapter, in which she asked why in Japan caring for the elderly was left only to the eldest son and his wife.) It was also a key reason that Japanese residents identified Filipina women as appealing brides and as more Japanese than women who had been born and raised in Japan. Some scholars have argued that in contemporary rural Japan the ie no longer plays a political-economic role, but has come to be an important organization for caring for elderly.[20] In this case, Filipina women's ideas about caring for their elderly in-laws, then, may be one point where discourses of the ie actually enabled *smooth relationships* (not tensions, as others have suggested) between Filipina women and their Japanese families.

Tessie also maintained a sense of self by managing her housework. One of the first days I was living at Tessie's home, I told her that I wanted to assist with her daily housecleaning. Reluctantly, she allowed me to help with her morning chores. Initially, I suspected that she was embarrassed to have me help. However, I soon realized that I could not keep up with her careful routine. Before long I took a seat at the kitchen table for a quick break. Embarrassed, I told Tessie that I would get back to work in a moment. "That's OK. I'll do the rest, you sit," Tessie insisted. After repeated protests on my part, Tessie conceded that she preferred to do these activities "her own way." She had learned to clean house both from her mother in the Philippines and during the years she had worked cleaning in a convent to receive a scholarship to complete high school. She said she felt incomplete when she did not get her chores done to her satisfaction. (Tessie also positioned herself in relation to Japanese women on these grounds, sometimes whispering that she did not think that they kept their homes very clean.)

Tessie, as I've mentioned, was also a very observant Catholic. She built a large Catholic altar with religious statues, rosaries, and other Catholic images and decorations on the *tokonoma* (a Japanese wooden alcove for displaying hanging scrolls and flower arrangements or bonsai trees) in one tatami room in her house. She prayed there daily. She also attended Mass at the nearest Catholic church in Matsumoto whenever possible, getting her husband to drive her and to wait in the car while she and their children went inside. In addition, she regularly organized Tagalog prayer meetings in the area, which, as I later discuss, women also viewed as opportunities to get together and "be Filipina." On her kitchen wall, Tessie kept a poster of the Ten Commandments with descriptions in English of the multiple ways each commandment should be abided in one's daily life. Tessie's younger sister had sent the poster from the Philippines, and Tessie once asked me to explain some of the more complicated words on it, explaining that she was doing her best to follow all of its proscriptions.

Tessie's religious faith might seem to contradict standard images of a good oyomesan. Not only did Tessie and other Filipina women associate Catholicism with life in the Philippines and maintaining a sense of Filipino identity, but also few Japanese people are Christian. In Japan, Christianity is often posited in contradistinction to Japaneseness. In fact, a number of Japanese residents stressed Japan's non-Christian roots with me, telling me that the difference between the United States and Japan was that "the U.S. is a Christian country and Japan is a Buddhist country." However, I found that most Japanese residents in Central Kiso did not view religion as a central tenet of personhood so much as a set of rituals or customary practices.[21] As I have mentioned, some men married to Filipina women in Central Kiso drove their wives and children well over an hour to Matsumoto so that their wives could attend church on Sundays. Moreover, Filipina women's Christianity (and in nearly all cases Catholicism) offered discourses of gender and kinship that in some ways resonated with Japanese residents' expectations about what it meant to be a traditional Japanese bride.[22] For example, Japanese community members often described Filipina women as similar to traditional Japanese women because they said that the women deferred to their husbands' desires and judgment. While women's treatment of their husbands was certainly shaped in part by their political-economic vulnerability in Japan, including their dependence on the men's sponsorship of their visas, the women's Catholic beliefs shaped their attitudes as well. Tessie circulated among her friends a book that her sister had sent from the Philippines entitled *Secrets Revealed! Twenty Ways to Use the Power of Prayer*. The book discussed biblical passages such as "Words to live by: Wives, submit yourselves unto

Figure 6. Some Filipina women in Central Kiso created Catholic altars in the *tokonoma* of their homes, September, 1999.

your own husbands as unto the Lord. For the husband is the head of the wife" (from Ephesians 5:22–25). A number of Filipina women in Central Kiso cited this and related Bible passages to me. In fact, ironically, several women told me that they made daily offerings of rice and incense to their Japanese families' *butsudan,* their Buddhist family altars, because their husbands had requested that they do so and these women were following the Bible's injunction that wives abide their husbands' requests.[23]

We might understand discourses of gender and kinship that discrepantly circulate in Japan and the Philippines but that resonate in aspects of their patriarchal constructions of masculinity and femininity as "resonant patriarchies." Although these discourses have different cultural foundations and genealogies, links and resonances exist between them. Tessie believed that she should ask her husband's permission before going out, and she respected his wishes that she not stay out late or drive in the snow. Tessie's husband once described her deferential attitude as characteristic of a *yamato nadeshiko,* an ideal traditional Japanese woman. For Tessie, however, it was a means of respecting her husband as a good Catholic wife. She also felt that her husband respected her wishes by taking her to church and supporting her efforts to financially assist her family in the Philippines. She felt that she should respect his wishes, in turn.

Although many Filipina women in Central Kiso suggested that they were frustrated with life in rural Nagano, some of these women's desires for upward class mobility, or what they called "a better life," were also in part fulfilled by their lives there. Tessie, for example, was proud that her husband was one of the few husbands of Filipina women in the region who worked in an office and could comfortably support her and their children. Once when we went out to dinner at a relatively pricey restaurant in town, Tessie pointed out that the restaurant was her husband's favorite. She added with pride that some young people at a nearby table had left after looking at the menu because it was too expensive for them. Tessie believed that Yoshimoto-san's financial situation enabled him to fulfill his role as a husband and father in ways that many Filipina women's husbands in Japan, and most men she had known in the Philippines, could not. As I've mentioned, other Filipina women in Central Kiso told me that they had been involved with men in the Philippines— sometimes for many years—when they met their Japanese husbands. When I asked why they had chosen to marry their Japanese husbands over their longer-term Filipino boyfriends, many of these women explained that their Filipino boyfriends had not proposed marriage and their Japanese husbands had jobs that would enable them to provide for a family in ways that their Filipino boyfriends could not. This statement did not reflect these women's desires for money so much as for financial stability and a particular, idealized kind of marital relationship with a man who could financially support his wife and children. In explaining their decisions, several of these women summarized a passage that they said was from Genesis in which God prescribed that as punishment to Adam and Eve for eating the forbidden fruit "the husband must work to feed the family, and the wife must be in the house to raise the children and give birth."

Studies of vernacular understandings of masculinity and femininity in the Philippines during the late 1970s and 1980s, a time when many Filipina women in Central Kiso were growing up there, argue that many in the Philippines defined highly valued traits for men and women in terms of their gendered roles in the family. Ma. Carmen C. Jimenez writes that in the Philippines a man is "regarded as most masculine when he is able to support his family adequately just as a female is regarded most feminine when she is able to fulfill her role as mother and homemaker satisfactorily. 'Ang lalake ang siyang haligi ng tahanan habang ang babae ang siyang ilaw nito' [The man is the foundation of the home, and the woman is the light inside]."[24] Jimenez also states that, according to many surveyed, the only acceptable (stated) reason for a married woman to work would be for the benefit of her family; a married woman was expected to find fulfillment and satisfaction in her role as mother and homemaker. Clearly class ideals shape these perceptions of masculinity and femininity (and likewise the desires to approximate them expressed by Filipina women in Central Kiso). Moreover, as Ocampo argues in the same volume, this study overlooks diversity within the Philippines, including a diversity of family forms.[25] However, what Jimenez's study suggests is that such discourses have long circulated within the Philippines and that domestic roles provide a means for crafting masculine and feminine selves in the country. For many Filipina women in Central Kiso, being a good wife, mother, and daughter-in-law was part of what it meant to craft a feminine self as a woman, a Catholic, and a Filipina. At the same time, the practices women associated with these roles also in some (but not all) ways resonated with their Japanese communities' understandings of what it meant to be an ii oyomesan.

"THAT'S HER JOB AS A WIFE!"

I found, too, that Filipina women in Central Kiso sometimes disciplined each other to behave in certain ways they saw as appropriate to a wife and mother—ways that happened to resonate with Japanese communities' ideas about what it meant to be an ii oyomesan. Again, these women did not necessarily do this because they were trying to encourage other Filipina women in the region to be ii oyomesan but because they had strong feelings about what constituted appropriate behavior for women. (These feelings reflected not only Catholic values but also class-based ideals that regularly circulate in mass media in the Philippines.) For example, Tessie frequently lamented that some Filipina women in the region spent too much time playing pachinko, sometimes borrowing (and not paying back) large sums of money to support their gambling habits. (She would say that spending all day in a pachinko parlor was "not good" for Japanese people as well.) Many of the Filipina women in Central Kiso that I knew best spoke critically of those Filipina women in the region who did not care for their children or husbands in ways they deemed proper. These women were also critical of other Filipina women whom they believed allowed their waged labor to interfere with their responsibilities toward their husband and children. Many Filipina women in Central Kiso agreed that a married woman with children should not work "at night" (in a bar). Many married Filipina women in the region did so anyway, justifying their decisions by saying that this work enabled them to support their families abroad. Although working in these bars was generally stigmatized within the Japanese community, some Filipina women's Japanese families in Central Kiso were sympathetic to the women's desires to help their families in the Philippines or, in some cases, needed their financial contribution and permitted them to do such work. However, many Filipina women with whom I spoke in Central Kiso (including those who worked in bars) maintained that, *ideally* (whether or not they viewed this as practical—or even desired such a life—for themselves), a woman (whether Japanese or Filipina) should remain in the house and care for her children while her husband worked outside the home.

Ruby was often the object of gossip among Filipina women in the region concerning what was not appropriate behavior for a wife, a mother, and, more generally, a woman. During the course of my fieldwork, she was going through mediation hearings for a difficult divorce, and her move out of her husband's house and into her own apartment coincided almost exactly with my move into the area. During my stay, I accompanied Ruby and two other Filipina women to Ruby's early mediation hearings to help translate the proceedings and offer support. Initially, these other Filipina women sided with Ruby in her custody battle. After the first meeting we shared our frustration with her husband's lawyer's claims that Ruby was not an adequate custodian for her child because, as he put it, she came from the Philippines, which was a "hot place" *(atsui tokoro)*, and therefore she did not know how to properly raise a child in a "cold place" *(samui tokoro)* like Central Kiso.[26] However, the other women increasingly changed their minds about Ruby's abilities as a mother after observing the way she ran her business and managed her personal affairs now that she was on her own.

Although most Filipina women with whom I spoke in Central Kiso did not believe that the climate of one's country of origin had anything to do with one's ability to care for a child, or that a Filipina woman could not properly raise a child in Japan, by midway through my fieldwork they unanimously agreed that Ruby was to blame for her marital problems and was not a suitable parent. These women spoke disapprovingly of Ruby's sexual promiscuity and of the fact that she spent the night at her boyfriends' homes or allowed them to stay over at her home with her daughter present. Tessie once complained that Ruby had brought her daughter to Tessie's house at seven at night, claiming that she would return for her by nine o'clock after her date; according to Tessie, Ruby did not return for her daughter until the following morning. Tessie and other Filipina women also said that they were "disgusted" that Ruby brought her five-year-old daughter to her bar while it was open for business. They said that this was a terrible thing to do, even if Ruby's husband neglected to pick up the child as agreed before she went to work. A number of Filipina women also strongly disapproved of the amount Ruby drank, and the fact that she sometimes passed out drunk in her bar or her car. They believed (perhaps accurately) that she was endangering herself, her child, and the reputation of all Filipina women in the region.

Tessie and other Filipina women also complained that Ruby did not keep up with requirements of her daughter's elementary school, stressing that parents' responsibilities only grew as children got older and that this would become a bigger and bigger problem. They complained that Ruby depended on other Filipina mothers at the school to find out if it was *bentō no hi* (lunch box day) or if her daughter needed to bring something special to class, explaining that Ruby claimed that she was too busy to read the notes the school sent home. (Ruby was only minimally literate in Japanese and was not fully literate in English, and because she was living apart from her husband she could no longer easily ask for his assistance.) These women also complained about what Ruby fed her daughter. One day Ligaya and some other women were at Tessie's home talking about some of Ruby's behaviors that they found troubling. Tessie started to complain that after Ruby had separated from her husband, she prepared only Filipino foods that she liked to eat and stopped preparing Japanese food for her daughter. This was a problem, Tessie said, not because Ruby was preparing Filipino food for her child but because Ruby's daughter was not accustomed to eating it (and thus did not like it). She explained that Ruby had prepared only Japanese food for her child and her husband when they lived as a family. Sometimes, Tessie added, Ruby gave her daughter only rice and *furikake* (Japanese dried seasonings for rice). Tessie stressed that children needed to eat vegetables and fish and that Ruby never prepared them for her child. Ligaya added that she had heard from Victoria that Ruby didn't even buy milk: "You need to give a child milk three times a day!" she maintained. Tessie piped in that Ruby gave her daughter only sports drinks and other drinks unsuitable for children. On another occasion, Malou shared an incident that had happened while Ruby was still married. She relayed how Ruby's husband had pulled from the refrigerator a pot of curry that Ruby had left uncovered for three days. Malou demonstrated how Ruby's husband had asked her: "Would you leave curry like this for three days in the fridge and expect me and the child to eat it?" Malou, Tessie, and Victoria agreed that Ruby was wrong in not being more attentive about such things. "That's her job as a wife!" Malou asserted.[27]

Tessie and the other women were partly responding to pressures and concerns regarding how Ruby's behaviors would reflect on all Filipina women in the region. In some ways, expectations that Filipina women be oyomesan set these women against themselves. As I have suggested, even while these women strategically performed their roles as oyomesan to challenge negative stereotypes of Filipina women, they had to distinguish themselves from other Filipina women (that is, to establish themselves as "exceptional Filipinas") to gain this recognition. Moreover, to demonstrate that they were ii oyomesan, Filipina women in Central Kiso were also expected, as my friend Ande suggested, to "forget" parts of their lives in the Philippines. Even in those cases in which these women empathized with other Filipina women's situations in Central Kiso, they had to in some sense resist not only being associated with these other women but also being judged by the standards that some of these women were setting.

However, the opinions that the Filipina women I knew best expressed about Ruby were also shaped by their ideas about how a wife, mother, and woman should behave. In their views, these standards—which took shape through their relationships and experiences in both Japan *and* the Philippines—applied not simply to Filipina women but to *all* women. These Filipina women viewed their roles as wives and mothers as not simply a form of labor but an occupation ("That's her job as a wife!"), and they took it very seriously. It was part of how the women constructed themselves as both women and Filipina.

BOUNDARY PRACTICES ENABLE RESISTANCE
TO BE MISREAD AS COMPLIANCE

One might say that in encounters between Filipina women and Japanese residents in Central Kiso, gendered domestic practices such as such as respecting and caring for elderly, preparing meals, maintaining a tidy home, and prioritizing one's husband and children, became a kind of "boundary object," or more aptly, a set of "boundary practices" through which members of these groups negotiated their relationships. The term "boundary object" comes from science studies scholars James R. Griesemer and Susan Leigh Star, who use it to refer to objects that "inhabit several intersecting social worlds" and are "both plastic enough to adapt to local needs and the constraints of the several parties employing them, yet robust enough to maintain a common identity across sites."[28] Boundary objects are sites of cultural meeting where difference is contingently leveled into something communicable. While these objects may mean different things in different cultural worlds, they share enough of a common structure that they are recognizable across these worlds. As points of common reference, they encode interlocking and diverging discourses, each with their own histories and agendas.

For some Filipina women and Japanese residents in Central Kiso, gendered everyday domestic activities were boundary practices that inhabited multiple and overlapping worlds of meaning. These practices assumed variant significance for members of these groups (and also within these groups, as suggested by Ruby's refusal to behave in the ways that a number of other Filipina women in the region found appropriate). However, the parallel structure of some of these practices made some Filipina women legible to some Japanese community members as ii oyomesan.

I found, too, that boundary practices were created not only through resonances between Filipina women's and Japanese residents' ideas about gender and kinship but occasionally through discrepancies in these ideas. That is, even when Filipina women self-consciously did things to resist the pressures their Japanese families placed upon them, their Japanese families sometimes misinterpreted these behaviors as acts of compliance and took them as evidence that a given woman was an ii oyomesan. For example, as I mentioned earlier, food preparation and consumption were key sites where tensions between being oyomesan and being Filipina emerged for these women. Some women's Japanese families enjoyed select dishes from the Philippines. Chicken adobo was popular among many women's families. Virgie's mother-in-law loved *biko* (Philippine-style rice cake) and tea with *kalamansi* juice; she would prepare these for herself. Other women's children also liked *leche flan*. However, most Filipina women's families were open to eating only select Filipino foods and only on occasion, and insisted that the women prepare and consume Japanese food almost exclusively in their homes. Many Filipina women's husbands complained that Filipino food was too heavy and greasy. One woman sadly demonstrated how her seven-year-old son pretended to stick his finger down his throat and gag whenever she asked if he would eat Filipino dishes. Many Filipina women's in-laws also objected to the women eating with their hands as some had done in the Philippines. As I mentioned, Cora told me that the first time she did this her in-laws scolded her, telling her it was unclean and disgusting. She never did it in front of them again.

As a result, women found alternative spaces where they could eat Filipino food and "be Filipina" in ways unacceptable to their Japanese families and communities. They would regularly organize prayer meetings and birthday parties that only Filipina women attended. In addition to preparing and eating Filipino foods at these events, women would speak Tagalog (sometimes a few would also converse among themselves in Bicolano or pairs of women would speak in other Philippine dialects); often they would play Filipino or U.S. American pop music; and sometimes they would dance and sing karaoke. To these gatherings, these women invariably brought plastic bags in which they excitedly took home leftovers. One woman told me that she had never done this in the Philippines: The difficulty of preparing these dishes in Japan was what had inspired her to do so there.

Some Filipina women in Central Kiso said that they did not feel comfortable eating in front of their in-laws and so they ate in their rooms or in other parts of the house away from them. Many of these women also cooked separate meals for themselves, eating them (or leftovers from parties and friends) with their hands (or with cutlery rather than chopsticks) after their families had finished eating or when their in-laws were not around. When their husbands went out at night (and in a few cases when the men were home), women held late-night cooking parties at their homes in which groups of them would prepare *ginataan, bopis,* and *dinuguan,* Filipino foods that their Japanese families tended not to like.

Consuming food is, of course, a performative practice of ethnic identity.[29] For Filipina women in Central Kiso these eating and gathering strategies were not only pleasurable but also a means of maintaining a sense of Filipina identity and a way to resist the pressures their husbands and in-laws imposed on them to be Japanese. Yet, ironically, some

Figure 7. Prayer meetings were occasions when Filipina women in Central Kiso felt that they could "be Filipina," March, 1999.

Filipina women's in-laws viewed the women as *similar* to traditional Japanese women and all the more ii oyomesan on account of these practices. As I explained in the previous chapter, Ana's mother-in-law Kawaguchi-san described how, in her day, the yome would serve her in-laws and husband first, offering them the choicest bits of food, and then eat alone after the rest of the family had finished. By compartmentalizing their Filipinoness into "appropriate" (and concealed) spaces, such as by eating Filipino foods and participating in other Filipino activities apart from their in-laws, Filipina women in Central Kiso thus reinforced notions that they were ii oyomesan. Their guarded resistance to the discipline imposed upon them became a form of compliance. In this way, Filipina women's Japanese families' misinterpretation—or willful disregard—of the women's desires to maintain a sense of Filipina identity was also important to how the women came to be identified as ideal traditional Japanese brides.

POINTS OF TEMPORARY ATTACHMENT — AND MISALIGNMENTS

Stuart Hall tells us that identification is a conditional and contingent process of suturing or articulating, whereby subjects interpellated into discourse "fashion, stylize, produce and 'perform' these positions" in situated and changing ways.[30] Hall's point is that our identities do not inhere in us as persons; they must constantly be reproduced in both language and practice as we produce ourselves as identifiable subjects/objects in the world. Moreover, Hall tells us, the process of reproducing identities also destabilizes and transforms them. Instabilities and inconsistencies emerge as different people invoke and reinvoke a given identity in different contexts at different points in time.

In developing his theory of identification, Hall draws on Judith's Butler's theory of gender performativity.[31] For Butler, gender is performatively produced as an effect of citational practices. That is, the citational repetition of gendered practices (e.g., wearing makeup, sitting with one's legs crossed, identifying a newborn infant as a girl) performatively makes gender "matter" and creates the illusion that it is fixed and stable. Butler is also interested in how the repetition of such practices produces a domain of exclusion or abjection, a category that is undesirable and uninhabitable and against which the normative subject constructs a gendered self. Building on Butler, Hall inquires into the kinds of exclusions that all processes of identification involve—the excesses and "other" sides produced when boundaries of identity are drawn. However, rather than placing the emphasis on the ways that the subject is constituted through language and convention, as Butler does, Hall stresses the need to ask: why, and under what conditions, "individuals as subjects identify (or do not identify) with the 'positions' to which they are summoned"?[32] For Hall, identities are points of temporary attachment—sites of suture—between those discourses and practices that interpellate us as subjects and those practices of self-constitution through which we produce ourselves as such.

In this and the previous chapter, I have drawn on Hall's and Butler's analyses to suggest that we understand those processes of identification through which Filipina women "came to matter" as ii oyomesan as processes of unequal encounter in which Japanese residents (and the Japanese state) interpellated Filipina women in such terms and these women in various ways responded.[33] However, I have also shown that these cultural encounters enabled some Filipina women to materialize as ii oyomesan not only because of the articulations—those sites of suture based in overlaps in meaning or forms of coercion and consensus—that developed in relationships between Filipina women and their Japanese community members, but also on account of the contradictions, ambivalences, and misunderstandings that developed between them. Filipina women's understandings of their roles in their Japanese families often differed in qualitative ways from the ways those roles were understood by Japanese residents in Central Kiso and Japanese immigration officials. These discrepant understandings both enabled Filipina women to fulfill their roles as oyomesan and unsettled what these roles meant. Yet the dynamics of these misunderstandings were not always abrasive; they were sometimes smooth and even frictionless.

Being oyomesan was not only part of how Filipina women maintained amicable relations with their Japanese in-laws and neighbors—as Cora put it, "avoiding their being able to say anything bad about Filipinas"— it was also part of how they maintained kinship relationships with their families in the Philippines and crafted senses of self as Filipina. By caring for their families (in both Japan and the Philippines), Filipina women I knew in Central Kiso presented themselves as good wives, daughters, and mothers and as Catholic, Filipina, and middle-class. They became breadwinners for their families in the Philippines and gained leverage in their Japanese families and communities. They also constructed senses of self in relation to other Filipina women, distinguishing themselves as different from them, and special when compared to them. Moreover, Filipina women in Central Kiso were sometimes identified as ii oyomesan by their Japanese community members even when the women were self-consciously trying not to conform to expectations that they do things the Japanese way. In this way, Filipina women were perceived as ii oyomesan through forms of cross talk and productive misunderstandings in which their resistance to the discipline imposed upon them was mistaken for compliance.[34]

Insofar as Filipina women were recognized as ii oyomesan by their Japanese families and communities, their embodiment of this role emerged on account of both the structural pressures these women faced and the alignments and misalignments between Filipina women's and Japanese residents' desires and agendas for their lives. These desires and agendas were culturally shaped by political-economic processes and cultural discourses of gender and kinship circulating in *both* Japan and the Philippines. The attitudes that Filipina women in Central Kiso held toward life in the region were also shaped by the contingencies of individual women's lives—a complex calculus of personal history, past encounters, personality, and the immediate circumstances of women's families in Japan and the Philippines. These factors prompted women like Cora, Tessie, Ana, and Ruby to sometimes respond to their roles in their Japanese communities in different ways.

Yet most Filipina women in Central Kiso with whom I spoke (including nearly all who were identified as ii oyomesan) expressed some degree of ambivalence about this role in ways that their Japanese families did not. There was an inherent tension in the fact that these women—who having left the Philippines in search of a better life were in some sense trying to reject the domestication involved in living both with their natal families and in their country of birth—ultimately could find some semblance of that better life only by performing what they and the Japanese community identified as a traditional domestic role. Being oyomesan at once opened and closed opportunities for these women's lives. Moreover, these women had to deal with contradictions not only between their own and their Japanese communities' desires for their shared lives, but also among their aspirations to help their families in the Philippines, be good wives, mothers, and daughters-in-law in Central Kiso, and find a measure of independence and adventure abroad. Their experiences in Japan were defined by the lived expression of these dissonant desires.

As I have shown in this chapter, these tensions were often in different ways and to various degrees managed, either self-consciously by the women themselves or through the very contingencies of their encounters in rural Nagano. In some cases, however, unbridgeable gaps also emerged—between Filipina women and their Japanese families, among the women themselves, and within the very dreams they hoped to find in Japan. These gaps prompted some of these women to run away. By focusing on stories of Filipina women who left their Japanese families in Central Kiso, the next chapter explores how these gaps were at once recuperated into and disrupted those processes through which some Filipina migrants in Central Kiso came to be viewed, and to identify themselves, as oyomesan.

CHAPTER 6

Runaway Stories

"It's lonely, isn't it?" Sharyn remarked. It was a grey afternoon, and we were sitting in the living room of her family's large, empty house. Located a ways up Route 19, the multiple-level structure sat beside the highway, looking out across the railroad tracks and the smattering of homes, trees, and fields that filled the cross section of the narrow valley below it.

Like most Filipina women married to Japanese men in the region, Sharyn had met her husband while working as an entertainer at a local hostess bar. She told me that she had been happy being a homemaker and was trying hard to be a good oyomesan, until she learned that her husband was having an affair with another Filipina woman working at a nearby club. Since discovering her husband's infidelity, Sharyn had grown increasingly distraught. Several other Filipina women we knew were concerned that she was close to a nervous breakdown. Worried about Sharyn's depression, these women had encouraged me to keep her company during the day when her husband and mother-in-law went to work. So, Sharyn and I were sitting on her living room couch. We were talking about her marriage as we kept an eye on her four-year-old son, Takefumi.

Sharyn explained that since she had confronted her husband about his affair their fights had become regular and mean-spirited. He had taken to calling her fat and unattractive, and he frequently accused her of marrying him for his money. His mother, with whom they lived during my fieldwork, seemed to think that Sharyn should overlook her son's infidelity:

Sharyn was his third wife and another divorce would be embarrassing for the family. Sharyn was deeply affected by her husband's accusations and found her situation at home unbearable. However, an observant Catholic, she was hesitant to get a divorce and create what she and other Filipina women in the region called a "broken family." She was also attached to her husband, who was the *shachō* (president, Jpn.) of a local construction firm. His occupation was much more lucrative and prestigious than those of other Filipina women's husbands who worked in construction or at pachinko parlors or bars. Sharyn told me a dramatic and romantic story about falling for her husband the moment he walked into the club where she had worked, and she proudly showed me photographs of the large home he had bought her family in Parañaque, a middle-class subdivision of Metro Manila. She was clearly having a hard time facing the possible end of a marriage that at one time had seemed to promise an ideal life.

Suddenly, after a pause, Sharyn rose and walked over to the front window. She beckoned to me to join her and told me to look out. Sharyn pointed a limp finger across the railroad tracks. She asked in Japanese, "See that house over there, in the not-so-far distance?" I nodded affirmatively. "I had a friend who lived there," she whispered, "a Filipina who I worked with at Club Fantasy." She told me that she and this woman used to look out their windows at each other during the day. They would wave to each other across the distance, and sometimes they would meet. The woman also had a little boy, very cute. But then two years ago, the woman had, in Sharyn's words, "run away." This woman had problems with her husband or mother-in-law (Sharyn wasn't specific), and she had left to work in clubs in Tokyo, planning to overstay her temporary spousal visa and remain in Japan. Sharyn didn't know where her friend was anymore, she told me. She hadn't spoken to this woman since she had run away. By the time her friend had left, Sharyn's relationship with her own husband had become strained, and Sharyn had wondered if she might also soon leave. With that, Sharyn ended her story, gazing out of the window for a few moments before she turned back into the room.

Throughout my stay in Central Kiso, stories about Filipina women who had married Japanese men in the region but who "ran away" from their Japanese families regularly surfaced in casual conversations among Filipina women I knew. The repeated mention of these women contrasted strikingly with a lack of discussion about those who had moved away because their husbands were transferred or had large gambling debts.

In these latter cases, Filipina women in the region either maintained friendships with those who had left or never bothered to speak about them at all. Stories about Filipina women who had run away, however, easily became the subject of reflection or gossip, even in cases when these women had been gone for years. I overheard conversations about them when I visited with different Filipina women at home, work, and other social gatherings. These women were discreetly mentioned as Filipina women in the region chatted and smoked during the breaks of the weekly government-sponsored Japanese class. They also came up during the Catholic prayer meetings, Masses, and counseling sessions that Sister Ruth and Father Art held. During the months I lived with Filipina-Japanese families in the region, I also noticed that Filipina friends discussed stories about those who had run away when they gossiped on the telephone. By the time I left Japan in early August 2000, I had heard stories about seven Filipina women who had run away from their Japanese families in Central Kiso, including two who had left for a time and then returned.

Before my fieldwork in Central Kiso, I had volunteered with a help line in Tokyo that assists Filipina migrants in Japan. Over the years I had worked with this organization, I had heard or read stories about Filipina women who had run away from Japanese husbands in other parts of the country.[1] However, I had imagined that these were simply isolated cases in which individual women were pushed to desperate measures to deal with extreme problems in their marriages. When I began my fieldwork in Central Kiso, I had not anticipated that running away would figure as prominently as it did in the lives and imaginations of so many Filipina women married to Japanese men in the region. Moreover, as I increasingly paid attention to the circulation of stories about Filipina women who had run away, I noticed that these narratives took different and sometimes conflicting forms. They figured for differently situated Filipina women in the region as either models or threats, or at different moments both, depending on personal factors that assumed shifting relevance, including the political-economic stability of women's families in the Philippines, women's past and present relationships with their families in Central Kiso, and their desires for and investments in their marriages and futures in Japan. In some cases, such as Sharyn's, stories about Filipina women who had run away signaled the possibility of escaping the anxieties, constraints, and limitations of married life in rural Nagano; in other cases these stories became a locus of criticism, a means for disciplining Filipina women in the region to strategically perform their roles as oyomesan.

In this chapter, I focus on running away as one means through which Filipina women in Central Kiso managed the dissatisfactions that emerged between their dreams and expectations for their lives abroad and the demands and constraints that they experienced in them. As I have suggested, these women's desires for their lives in Japan, including their understandings of marriage, were in some ways compatible with those of their Japanese husbands and families. Many of these women learned to manage a Japanese household, worked in their Japanese families' businesses, and participated in local cultural activities and the PTA at their children's schools. They stressed the importance of caring for elderly, and they expressed desires to be good, loving Catholic wives and mothers. These were roles that their lives as oyomesan enabled. Many Filipina women also told me that they found pleasures in their marriages, which in some ways resonated with their image of a desirable "modern" life. They spoke with pride of their husbands' ability to financially support them, and they enjoyed caring for their homes and shopping in the large discount stores in nearby cities. However, as I have also suggested, these women's dreams and goals for their lives were in other ways irreconcilable with their lives in Central Kiso. Some of these women also faced serious and destructive problems in their marriages. Running away and the circulation of stories about it offered important means through which these women negotiated the discrepancies between their desires for their lives abroad and the realities of their experiences in rural Nagano.

In focusing on the ways that running away figured for Filipina women in Central Kiso, then, I am drawing attention to the disappointing gaps that form within cultural encounters and the ways that they, too, shape the dynamics of cultural processes in a globalized world. I use the word *gaps* to refer to the incompatibilities that emerged as Filipina women negotiated their dreams and expectations for their lives abroad with their everyday experiences. In this understanding, gaps are those irreconcilable spaces of frustration, danger, and possibility that develop as discrepant genealogies of meaning and desire come into productive relation. Such sites of difference figured in cultural processes in Central Kiso in uncertain, yet transformative, ways.[2]

Insofar as running away involves legally and socially unsanctioned forms of movement, it can in some sense be understood as a form of what Foucault and others have called "resistance."[3] Resistance frameworks have been useful for revealing the limits, fractures, and fragility of power as it shapes migrants' lives. Scholars have stressed that members of migrant and immigrant groups do not passively assimilate to their communities of settlement but actively negotiate the demands and promises of them.[4] These scholars have explored the actions that migrants take, both individually and as a group, to negotiate, resist, and challenge the unequal relations of power that shape their lives abroad.[5]

As I will show, running away stood in the face of Japanese immigration laws and the demands that Filipina women's Japanese families placed on them. It offered some Filipina women an alternative strategy for supporting their families in the Philippines and crafting lives in Japan. Filipina women who ran away depended on personal networks of Filipina friends or relatives to find work and places to live. This was a strategy that enabled these women to survive in the margins of the Japanese state, independent of Japanese husbands and families.

However, to focus on action in terms of resistance is to approach it solely from the standard of structures of power—that is, as a unified and directed individual or collective response to power and exploitation.[6] Following feminist critiques of resistance frameworks, I am also interested here in the ambivalent ways that forms of action like running away became possible and preferable for Filipina migrants in Central Kiso through, or in spite of, their relationships with each other.[7] I also want to consider the unsettling and sometimes unexpected social effects such practices produced in these women's and their Japanese community members' lives.

To do so, I focus on the ways that Filipina women's dissatisfactions took on a kind of *runaway agency* in Central Kiso, assuming a social momentum that exceeded any individual woman's decision to leave her Japanese family and becoming an uncertain and thus unsettling social force in the lives of other Filipina women in the region and, correspondingly, in their Japanese communities. I argue that running away occupied an important but ambivalent place in the lives and imaginations of Filipina women in Central Kiso because it reflected at once the dreams and the instabilities of their lives and futures abroad. That is, running away was a preoccupation for these women, even though relatively few of them actually did it, because it resonated in ambivalent ways with features many of these women recognized in their lives: the possibility of finding something better in Japan for themselves and their families in the Philippines and the awareness that their prospects for realizing such dreams were always uncertain and sometimes even dangerous.

As I will show, running away was significant in Central Kiso because it created senses of both identification and tension among Filipina women and between them and their Japanese families. When these women circulated stories about those who had run away, they not only evoked running away as a strategic practice. They also used it chronotopically to evoke a space-time that existed outside the constraints of both the home and the nation and that suggested at once the dream and uncertainty of finding alternative ways for building a life in Japan.[8] Dangerous dreams of other worlds have long been part of Philippine history.[9] Filipina women's decisions to go abroad as migrant laborers are themselves one form such dreaming takes: a dreaming of, what Neferti Tadiar refers to as, "the creative potential of Filipina women gathering outside their 'home.'"[10] For Filipina women in Central Kiso, stories about women who had run away reflected at once the risky dreams that initially inspired these women to leave their homes in the Philippines and go to Japan and the disappointing gaps that developed as these women, paradoxically, tried to realize these sometimes undomesticatable dreams through the domestic path of marriages to rural Japanese men.

In what follows, I explore both the practice of running away and the "social life" of narratives about it as they circulated among Filipina women in Central Kiso. Following Arjun Appadurai's suggestion that an object's meaning and significance are produced through its circulation and use (and Julie Cruikshank's extension of this idea to stories and narratives), my aim here is to demonstrate not only how the practice of running away transformed the lives of women who left, but also the ways that narratives about these women reverberated in the region and figured in the lives of those left behind.[11] In recent years, scholars have explored forms of agency that exceed or stand apart from those attributable to individual human subjects or collectivities.[12] These studies have drawn our attention to the active and uncontainable ways that nonhuman actors and social and material processes shape people's lives. The runaway agency assumed by Filipina migrants' dissatisfactions did not simply reflect individual women's experiences or the cultural logic of a single Filipina diasporic community. Rather, it was a reverberating effect of the diverse and relational ways that running away figured for different Filipina women and members of their Japanese communities in Central Kiso. In this sense, it was a form of agency that cannot be attributed to any individual woman's decision to run away, even if it in part expressed itself through her actions. It emerged through the disappointing gaps that formed in Filipina migrants' and Japanese residents' unequal encounters abroad.

I'll begin by considering why running away became both an appealing and terrifying option for Filipina women in the region. I then turn to three ways that running away figured in the lives of Filipina women and their Japanese communities in Central Kiso. I first consider how Filipina women who ran away created extradomestic spaces: underground spaces that both lay outside the domestic boundaries of these women's lives in rural Japan and circumvented and challenged the legal boundaries of the Japanese nation. Second, I examine the ways that those women who remained with their Japanese husbands in the region circulated stories through *tsismis* (rumors or gossip, Tg.) about other Filipina women who had or were planning to run away. Finally, I consider how running away became both an intended and unexpected leveraging tool through which some of these women negotiated the conditions of their domestic situations, both to their advantage and to their peril. I maintain that while running away was interpreted in different ways by different Filipina women and their Japanese family and community members, it in all cases shaped those "processes of identification" through which these women negotiated, reproduced, and transformed what it meant to be an ii oyomesan in the region.[13]

A DISCOVERY PROMPTS A DEPARTURE

To illustrate how running away offered both a terrifying and hopeful option for Filipina women in Central Kiso, let me first say a bit more about what happened to Sharyn:

Sharyn ran away approximately five months after the day I spent at her house. She left in the middle of the night with her son and a few suitcases. During the weeks before her departure, she had become more and more distraught, unable to decide whether or not to file for divorce. I accompanied Sharyn to consult with a divorce lawyer in Matsumoto about her situation. I also put her in touch with a Filipina counselor at a help line for Filipina migrants in Japan. While the lawyer and the counselor were willing to assist her, both also cautioned her that divorce would not be an easy option.

First, they explained that she might have difficulty getting custody of her son, who was a Japanese national. They explained that in divorces between Filipina-Japanese couples, Japanese family courts tended to favor the parent who could give children the most economically stable and culturally normative (that is, middle-class Japanese) upbringing. They cautioned Sharyn that because her mother-in-law was still young and active enough to care for her grandchild, the courts might assign custody to her husband. At the time, the courts had not been known to favor Filipina women who worked in bars, and Sharyn did not think she could find another job lucrative enough to support herself and her child.[14] Second, the lawyer and the counselor both explained that even if Sharyn were awarded custody, she would need to provide "material evidence" of her husband's affair to win damages. Third, the help-line counselor warned Sharyn that because she did not yet have permanent residency, if she did not gain custody of her son she might have a problem receiving a visa to remain in Japan.

As I have mentioned, spousal visas in Japan are *temporary* residence visas. They are issued in graduated periods of six months, one year, and three years. Renewals are dependent on the sponsorship of one's Japanese spouse; they cannot be reissued if one gets a divorce. Since 1997, foreign nationals whose children are Japanese citizens have been eligible for renewable one-year (and occasionally three-year) visas as parents of Japanese nationals. Filipina women who have children with Japanese men can apply for these visas if they get a divorce. However, at the time when Sharyn was contemplating divorce, a Filipina woman had to become her child's legal custodian and demonstrate that she was financially able to support herself and her child to receive this permit.[15] Thus, if Sharyn did not gain custody of her child, and if she still wished to remain in Japan to work or remain close to him, she would have had no choice but to overstay her visa when it expired in a year.

Soon after her visit to the lawyer, Sharyn began to experience severe stomach pains and to hallucinate, seeing the walls and ceilings of her home moving away from her. She and some of our Filipina friends became convinced that she had been "bewitched" (*kinulam,* Tg.) by her husband's mistress. These friends decided that Sharyn needed to return to the Philippines to see, what they called, a *kwak-kwak doktor* (healer or witchdoctor, Tg.). Sharyn tied small plastic charms with images of the Virgin Mary around her waist. She contacted her mother in the Philippines, who visited a kwak-kwak doktor there on her behalf and, upon the recommendation of the help-line counselor, Sharyn began psychiatric treatment at the local hospital, eventually receiving prescription sedatives. Although still unsure about whether or not she would file for divorce, around this time Sharyn also became obsessed with obtaining material evidence of her husband's infidelity. She started going through her husband's things, collecting receipts from gas stations and love hotels. The day Sharyn ran away, she had discovered a videotape of her husband and his girlfriend at a love hotel having sex. In a state of panic, she called Tessie. Later that night, Tessie and I picked up Sharyn and her son and brought them back to Tessie's. At Sharyn's request, Tessie called a former mama-san of hers in Nagoya. Tessie's husband, Yoshimoto-san, arranged for Sharyn to work at this woman's bar. He also arranged for Sharyn and her son to live in the apartment provided for their employees. The next day, Tessie and I, sworn not to reveal Sharyn's whereabouts to other Filipina women in the region, drove her to the train station.

A HOPEFUL BUT CHANCY OPTION

In retrospect, I realized that Sharyn had foreshadowed her own departure when she had told me about her friend who had left. But the day at her home when she relayed that story to me, neither Sharyn nor I could have known with any certainty how her life might unfold. Rather, Sharyn's story about her friend had suggested that running away was a means that some Filipina women in the region used for dealing with their marital problems. Her friend offered an example that under certain circumstances—which Sharyn hoped not to face—she might decide to follow.

Most Filipina women in Central Kiso recognized running away as a strategy for dealing with marital problems. Many also said that they wondered if in the future they too might confront a situation that had driven another woman to leave, or they recalled times in the past when they almost did. These women suggested a number of reasons why a Filipina woman might want to leave her Japanese husband. These ranged from the pressure placed upon them by their Japanese families to do things the Japanese way, to their Japanese families constantly criticizing them or not supporting their desire to send money to the Philippines. A number of these women struggled with the limitations their Japanese families placed on their mobility. For example, some Filipina women's Japanese families restricted these women's daily activities and required that they ask for permission before going out, particularly in the evening. A few Filipina women in the region were discouraged from socializing with other Filipina women in the area, and at least one woman was for a time forbidden to return to the Philippines, even to attend a sibling's funeral. A number of Filipina women in Central Kiso also complained of loneliness and geographic isolation and that their Japanese families treated them "like a maid." Others, like Sharyn, were upset by their husbands' infidelities or lack of affection. Still others faced verbal or physical abuse.[16]

Yet the options available to Filipina women in Central Kiso for managing their marital problems were extremely limited. This is in part why running away figured so centrally as both a real option and an item of gossip. Some Filipina women in Central Kiso—women like Cora and Tessie who identified as "lucky"—could openly talk to their husbands and in-laws about their needs and desires and expect some degree of support from them. However, if Filipina women's Japanese families were not receptive to their requests, these women had few resources for managing even serious grievances.

As I have mentioned, the local public health nurses in Central Kiso had organized a support circle for foreign mothers in the area. However, this group offered only a place to share concerns, not a means for addressing them. Moreover, few job opportunities existed in Central Kiso for Filipina women to work full-time and support themselves if they left their husbands and remained in the region. Spousal and child support in Japan can be limited. For example, the lawyer whom Sharyn and I visited told us that even given Sharyn's husband's relatively large assets, her spousal support would likely be limited to a one-time payment that would likely not exceed ¥3,000,000 (about $28,500) and child support would likely hit a maximum of ¥50,000 (about $476) a month.[17] The small population in the area (under two thousand people in Sharyn's village; seven to eight thousand in nearby towns) would also make it difficult for her to move on from her relationship, or to escape gossip, if she remained in the region.

The Japanese state has also not been particularly supportive of foreign women who want to leave their Japanese husbands. In many ways, as Rhacel Parreñas tells us, Filipina migrants live in the margins of a citizenship regime in which they are only partial citizens.[18] There are a handful of shelters in urban parts of Japan where women can receive counseling and legal assistance to file for divorce. However, although I was in regular contact with staff in organizations in Tokyo and Nagano City who were part of these networks, I never heard from them that a Filipina woman from Central Kiso had gone to a shelter. When I worked at one of these shelters, I found that foreign women staying there were frustrated with both the limited financial support they received from the Japanese government and the restrictions on their movement. Many Filipina women in shelters were also discouraged by the limitations on their ability to work while they resided in a shelter, which made it difficult for them to send money to their families in the Philippines or plan for the future. As a result, even if women like Sharyn contacted shelter counselors before they ran away, a fair number of Filipina women who left their Japanese husbands avoided approaching them entirely. Instead, these women ran away and relied on personal networks to find work in other parts of Japan. Developed both through relationships in the Philippines and through previous work in bars, these networks became informal and underground resources for crafting alternative lives in Japan.

For Filipina women married to Japanese men in Central Kiso, running away was a practical strategy for dealing with domestic problems for two reasons. First, running away enabled these women, the overwhelming majority of whom were Catholic, to avoid making the morally unsanctioned (and thus often emotionally difficult) decision to divorce their husbands. And, second, it allowed them to defer—at least for a time—officially giving up their legal claims to remain and work in Japan as spouses of Japanese nationals (which would happen if they got a divorce). However, Filipina women who ran away technically violated the terms of their spousal visas and thus were vulnerable to deportation. In 2002, the supreme court of Japan ruled that foreign nationals do not satisfy the requirements of a spousal visa if their marriages do not have a tangible shared-living basis.[19] Yet, because running away kept open the possibility that a woman's marriage could be mended, Filipina women who did so could also hold on to the possibility of maintaining their spousal visas and their identities as wives. These women also would not immediately lose their visas if their husbands did not send the police after them or they simply did not get caught. (Of course, they would lose these spousal visas when these visas expired.) So running away to work in hostess bars in other parts of Japan became a chancy means for maintaining legal and social status and supporting one's family in the Philippines while extricating oneself, at least temporarily, from an unhappy or destructive marriage.[20]

In the remainder of this chapter, I turn to how the at once hopeful and dangerous possibilities that running away offered created runaway social effects in Central Kiso, becoming part of the very ambivalent processes by which some of these women came both to be identified as ii oyomesan and to rework what this meant. I consider three ways that running away figured in these processes and the possibilities these women imagined for their futures: (1) the creation of extradomestic spaces; (2) the circulation of gossip; and (3) the development of negotiating strategies.

THE DANGERS AND POSSIBILITIES
OF EXTRADOMESTIC SPACES

One reason that running away figured so centrally in the lives of Filipina women in Central Kiso is that it suggested the possibility of creating alternative, *extradomestic spaces* in the interstices of marriage and immigration laws in Japan. In describing the worlds Filipina women inhabited when they ran away as extradomestic spaces, I'm playing on the way that *domestic* can mean both "national" and "of the home" and on the links between these two meanings that feminist scholars have shown us.[21] Extradomestic spaces are clandestine, underground worlds that Filipina migrants who run away create through personal networks to enable their day-to-day survival. They lie outside the gendered domestic space of the home that is legally permitted to foreign wives of Japanese nationals. Moreover, because such spaces are under surveillance by police looking for migrant laborers who have entered Japan through (what they call) "fake marriages" *(gizō kekkon)*, extradomestic spaces are also key sites through which the domestic (that is, national) boundaries of the Japanese nation are asserted.

In this sense, extradomestic spaces might be understood as akin to what Susan Coutin has called "clandestine spaces," territorial gaps in a nation-state occupied by those who are physically within its borders yet legally considered outside of it.[22] Clandestine spaces, like extradomestic spaces, are liminal spaces of hidden yet known social worlds. Coutin focuses on clandestine spaces as sites of transit or passage through which Salvadoran migrants travel on their way to U.S. citizenship. However, for Filipina wives of Japanese men, extradomestic spaces were alternative spaces where one could settle for a while, sometimes for upward of ten years, and craft an underground life in Japan while supporting one's family in the Philippines.

When Filipina women ran away from Central Kiso they often went to urban parts of Japan and found jobs in hostess bars through friends, relatives, or prior employers. As I have explained, most Filipina women in the region had worked in bars before their marriages. Despite the stigma attached to these jobs, many of these women suggested that they enjoyed aspects of this work, describing it as a time when they felt independent, and sometimes glamorous, and enjoyed relatively large salaries.[23] When Filipina women ran away to extradomestic spaces, they enjoyed similar pleasures. They lived and worked in communities of Filipina women, freely sent money home to their families in the Philippines, and, in contrast to their married lives, did not have husbands or mothers-in-law telling them what to do.

However, as both Sharyn's story and other conversations I had with Filipina women in Central Kiso suggest, inhabiting an extradomestic space was also a terrifying prospect. First, running away could be socially stigmatizing. In the Philippines, running away from a foreign husband suggested that a woman had made a foolish choice, married for the wrong reasons, or was not upholding the sanctity of marriage. Moreover, running away could be dangerous. A woman could wind up with a bad boss or get unlucky with pushy, demanding, or even violent customers. Every Filipina woman I know who has worked in bars in Japan has stories about such men.

In addition, because Filipina women could not renew their spousal visas without the sponsorship of their Japanese husbands or families, those who ran away would eventually lose their visas if they remained underground. Stories about the tragic fates of Filipina migrants living in Japan without government issued visas—stories of arrest, rape, or sudden and unexplained death—circulate widely in both Japan and the Philippines. All Filipina women in Central Kiso were likely familiar with these stories. A number of them spoke of friends, relatives, or acquaintances who had tragic experiences, and occasionally even died, while living without documentation abroad. The very uncertainty of what one might find in extradomestic spaces meant that one could never quite be sure where running away would lead.

THE DISCIPLINE OF TSISMIS

If the uncertain possibility of running away and living in an extradomestic space informed the ways Filipina women made sense of their lives in Central Kiso, the departures of other Filipina women could also impact their day-to-day lives in the region. A second way that running away impacted these women's lives and marriages, then, is that stories about women who ran away circulated in tsismis. As a subject of gossip, these stories were a medium through which Filipina women who remained in Central Kiso negotiated among themselves what it meant to be oyomesan—what a woman should endure, and what were grounds for moving on. The very circulation of these stories influenced the ways that these women made sense of their lives and relationships in multiple and sometimes ambivalent ways.

Stories about Filipina women who ran away were pervasive, and women like Sharyn were aware before they got married that problems might develop with a Japanese husband. However, on account of romantic courtships, or for other practical reasons, these women had decided to overlook such concerns. Similarly, many Filipina women I met in Central Kiso said that one should endure marital problems, at least up to a certain point, both for moral reasons (to respect the sanctity of marriage) and for practical ones (to not rock an already fragile boat). These women knew that many Japanese community members did not completely trust them and that some Japanese residents believed that Filipina women came to Japan to financially exploit Japanese people. As Cora sometimes complained, "When Japanese community members see something that one Filipina has done, they think all Filipinas are like that." Thus, Filipina women who planned to remain with their husbands worried that another Filipina woman's departure might reflect negatively on all Filipina wives in the region and prompt their own Japanese family or community members to treat them harshly. These concerns often played out in tsismis.

First, Filipina women in Central Kiso gossiped about other Filipina women who were having problems in their marriages and might be contemplating leaving. In these cases, tsismis (which often got back to those who were the object of it) was a means of trying to influence these women's decisions. For example, before Sharyn left, tsismis circulated among other Filipina women in Central Kiso about whether or not her emotional distress was justifiable. Rumors spread that Sharyn's husband had married her only because she had gotten pregnant. Some Filipina woman in the region suggested that Sharyn needed to accept that her husband was a womanizer—as one of these women put it, she needed "to understand the character of her husband"—and not to nag him about it. Tessie wasn't sure if she agreed, but she did think that Sharyn knew what she was getting into before she started dating the man she married: he had openly told her that his first two (Japanese) wives left him because they had tired of his philandering. There were also rumors, Tessie explained, that Sharyn had for a time permitted his affairs, and that she was being unreasonable in suddenly changing her mind. Gossip spread that Sharyn was profligate with her husband's money and had spent upward of tens of thousands of dollars on a recent trip to the Philippines. Some speculated that she had used *shabu* (methamphetamines, Jpn. and now also Tg.) while she was there. Others suspected that Sharyn was upset solely because her husband had started curtailing her extravagant spending.

Through this gossip, Filipina women in Central Kiso evaluated Sharyn's domestic situation and debated what were legitimate and illegitimate reasons for her and other women to leave their spouses. Some compared Sharyn's situation with that of another woman named Deedee. For more than eleven years, Deedee had been contemplating running away from a domestic situation that was severely abusive, both physically and emotionally. Many Filipina women in Central Kiso who knew about Deedee's situation agreed, if not advocated, that she run away. However, they took different positions when women's situations were not so clearly and grossly abusive. Tessie once explained, "Sharyn is still lucky. Her husband doesn't beat her. She has no financial problems." She relayed a conversation she had recently observed between Arli and Sharyn: "The other day, Arli and Sharyn were at my house and they were talking about their lives. Arli was telling Sharyn she's lucky. Arli's husband doesn't even give her money for the doctors' bills!" Tessie explained that Arli had advised Sharyn to stay with her husband. She then added her own perspective: "Sharyn cannot handle the responsibility of supporting herself and her child alone." Like Tessie, few Filipina women in Central Kiso with whom I spoke thought that Sharyn would be justified in running away, and some even tried to dissuade her from leaving.[24]

Second, Filipina women in Central Kiso also gossiped about those who had left. In these cases, tsismis was a means of managing the implications of other Filipina women's departures for what it meant to be a Filipina in Central Kiso. For instance, one day Ligaya and I were standing over her kitchen table, slicing cucumbers and cabbage for a simple *tsukemono* (pickled vegetable, Jpn.) dish for dinner, when she brought up Star's recent disappearance. Ligaya explained that she had heard that Star had run away because her husband had refused to give her a large sum of money to send to her family in the Philippines. According to Ligaya, Star's husband had also told Star that his family had been shocked when they had recently learned about her job at a nearby hostess club. They did not believe that it was appropriate for Star, a married woman with a baby, to be working at night in a bar. Encouraged by his family, Star's husband had insisted that she quit. So Star had taken her baby and run away.

Ligaya and Star were not close friends. They were acquaintances who had friends in common. Unlike Star, Ligaya, as I have mentioned, had been introduced to her husband through a marriage mediator in the Philippines. She was one of four Filipina women I knew in the area who had never worked as an entertainer. She came from a large, middle-class family in the Philippines, and she prided herself on never having set foot in a hostess bar. Things had worked out well for her. The man she married was a generous and dedicated partner. He told me that he credited Ligaya with opening him up as a person and changing his life for the better. Ligaya and her husband agreed on a household division of labor, and he was committed to fulfilling her desires and expectations of him (including supporting her desire to send money to her family in the Philippines).

Ligaya told me that she strongly disagreed with Star's decision. She did not think that married Filipina women should work in bars, and she complained that many Filipina women come to Japan "simply so things will become easier, just so they can have an easier life." Ligaya felt that many Filipina women in Japan were selfish and lazy. "Why can't they make even just a little effort?!" she complained in frustration one day. In her view, these women should make every effort to ensure the success of their marriages. She prided herself on being a capable wife and mother and took pleasure in her community involvement and her competency at managing things the Japanese way. Gossiping about Star, thus, enabled Ligaya to distinguish herself from her and from other Filipina women in the region. Through tsismis, Ligaya defined what she thought it meant to be a responsible wife, mother, and daughter-in-law in the region and to assert that *her* Filipinoness did not make a difference (at least not a negative difference) in the way she managed her roles in her Japanese family.

Feminist anthropologists have argued that gossip is a means through which women not only protect their interests but also wield power over their lives and local decisions in their communities.[25] In the Philippines and within the Philippine diaspora, gossip can both provide a basis for constructing a sense of national identity and reveal the fractures within it.[26] Through tsismis, Filipina women in Central Kiso established standards of behavior for other Filipina women in the region. Yet, as Vicente Rafael tells us, just as gossip is a powerful tool for imagining events and identities, it is also epistemologically empty.[27] Because gossip precludes a full accounting of the epistemological and ethical bases of its claims, it is always an uncertain and uncontainable narrative form. As Filipina women in Central Kiso circulated gossip about women who ran away, these stories took on a runaway agency, shaping how different Filipina women came to understand their situations and their relationships with others in the region in various and shifting ways. In some cases, tsismis about women who had run away inspired these women to identify with other Filipina women in the region and even to run away themselves. In other cases, however, it offered a means for criticizing other Filipina women in the region and differentiating oneself from them. Depending on these women's situations, which themselves sometimes changed, running away, and gossip about it, became part of the very uncertain processes through which Filipina women in Central Kiso defined their roles in their Japanese communities, their relationships with each other, and what it meant to be a Filipina oyomesan in Japan.

UNEXPECTED RETURNS SOMETIMES FOLLOW

The third way that running away—or the option of it—shaped Filipina women's day-to-day lives as oyomesan is that it affected how some Filipina women's Japanese family members treated them. In some cases, Filipina women in Central Kiso ran away temporarily, returning to Central Kiso after several months or a couple of years. In these cases, running away (or the threat of it) could become a means by which some Filipina women in Central Kiso negotiated their roles in their Japanese households and communities. Yet because these women could not anticipate how their Japanese families would respond if they returned, running away was not an easily manipulated or controlled negotiating tool, and again it could produce unpredictable, runaway effects.

Most Filipina women's Japanese husbands and families depended on these women's domestic, and in some cases also waged, labor. In addition, some of these men cared deeply for their wives, whether or not they communicated this to the women. Other men's pride was injured when their wives left, and their families were embarrassed within the community. As a result, some Filipina women's Japanese husbands and in-laws worried that their Filipina wives and daughters-in-law might leave. They sometimes took steps to ensure that this would not happen or, if it had happened once, that it would not happen again. In this way, just the *prospect* of running away could serve to encourage Filipina women's Japanese family members to be both more attentive to these women's needs and more controlling of their movements.

For example, running away enabled Shayrn to negotiate the terms of her relationship with her husband in ways that fulfilled some of her dreams for her life abroad. The last time I saw Sharyn before I left Japan in 2000, she was driving a new powder blue Toyota Starlet, and she and her son Takefumi were sharing a compact but stylishly decorated one-bedroom flat in Nagano City, where she had later moved from Nagoya. Sharyn had gotten her husband to agree to pay for the car and apartment, provide her with a modest living allowance, and perhaps most importantly sponsor her application for permanent residency, as long as she agreed not to file for divorce. While Sharyn kept in regular contact with only one Filipina woman in Central Kiso, she was occasionally sighted in the area, driving her new car and wearing a fashionable outfit or new haircut. She told me that she suspected that her husband preferred to remain married, but to have his wife far enough away that he could meet other women as he pleased. Although divorce carries less social stigma in Japan today than it did in the past, a third divorce for him would push the limits of social acceptability in the rural region. Sharyn was not close with many of her neighbors in her village, and she explained that they might not have even realized that she was working in a bar in another city in Japan as opposed, for example, to being on an extended stay visiting her mother in the Philippines. Sharyn also told me that she had not ruled out the possibility of moving back in with her husband, but that she was not yet ready to return full-time to her life in the region. In the meantime, she was working at a hostess club, using her salary to supplement the stipend her husband gave her, and saving for the future . . . just in case.

When I saw Sharyn again several years later, she had returned to her husband. She had convinced him to open a bar for her in a nearby regional city where she could work as a mama-san, long a dream of hers and of some other Filipina women I knew. She told me that she was not sure if she would stay with her husband long-term, but she had decided to overlook his infidelities for the time being.

However, not all cases in which Filipina women ran away and then returned to their husbands had such favorable outcomes for the women involved. For example, in another case in Central Kiso, a woman named Dely ran away and then suddenly returned after nearly nine months. Initially, I heard that Dely's in-laws were being careful not to upset her out of fear that she might leave again. Dely's Japanese family had a small grocery business, and they depended on her labor. A mutual friend (and the only person in Central Kiso to whom Dely had revealed her whereabouts) disclosed that Dely had been working in a bar in Nagoya because her Japanese family would not allow (and perhaps could not afford) for her to send much money to the Philippines. This friend explained that Dely was also tired of her in-laws' constant criticism and brother-in-law's verbal and physical abuse. Dely also had wanted to complete building a house for her parents in the Philippines, and she had remained away until she had saved enough to do so. However, even after Dely had returned to Central Kiso, she had hidden her actual whereabouts during her absence from her husband and in-laws. She told them that she had gone back to the Philippines because she had been homesick, and her prolonged absence became a bargaining chip, a tool for negotiating the terms of her domestic situation. I heard too that upon learning of Dely's absence, some other Filipina women's in-laws similarly became cautious in their treatment of their daughters-in-law. They did not want to do anything that might prompt the women to leave. But a few weeks later, I learned from a mutual friend that despite Dely's desires to the contrary (she had not ruled out leaving once more, possibly for good), her husband had decided that she should get pregnant again. This friend suggested that Dely's husband had been forcing himself on Dely, telling her that if she had another child to care for she would be less likely, or able, to leave again.

UNDOMESTICATED DREAMS
AND EXTRADOMESTIC WORLDS

In this chapter, I have suggested that the gaps and instabilities that Filipina women face in trying to realize their dreams for a better life in their encounters abroad sometimes took on a runaway agency, assuming a social force that created uncontainable and sometimes unexpected effects in these women's lives and in their communities. This runaway agency cannot be grasped simply in terms of the will or actions of an individual or a collective subject. Rather, it is the unsettling, uncertain, and not always predictable agency of that dialogic or in-between space between discourses and subjects. It must be understood in regard to the ways that Filipina women's understandings of their lives and their actions took shape through the unequal dynamics of their encounters abroad, including their relationships with each other.

By offering the prospect of extradomestic worlds, running away was both practically and figuratively one of the processes through which some Filipina women crafted lives in Japan. First, because stories about women who run away from unhappy jobs or situations abroad circulate widely in the Philippines, Filipina women who were planning to marry Japanese men knew that if things were unbearable in their marriages, running away was always an option, even if it was an uncertain and dangerous one. In this way, the possibility of running away contributed to at least some women's decisions to marry Japanese men, just as it enabled women in unhappy marriages to continue to support their families in the Philippines while living apart from their husbands. And for those Filipina women who did not have the desire or the ability to leave their Japanese husbands, stories about women who ran away became part of the processes through which they crafted identities as new citizen-subjects in Japan.

Second, because the extradomestic spaces Filipina women inhabited when they ran away were not only hopeful but also dangerous, running away was a terrifying and unstable—not entirely predictable, but also not entirely unpatterned—means for these women to transform their lives. Filipina women in Central Kiso agonized over their decisions to leave, were sometimes suddenly prompted to do so, sometimes rethought their decisions and returned to their Japanese families, and in some cases simply decided to go back to the Philippines.

Third, because stories about Filipina women who ran away suggested not only the dangers but also the possibilities of extradomestic worlds, they kept alive the dreams of a better life that had initially inspired many of these women to go abroad. As Filipina women in Central Kiso circulated these stories, they staked out unsettling positions of faith or skepticism toward the possibilities and limits extradomestic worlds offer. These dreams of other worlds were both created and constrained by the material conditions of these women's lives in Japan and the Philippines. They unsettlingly kept alive the possibility that women might find something better for their lives and thus assumed a kind of runaway agency that shaped the lives of Filipina migrants and their Japanese communities.

Fourth, although many Filipina women who ran away from Central Kiso left their Japanese husbands in part so that they could better support their families in the Philippines, as I have suggested, some Filipina women in the region also expressed frustration with the expectations of their families back home. In this regard, we can also read in Filipina women's decisions to run away (in some sense mirroring their decisions to leave the Philippines, which can sometimes also be interpreted as a form of running away), a desire to leave the familiar (and familial) bonds of the domestic behind.[28] Even if a Filipina woman initially leaves her Japanese family so that she can better support her family in the Philippines, once she has run away and gone underground, she can more easily avoid contact with her Filipino family, if she so chooses.

Earlier in this book, I suggested that we think about Filipina migration to Central Kiso not in terms of a back-and-forth movement between home and abroad, but as part of a broader process of continuing or moving on along the road to one's dreams. In this light, we might look to narratives about Filipina women's departures as stories not about women who "ran away" so much as about women who "ran on"—or, as one Filipina woman in Central Kiso suggested of another who had left, "escaped"—as they looked for other possibilities for their lives. And by extension, rather than asking how we might make the world a safer *home* for migrants and other marginalized groups, we might think about what it would mean to create a world where it is easier to live undomesticated lives.

Many studies of migrants' resistance, and particularly of those who are Filipina, have stressed the limitations of migrants' efforts in the face of hegemonic structures of nation-states and global capitalism. By drawing attention to these limitations, scholars highlight the vulnerabilities migrants face in their lives abroad. Clearly, Filipina women in Central Kiso were vulnerable. The problems they faced in their lives in rural Nagano were shaped by their vulnerabilities within Japanese immigration law and histories of unequal political-economic relations involving Japan, the Philippines, and the United States. Yet here I have chosen to highlight the both constraining and enabling ways that, in at least some cases, the dissatisfying gaps that emerged in women's lives abroad reflected unresolved desires for something and somewhere better. In the cases I have explored, running away suggested the uncertain possibility of someday finding that "elsewhere"—a possibility that had inspired many of these women to come to Japan in the first place. It thereby exerted a runaway agency, informing what it meant to be a Filipina oyomesan in Central Kiso and becoming a palpable and unsettling force in the lives of Filipina women and their Japanese communities there.

Epilogue

I'll end this book just as I began it: somewhere in the middle—in the middle of ongoing social processes; in the middle of long histories of unequal relations among people in Japan, the Philippines, and the United States; and in the middle of a conceptual and practical zone of encounters among Filipina women, their Japanese communities, and me.

After being away from Central Kiso for nearly five years, I returned for a visit in 2005. That year and every following year that I have gone back (in 2006 and 2007), I have found that people's lives in the region have changed. Some of these changes have been big, and some have been subtle. Some have reinforced trends I noticed before; others suggest shifts away from those trends. In some cases I have anticipated the transformations, but in other cases they surprised me.

Among the changes I have learned about over the last several years are developments in the lives of some of the Filipina women who are mentioned in this book:

Sharyn, as discussed in the last chapter, had returned to her husband and convinced him to make her a mama-san.

Deedee finally got permanent residency, divorced her abusive husband, and moved to Osaka, where she was working in a hostess bar.

Dely had a new little boy.

Malou was no longer working in clubs. Because of liver problems, she could no longer drink, which made bar work difficult. Instead, she was working in a pachinko parlor. "It's better," she explained, "because the wages are low, you have to work hard. So you appreciate the money you make and don't spend it carelessly."

Ana's mother-in-law had passed away, and Ana had started working in a local bar at night. She told me that her father-in-law did not know that she had taken the job and that she had done so more to stave off boredom than out of financial need. Ana, if you recall, was one of the Filipina women in the region whom I most often heard described as an ii oyomesan, and I heard some surprised (and skeptical) whispers about her moonlighting from both Japanese and Filipina friends.

Ruby's bar, Sampagita, had failed. She had left her patron and business partner, Suzuki-san, and married another local Japanese man, who had since died and left her with a significant sum of money, a monthly pension, and a large, new home. She was driving a used BMW (one of the only European cars I ever saw in the region) and had gone through most of the money her husband had left her. To Tessie's distress, Ruby used the pension she had inherited to play pachinko and throw parties, begging loans from friends for necessities to last through the month. Tessie and her husband speculated (with disapproving nods) that it was just a matter of time before Ruby sold her house and ran through that money too.

Arli's husband had died of a stroke, leaving her to care for their three children alone. She was struggling.

Babs, the controversial mama-san at Club Fantasy, had closed her hostess bar, and she and her husband had moved to another town. Nobody with whom I spoke had contact with them. Some suggested that they were glad to have seen them go.

Pearl (who was Mika's grandmother's sister's granddaughter-in-law) had suddenly and unexpectedly died. She had only been in her early forties, and some of the Filipina women who knew her well were clearly shaken by her unexplained passing.

Cora's Japanese household's produce business had folded. With a mixture of frustration and pride, she told me that she was now working two jobs, one in a factory and one in a bar, to help put her eldest son, Shinji, through college. He was the first in his family to go (on both Cora's and her husband's sides). He was studying English and international relations, with an emphasis on the Philippines, and was enthusiastic about it all.

And Tessie? Tessie had gotten into direct sales of beauty products. She explained that unlike piecework, factory work, or bar work, this was, in her words, "a career with a future." She also told me that her attitude toward Japanese people had changed some. Through her direct sales training she had developed a community of close Japanese women friends.

Her Japanese language skills had gotten quite good, and she said with excitement that through her new job, she was learning not only about beauty but also about how to become a balanced person and to withstand the vicissitudes of life, regardless of what happened.

Along with the changes in individual women's lives and attitudes, more general political-economic shifts, including a further decline of the local political economy, have also affected life in the region. Since the Japanese government began adopting rural decentralization policies in 1999, it has cut subsidies and moved funds away from construction and other projects that brought money into rural areas. Grappling with these cuts and facing increasing depopulation, in 2005 the towns of Kisofukushima and the villages of Kaida, Mitake, and Hiyoshi merged to form Kiso Town (with a population that year of around 13,900 people). As a result, all but one local government office closed, many administrative positions were cut, and those who had previously worked in government offices in outlying areas had to begin commuting long distances each day to work. A number of local residents with whom I spoke were concerned about the loss of not only jobs but also town and village identities. Local government officials were struggling to come up with new ways to make the region economically self-sufficient. Longtime residents expressed increasing pessimism about the future of the region.

In addition to the worsening of the local economy, since I left Central Kiso in 2000 many Filipina hostess bars in the region have closed because they have not been able to hire Filipina entertainers. In its 2004 annual "Trafficking in Persons Report," the U.S. State Department identified entertainer visas as a key route through which Filipina women were being trafficked to Japan. The report ranked Japan on the "Tier 2 Watch List," criticizing it harshly for its approach to human trafficking, ranking it below nearly all countries in Europe and North America, and threatening economic sanctions if it did not take steps to deal with the issue.[1] The Japanese government quickly changed the requirements for entertainer visas, making them much more difficult to obtain. Many Filipina women who would have qualified for such visas just a few years back no longer could. By 2006, the number of Philippine nationals entering Japan on such visas had dropped precipitously (from more than 83,000 in 2004 to fewer than 8,700 in 2006).[2] The few remaining Filipina hostess bars in Central Kiso began to exclusively hire "part-timers"—married Filipina women who work a few nights a week. (In a dovetailing development, as the local economy had taken a turn for the worse,

an increasing number of married Filipina women had begun to work in
local bars, sometimes to help support their families in Japan.)[3]

Surprisingly, despite the worsening of the local economy and the de-
creased number of Filipina hostess bars in the area, the number of Philippine nationals in Central Kiso has continued to rise. As I mentioned earlier, a number of Filipina women married to Japanese men in the region
had children in the Philippines from previous relationships with Filipino
men or Japanese men they met before their husbands while working at
hostess bars in other parts of Japan. With the support of their Japanese
husbands and in-laws, some of these women have brought these children
over to join their Japanese families in Central Kiso. I met some of these
children when I visited the area in 2006 and 2007. Some, especially those
who came at a young age, seem to have smoothly adapted to their new
lives in the region. They quickly learned to speak Japanese and were en-
rolled in local schools. However, others, and particularly teenagers who
had previously been living in Metro Manila, were not doing as well. A few
of them told me that they remained in Japan only because their mothers
insisted that more opportunities for their futures could be found there.
They dressed in fashions from the Philippines, listened to Philippine pop
music, and said that more than anything they wanted to return "home."

While these children and teenagers account for a small portion of the
increase of Filipinas/os in Central Kiso, a number of Filipina women in
the region told me that the growing presence of Philippine nationals in
the area should, more than anything, be attributed to a recent rise in *omiai
kekkon* (mediated marriages) between Filipina women and local Japanese
men. In the past, I had seen scandalous stories in Japanese mass media
about police breaking up rings that promoted marriage in exchange for
visas. I had also heard skeptical and snide comments from people in the
Philippines who questioned Filipina women's motivations for marrying
Japanese men (recall, for example, Ligaya's niece Mely's assertion cited in
chapter 2 that Filipina women go to Japan just so they can "marry a rich
Japanese"). This time, however, Tessie and other Filipina women in the
region suggested with dismay that spousal visas have become one of the
few available options left for Filipina women looking to come to Japan
to work. They explained that an unprecedented number of women in the
Philippines were marrying Japanese men to acquire visas that would enable
them to work in Japan. Indeed, the number of marriages between Philippine and Japanese nationals jumped from 5,430 in 2004 to 8,601 in 2006.

As I sat at Tessie's kitchen table chatting with Tessie, Leny, and some
others, Tessie pulled out a sheet of government statistics indicating that

218 Philippine nationals now lived in the Kiso Valley.[4] In the past, Filipina women on entertainer visas had accounted for a significant portion of the number of Philippine nationals residing in the region. Tessie presumed that because most of the hostess bars in the area had closed, wives of local men who had mediated marriages now accounted for the balance of this number. She could think of at least seven Filipina women who had omiai kekkon with local men over just the past few months. She explained that most of these women were significantly younger than the men they married. "How could these women marry a man they hardly had met?" Tessie wondered aloud. Leny added that she had been shocked to hear stories of Filipina women who had *paid* Japanese men to marry them to obtain spousal visas, which would enable them to work full-time in Japan. Others shared rumors of Filipina women who married local men with the intention of running off.

These women recognized the financial strain that the change in entertainer visa requirements was having on people in the Philippines. They recognized, too, the vulnerabilities women who entered these marriages faced. However, they were also concerned about how these new migration patterns would impact perceptions of their own marriages and of themselves as Filipina, as well as about how these relationships reflected on the sanctity of marriage more generally.

Tessie and others said too that they were glad that fewer Filipina women were coming to Japan to work in bars. Despite their own previous, and in some cases current, work in them, these women expressed concern about how much riskier coming on entertainer visas had become over the past decade because bar owners' and customers' expectations had changed. Ana mentioned that she thought that, for their own good, Filipina women should not come on entertainer visas because the work was morally compromising, and the women could find themselves in undesirable and even dangerous situations with customers. Others commented about how the behavior of Filipina women who had recently come on such visas negatively impacted perceptions of Filipina women in the region. Cora complained that those who had been coming on entertainer visas since the late 1990s dressed inappropriately when walking through town, wearing clothing that was too revealing and made no sense given the cold weather. Tessie reiterated a comment that I had heard her make more generally in the past about other Filipina women: most recent Filipina entertainers had come only for money and flashy things. These women easily got hooked in a vicious consumption pattern. After working in Japan and returning to the Philippines, in a month they blew all the money they had made, giving them no choice but to go back to Japan and work again. "They didn't have a dream," Tessie explained, shaking her head in disappointment. She echoed a sentiment she had shared when telling me her story, "You have to have a dream."

By distancing themselves from more recent Filipina migrants, Tessie, Cora, and others both reinforced the adoption of their own roles as wives, mothers, and daughters-in-law and indicated that they have come to feel more established in their lives in Central Kiso. Like a number of other Filipina women in the region, they also suggested that they felt a greater sense of investment in their communities. Many of these women have children who are now in or approaching middle school and high school, and in a few cases even college. Some of these women are involved in their children's schools and other local activities, such as neighborhood groups and *taiko* (drum) circles. Like Tessie, they have become more fluent speakers of Japanese, grown accustomed to their lives in rural Nagano, and developed friendships with Japanese residents. In some cases, their in-laws have passed away, relieving some of the pressures they faced in their homes. A number of them mentioned positive shifts in how their Japanese families and neighbors treated them. Cora, for example, said that she didn't feel as much discrimination as she had in the past. When I asked Tessie if any Filipina women I remembered from my first fieldwork had since run away, she could not think of any additional women who had, or at least who had stayed away.

However, I would caution against assuming that these Filipina women are following some smooth trajectory of assimilation. Even if they are more comfortable with their situations in Central Kiso, they have become so in part because the growing presence of Filipina women in the region has transformed life there. Moreover, many Filipina women in the area with whom I spoke still described feelings of restlessness. Consider Ana's choice to return to bar work to stave off boredom. Many also still spoke of other dreams for their lives. Some of these women mentioned plans to someday retire with their husbands to a beautiful home in the Philippines. Others suggested they wanted at some point to move to an urban part of Japan. Still others simply said that they hoped someday to find themselves living somewhere better.

I began this book by asking how it was possible that Filipina migrants, who were widely disparaged as prostitutes and foreigners, had come to be described by Central Kiso residents as ii oyomesan. I also asked how, why, and to what ends Filipina women performed this role. In the previous six chapters, I have tracked those everyday, relational, and dialogic processes of encounter through which Filipina women have come to be identified and to identify themselves as Japanese brides and daughters-in-law. I have traced how these women's desires for glamour, mobility, and political-economic stability came into productive relation with local Japanese residents' ambivalent longings to be part of a modern, wealthy, and cosmopolitan Japanese nation. I have considered how Central Kiso residents' experiences of marginality within dominant discourses of affluent and modern Japaneseness informed their investments in identifying Filipina women as ideal, traditional Japanese brides. I have also explored how Filipina women come to be described in such terms through their strategic and inadvertent performances of those behaviors that Central Kiso residents recognized as the Japanese way. Finally, I have considered the unsettling gaps that emerged in cultural encounters among Filipina women and their Japanese communities, and I have suggested that these gaps themselves became part of the processes through which these women came to be identified and to identify themselves as oyomesan.

At stake in the approach to cultural encounters I have laid out is the way we understand the dynamics of cultural and social process in the contemporary interconnected world. The ethnographic narratives that I have offered do not present a single or unified view of relationships among Filipina women and their Japanese communities. Rather, they highlight the relations of power through which these relationships have developed and become meaningful in multiple and sometimes conflicting ways. The desires that Filipina women and Japanese residents brought to their interactions were configured within larger histories and political-economic relations among Japan, the Philippines, and the United States. Through the contingencies of their encounters, these desires aligned and misaligned in ways that both reinscribed and transformed cultural meanings and identities.

Over the past decade, nation-states such as Japan and the United States have increasingly tightened regulations on migration. National governments have established ever more restrictive terms of national inclusion. These policies affect people's lives in material ways. But the terms of national belonging are also negotiated on multiple and interactive levels through relationships among people who live in the overlapping margins of nation-states. If we overlook these everyday processes, we miss some of the intimate and contingent dynamics through which meanings of culture and identity are made and remade. This book has explored the ways that Filipina migrants and rural Japanese residents reproduced and transformed meanings of Japaneseness and Filipinaness as they negotiated terms of national identity and belonging through their shared daily lives. As their encounters redefined these terms, they produced unexpected outcomes at the level of everyday practice: elderly Japanese women found themselves preferring Filipina daughters-in-law to Japanese ones. Rural Japanese men adopted their wives' Filipino children and raised them as their own. Filipina women learned to prepare traditional Japanese foods, raised Japanese children, and came to be identified and to identify as ii oyomesan. Some of them became Japanese citizens. The lives people found themselves living were not the ones they had dreamed for themselves. Their encounters were shaped by inequalities and rested on compromises. Their relationships produced not only pleasures but also dissatisfactions and violence, reflecting the ways that people unequally situated on the margins of larger configurations of power negotiate a world that is not much in their control.

However, the very ambivalences that members of these groups felt toward their lives became transformative forces in their relationships, reshaping the ways they saw the world and the choices they made in it. Insofar as this book has traced these processes of transformation, it cannot be read as offering timeless or fixed truths about Filipina migrants, Japanese residents, or life in Central Kiso. The stories I have relayed in the previous six chapters could not unfold in the same way today. The shift in requirements for entertainer visas has meant that Filipina women married to local men now staff the few remaining Filipina hostess bars in the region; these bars are thus no longer the same sites of encounter they were in the 1980s and 1990s. Most Filipina migrants coming to the region have mediated marriages with local men, possibly because they have few other avenues to acquire work visas. A significant number of Chinese women have also begun coming to Central Kiso through omiai kekkon, and local residents now positively compare Filipina women to them. These changes are affecting the kinds of encounters occurring in the region today, which will in turn shape those that follow. What it means to be "Japanese" and what it means to be "Filipina" will continue to be renegotiated as discrepantly located discourses, histories, and forms of meaning and desire come into productive relation through the contingent and intimate dynamics of everyday life in zones of encounters.

Registered Philippine Nationals in Central Kiso by Year (1981–1999)

Year	Number of Nationals
1981	7
1982	6
1983	5
1984	6
1985	12
1986	13
1987	36
1988	40
1989	53
1990	108
1991	168
1992	138
1993	161
1994	185
1995	125
1996	142
1997	137
1998	156
1999	189

Note: This table is based on unpublished data provided by the Nagano prefectural government. These numbers represent those Philippine nationals registered in the region of Kiso County that I call Central Kiso. Data was first collected in the year 1981. Breakdowns along lines of gender and residency status were not available. Based on conversations with Filipina women and Japanese residents in the region, I assume that until the mid-2000s the overwhelming majority of registered Philippine nationals in the region were Filipina women with entertainer visas. Beginning in the mid-1980s, wives of local Japanese men also started to constitute a growing portion of those registered including approximately 60 by 1998.

Registered Philippine Nationals in Japan on Entertainer Visas by Year (1980–2006)

Year	Number of Nationals
1980	8,509
1981	12,048
1982	9,125
1983	8,395
1984	11,972
1985	17,861
1986	26,029
1987	36,080
1988	41,423
1989	32,719
1990	42,867
1991	57,038
1992	51,252
1993	42,805
1994	53,996
1995	24,212
1996	19,063
1997	31,774
1998	36,777
1999	46,000
2000	60,933
2001	72,230
2002	75,285
2003	80,563
2004	83,295
2005	48,142
2006	8,673

Note: Data from 1980–2003 is cited in JNATIP and F-GENS (2005). See Hōmushō Daijin Kanbō Shihō Hōseibu (2005, 2006, and 2007) for data for 2004, 2005, and 2006, respectively.

Notes

INTRODUCTION

1. "Central Kiso" is not an officially recognized region. It is the name I have given to a cluster of mountain towns and villages in Kiso County that includes the towns of Kisofukushima and Agematsu and several nearby villages.

2. In Tagalog, *ate* is a title or term of address, meaning "elder sister." It is used to show respect not only by younger siblings to older ones, but also among cousins, neighbors, and other members of one's community or group.

3. For historical discussions of kokusai kekkon in Japan see Higurashi (1989), Kelsky (2001), Koshiro (1999), and Shukuya (1988).

4. I identify Japanese words with "Jpn." and Tagalog words with "Tg."

5. By *discourse* I mean, following Michel Foucault (1977a), a configuration of statements and practices through which something can be identified and known. A discourse is a social formation that produces the very object of knowledge that it claims to represent. It does this by establishing the language and conditions (what I call the "terms") through which this object can be identified. A discourse is also a site for the production of subjectivities that works by delimiting the terms of possibility for certain modes of being.

6. Bakhtin (1981a: 284).

7. A dialogic approach to encounters differs from those that use transactional models (Thomas 1991) or focus dialectically on the transformation of self-contained structures of culture (Sahlins 1981, 1985). As I explain later, I am interested in the intimate and interactive dynamics through which cultural ideas and practices come to be knowable and relationally formed. Dialogic processes may include forms of "transculturation" in which a disadvantaged group selectively borrows cultural ideas from another (Ortiz 1995; Pratt 1992); however, they cannot be reduced to this practice. See Meyler (1997) for a discussion of how Bakhtin's notion (1981a) of the dialogic differs from a dialectical approach.

8. Like all encounters, those I describe also rest on exclusions. They foreclose certain forms of relationships and modes of desire and subjectivity (Clarke 2007; Lowe 2006; Stoler 1995, 2002, 2006).

9. Rizal (1887/1996).

10. Cannell (1995: 225, italics added). Sally Ann Ness (1992) has also demonstrated the ways a long history of foreign influence shapes the meanings and forms of the *sinulog* dance tradition in Cebu City.

11. Rafael (1995: xv).

12. Nihonjinron is a genre of writing that became popular in Japan during the late 1970s and early 1980s. Literally "discussions of the Japanese," this body of literature stresses the uniqueness, purity, and superiority of the Japanese people, sometimes citing Japan's island geography as a reason for Japan's uniqueness. For critiques of Nihonjinron and other essentialist literatures on Japan see Befu (1993), Dale (1986), Oguma (2002), Mouer and Sugimoto (1986), and Yoshino (1992). Ironically, the Philippines is also an archipelago and, at that, one farther than Japan from the nearest continental land mass.

13. Many scholars have written about the ie as a definitively Japanese form of domestic organization tied to a rural way of life; see in particular Fukutake (1980) and Nakane (1967). Some have also stressed its continuing practice in rural Japan (Ueno 1987). Dorinne Kondo (1990) has taken a more critical approach to such arguments and explored the place of the ie in family firms in downtown Tokyo.

14. For scholarly discussions of rural nostalgia in contemporary Japan, see Ivy (1995), Kelly (1986), Robertson (1998a), Scheiner (1998), and Tamanoi (1998). For discussions of descent-based ideas about race in Japan, see Dower (1986), Koshiro (1999), Oguma (2002), and M. Weiner (1994, 1997a).

15. Work in a number of different fields has discussed marriage as an institution that reproduces social organizations, including earlier anthropological work that approaches marriage as a fact of social structure (e.g., Evans-Pritchard 1990; Levi-Strauss 1969); feminist critiques of these ethnographic studies (e.g., Rubin 1975; A. Weiner 1983); and feminist analyses of politics and nationalisms (e.g., Collier, Rosaldo, and Yanagisako 1997; Pateman 1988; Visweswaran 1994).

16. Anderson (1991).

17. Winichakul (1994).

18. Baty (1995), Mankekar (1999), and Rofel (1999).

19. See, for example, Chatterjee (1993) and Guha and Spivak (1988). See also Dirks (1990) for a related argument.

20. Ivy (1995).

21. Anzaldúa (1987), Rosaldo (1993), and Tsing (1993).

22. Stewart (1996).

23. Gilroy (1993).

24. Appadurai (1996).

25. Ong (1999).

26. Gupta and Ferguson (1997).

27. Brown (2005), Clarke (2004), Espiritu (2003), and Gopinath (2005). See also Bakrania (2004), Brennan (2004), Constable (1997, 2003), Kelsky (2001), Manalansan (2003), and Parreñas (2001).

28. See Bhabha (1994) for a related discussion of contingency as it shapes the temporal and spatial contradictions that condition agency.

29. Coutin (2003, 2005), and de Genova (2005).

30. Comaroff and Comaroff (1991), McClintock (1995), Povinelli (1993), M. L. Pratt (1992), Stoler (1995, 2002), Cooper and Stoler (1997), Rafael (1988), Taussig (1987), Taylor (1984), Uchida (2005a, 2005b), and Van der Veer (2001).

31. Rafael (1988: 218).

32. M. L. Pratt (1992).

33. Stoler (1995, 2002).

34. The reference to modernity "at large" is from Appadurai (1996).

35. Ong (2006).

36. Tsing (2005).

37. Tsing (2005: 6).

38. Clarke (2009).

39. My use of the term *intimate* draws from Stoler (1995, 2002, 2006), Wilson (2004), Povinelli (2006), and Lowe (2006).

40. I take the idea of the "in-between" from Homi Bhabha's reading of Jacques Derrida: "The address to nation as narration stresses the insistence of political power and cultural authority in what Derrida describes as the 'irreducible excess of the syntactic over the semantic.' What emerges as an effect of such 'incomplete signification' is a turning of boundaries and limits into the *in-between* spaces through which the meanings of cultural and political authority are negotiated" (Bhabha 1990: 4, italics in the original; see also Bhabha 1994, 1996). The quotation from Derrida in the passage is in Derrida (1981: 221).

41. According to statistical records provided by the Nagano prefectural government, in 1999 an additional 129 Philippines nationals (for a total of 189) were registered in the portion of Kiso County that I call Central Kiso. (Two others were registered in other parts of Kiso County for a total of 191 in the county that year.) The overwhelming majority of Filipina women who were not wives of Japanese men were presumably on entertainer visas, working in local hostess bars. A few may have been family members of Filipina wives who were visiting the region on temporary visas. In other parts of Japan, some Philippine nationals enter on training visas and are employed in factories; however, I never heard of such a case during my primary fieldwork in Central Kiso.

42. I mark the terms "companions" and "hostesses" in quotation marks here for two reasons. First, in Japan the term *konpanion* had for a time become a politically correct replacement for the term *hosutesu*. However, *hosutesu* is much more commonly used in Japan, as is *hostess* in the United States. I acknowledge that hostess is a gendered term. However, it is a recognized job category in Japan, and English lacks a gender-neutral equivalent. Second, Filipina women working in bars refer to this work in different terms than the Japanese public. In the Philippines, Philchime and the Overseas Employment Agency refer to these women as "overseas performing artists" (OPAs). Women who have legal contracts sometimes speak of themselves as "talents" and distinguish themselves as either "dancers" or "singers," rather than considering themselves "hostesses." Job responsibilities depend on the club where one is employed, and especially on one's

boss or mama-san. I discuss Filipina women's labor in bars in more detail throughout this book. For descriptions of bar work for Japanese women, see Allison (1994), Jackson (1976), and Mock (1996).

43. Filipina women have consistently and overwhelmingly constituted the largest group of foreign women entering Japan on entertainer visas. For a general discussion of migration trends in Japan over the past few decades, see Douglass and Roberts (2003).

44. JNATIP and F-GENS (2005: 29). These numbers did not steadily increase but to some degree fluctuated during given years on the basis of changes in visa laws and widespread media stories in the Philippines about the tragic fates of Filipina migrants in Japan. For a discussion of these policy changes and some of these stories, see Tyner (2004). These figures represent numbers of Filipina women legally registered in Japan. NGO workers in Tokyo once told me that if one included those women working and living in Japan without government issued visas, the numbers would likely double.

45. One bar opened and several closed during the course of my research, hence the ambiguity in numbers.

46. As a result, most outsiders did not necessarily associate bars with the region, and many were surprised to learn there were so many. I remember the reactions of Japanese friends and scholars from Tokyo when they learned about the sizable population of Filipina women working in the area. Both Father Art and Sister Ruth, Filipina/o missionaries and activists who first introduced me to the region, expressed astonishment as well.

47. Bello et al. (2005).

48. This summary is consistent with that in Constable (1997). For other discussions of migration from the Philippines, see also Battistella and Paganoni (1992), Chant and McIlwaine (1995), Choy (2003), Espiritu (2003), Parreñas (2001), G. Pratt (2004), and Schirmer and Shalom (1987). Kale Fajardo (2004) also has a provocative critique of "waves" migration models on account of the ways they overlook migration patterns that are not land-based.

49. These texts were published by scholars and journalists in Japan and the Philippines. See, for example, Ballescas (1992), DeDios (1990, 1992), Nīgata Nippōsha Gakugeibu (1989), Higurashi (1989), Hisada (1989), Furusawa (1992), Matsui (1989), Shukuya (1988), Sato (1989), and Usuki (1988).

50. The expression "institutionalized oppressions" is from Tyner (1996). Here I am referring to writings about Filipina migrants not only in Japan but also elsewhere. These include Burgess (2004), Constable (1997, 1999, 2002, 2003), Law (1997), Nakamatsu (2003), McKay (2003), N. Suzuki (2000, 2002a, 2002b, 2003, 2004, 2007), Parreñas (2001), Piper (1997), G. Pratt (2004), Roces (2003), Tyner (1996, 2004), and Yea (2004).

51. Discussions of these marriages can be found in Burgess (2004), Furusawa (1992), Higurashi (1989), Kuwayawa (1995), Nakamatsu (2003, 2005), Sato (1989), Satake and Da-anoy (2006), and Shukuya (1988), among others. See Sataake and Da-anoy (2006), N. Suzuki (2002b), and Nakamatsu (2005) for critical analyses of popular representations of rural brides. In 1990, after the Philippine government banned mass interviews for potential marriage partners,

Japanese farmers began to look to Korea, Sri Lanka, and China for potential spouses.

52. See Knight (1995) for a discussion of the difficulty of finding brides in rural Japan and local strategies to assist men living there.

53. Pachinko is a gambling game something like a cross between pinball and slots.

54. Studies of Filipina migrants in rural Japan have tended to frame their analyses in terms of *all* foreign brides or foreign rural brides in the country (e.g., Burgess 2004; Higurashi 1989; Nakamatsu 2003; Sato 1989; and Shukuya 1988, among others). Other scholars associate Filipina wives of Japanese men with other groups of marriage migrants around the world or with other migrant women in caregiving labor markets such as domestic labor and the sex industry (see, for example, Constable 2003, Piper and Roces 2003, and Parreñas 2001). Even in Central Kiso, I might have taken a broader approach to kokusai kekkon. In addition to the large number of Filipina women in the region, two Rumanian women and a number of Chinese women (I knew six, most from Harbin) had married local men. I interviewed some of these women. Yet while the contexts through which Chinese and Rumanian women come to Central Kiso invite comparisons with those from the Philippines, differences among them have also created variations in their migration patterns and experiences. While for a very brief period one bar in the region hired Rumanian women, and while there may be some political-economic parallels between contemporary postsocialist Rumania and the postcolonial Philippines, these migrations developed through distinct locally situated histories. Moreover, Rumanian women are positioned differently in Japan because they are white and European. Most Chinese women come through arranged marriages, and Central Kiso residents sometimes describe their appeal as brides in terms of Japan's colonial history in China and the fact that there is a significant population of Japanese in the southern part of Kiso County who spent part of their lives in Manchuria (*Nagano Nippō* 1999). Parallel reasons were never given for why Filipina women were appealing brides. Moreover, although a few Filipina women in Central Kiso had arranged marriages, many Filipina women there told me that they could never imagine marrying a man they had only just met.

55. For example, Tomoko Nakamatsu (2005) points out that in their representations of potential foreign brides, marriage agencies target men of different class positions and who live in rural and urban areas in different ways. Clearly, there are both overlaps and divergences in how these marriages play out for differently situated men in Japan.

56. I draw in particular from Basu et al. (2001), Burgeson (2001), Gibson-Graham (1996, 2006), Ong (2006), Rofel (1999), and Tsing (2000b, 2005). Inda and Rosaldo (2002) also stress the importance of exploring the "situated and conjunctural nature" of globalization through the contradictions that emerge within the very localized articulations of its practices.

57. I focused my research on the region of the Kiso Valley I call "Central Kiso" for several reasons. First, Filipina women in Kiso County lived almost exclusively in this part of the region, and primarily in the towns of Agematsu and Kisofukushima, where the majority of Filipina bars were located. Moreover,

these women seemed to limit their everyday social contact to Filipina women within or near this area. In addition, I noticed that some Japanese residents shared overlapping cultural practices—for example, certain pickle-making styles—and kinship ties with others within this portion of the valley. Topographical features also shaped people's lives in this area in similar ways. While those living in villages to the north and south of Central Kiso could easily commute for work to the cities of Shiojiri and Nakatsugawa, which respectively bookend Kiso County, for those living in the central swath of the county, a daily commute was impractical, if not treacherous. As a result, Kisofukushima and Agematsu are economic and administrative hubs for people living in the ring of villages around them.

58. The term "power-geometry" is Doreen Massey's. Her emphasis, like mine here, is on *"place as meeting place"* (1999: 22, italics in original).

59. Ghosh (2005).

60. For discussions of "third spaces" see Gutiérrez (1999), Soja (1996), and Bhabha (1994).

61. I borrow the expression "cartographies of desire" from Greg Pflugfelder (1999).

62. The passage from which I take this expression (and base my epigraph on) can be found in Ghosh (2005: 228).

63. I take "relational ontologies" from Karen Barad (2003, 2007). The expression "co-constituitive relations of significant otherness" is from Donna Haraway (2003). See also Noel Castree (2003) and Sarah Whatmore (2002) for related discussions.

64. See Befu (1993), Christy (1993), Dale (1986), Fujitani (1992, 1993, 1996), Ivy (1995), Lie (2001), Morris-Suzuki (1993, 1998), Robertson (1998b), Ryang (1997), Sakai (1997), Mouer and Sugimoto (1986), Nakamura (2003, 2006), S. Tanaka (1993), Tamanoi (1998), Yoneyama (1995), and Yoshino (1992).

65. For discussions of differences based on class see Gill (2001), Fowler (1996), and Kondo (1990). Discussions of ethnic difference within Japan can be found in Lie (2001), M. Weiner (1997b), and Siddle (1996, 1997). To understand the role that geographic or regional differences play, particularly as they are manifest in rural/urban divides, see Kelly (1986, 1990), Tamanoi (1998), and Robertson (1991). Ethnographic attention to the role of gender and sexuality in shaping people's experiences in Japan is explored in Allison (1994, 2000), G. L. Bernstein (1983), Kelsky (2001), Kondo (1990), Robertson (1998b), and Tamanoi (1990, 1998). See Karen Nakamura (2003, 2006) for a discussion of the experiences of deaf people in Japan.

66. See Tamanoi (1990) for a critique of the silencing of women's voices in the anthropology of Japan.

67. See Ching (2001), Christy (1993), Dower (1986), Lie (2001), S. Tanaka (1993), M. Weiner (1994, 1997a), and Siddle (1996). For discussions of the ways that imperialist legacies shape life in contemporary Japan, see Chung (2004), Field (1993a, 1993b), Morris-Suzuki (1998), Ryang (1997, 2005), and Yoneyama (1995, 1999).

68. See Ivy (1995), Kondo (1997), Sakai (1997), and Tobin (1992) for discussions of the ways that the West or Western consumer products are incor-

porated into, and reinterpreted in, in Japan. See also Kelsky's (2001) study of internationalist Japanese women; Anne Allison's (2006) recent work on Pokemon in the United States and Japan; and Theodore Bestor's (2004) exploration of links between fish markets across the globe.

69. Discussions of the experiences of other immigrant, migrant, and ethnic minority populations in Japan can be found in Christy (1993), Douglass and Roberts (2000), Linger (2001), Maher and MacDonald (1995), Roth (2002), Ryang (1997, 2005), Siddle (1996, 1997), N. Suzuki (2002a, 2002b, 2003, 2004, 2007), Tsuda (2003), M. Weiner (1997b), and Yamanaka (1993).

70. Many studies of these groups have focused on the transnational dimensions of the lives of those in the Philippine diaspora. Linda Basch, Nina Glick Schiller, and Christina Szanton Blanc have explored the ways that Filipina/o transmigrants in the United States participate in nation building in the Philippines as they engage in political, social, and economic activities from overseas (1994). Others stress the ambivalences that Filipina/o migrants face as they reconcile their connections to their homelands with the demands and promises of their current homes (Constable 1997, 1999; Espiritu 2003; Law 2001; Manalansan 2003; Parreñas 2001; G. Pratt 2004; Roces 2003). Martin Manalansan (2003) considers how gay Filipino men in the United States negotiate between different sex and gender traditions as they craft diasporic subjectivities. Yen Li Espiritu (2003) explores how ideas and practices of home figure in the ways that Filipina/os in the United States craft lives and selves.

71. Burgess (2004), Constable (1997, 1999, 2003), Law (1997), Nakamatsu (2003), McKay (2003), Parreñas (2001), G. Pratt (2004), Roces (2003), Satake and Da-anoy (2006), N. Suzuki (2002 a, 2002b, 2003, 2004, 2007), Tyner (1996, 2004), and Yea (2004).

72. Clifford (1988), Clifford and Marcus (1986), Dumont (1992), Harding (2000), Kondo (1990), Marcus and Fischer (1986), Rosaldo (1993), Stewart (1996), Tsing (1993), Trinh (1989), and Visweswaran (1994).

73. Visweswaran (1994).

74. Clifford (1997: 69, italics in original).

75. See John (1996) and see also Clifford (1997: 82–88).

76. For historical discussions of the U.S. colonial presence and its legacies in the Philippines, see Constantino and Constantino (1978), Rafael (2000a), Salman (2001), and Schirmer and Shalom (1987).

77. Sturdevant and Stoltzfus (1992).

78. I borrow the term "provincialize" from Dipesh Chakrabarty (2000) to suggest that examining the role of the United States in Central Kiso is at once indispensable and inadequate for understanding the situation of Filipina migrants and their Japanese communities. I use "dislocations" in the way that Naoki Sakai (1997) suggests that the United States/West in some sense always comes into being in Japan (and I would add the Philippines) as an allocation of difference.

79. Trask (1999).

80. Stewart (1996: 5).

81. Abu-Lughod (1993), Kondo (1990), Stewart (1996), Trinh (1989), Tsing (1993), and Visweswaran (1994).

82. The expression "studying up" is famously Laura Nader's (1972).

83. See Mohanty, Russo, and Torres (1991) and Narayan (1997) for discussions of the ways that race, class, and nationalisms shape not only the lives of these women but also the studies of them.

84. Gordon (1997): 4–5.

PART ONE

1. The expression "setting trope" is Dorinne Kondo's (1990).

2. Foucault (1990) challenges psychoanalytic traditions that identify desire as the product of originary loss and the attachments that follow from it. He argues that subjects are not defined by their desires but that desires emerge through those productive relations of power that name, delimit, and give social meaning and possibility to them. Foucault is concerned primarily with sexual desire. However, Ann Laura Stoler (1995, 2002) has expanded our understanding of Foucault's argument by introducing questions of race, class, gender, and colonialism. I am drawing here on her reading as well as that of Judith Butler (1997b), who builds on Foucault to explore desire as an interface between the social and the subjective.

By approaching desires as historically and culturally constituted, I do not mean to foreclose the possibility of a historically and culturally grounded psychoanalytic reading of them. Examples of such readings can be found in Allison (1994, 2000), Ivy (1995), and McClintock (1995). Scholars in both Japan and the Philippines have also developed psychoanalytic traditions that challenge the hegemonic categories of those developed in the United States and Europe by offering culturally and linguistically specific ones (for well-known work on Japan see, for example, Doi 1973 and on the Philippines, see Enriquez 1992). I mention some of the concepts developed in these fields in the pages that follow. However, here I am interested more in tracing the multiple, and sometimes contradictory, cultural and historical forces that inform people's desires than in considering how their desires define them as individuals. I also worry that in some cases a psychoanalytic perspective assumes a single national psychological subject and does not leave enough room for considering the differences of gender, class, ethnicity, region, positioning, and experience I hope to emphasize.

3. See Rofel (2007).

4. See Haraway (1997) and Castañeda (2002).

CHAPTER 1

1. For discussions of prostitution as a reflection or form of violence against women see Barry (1979), Dworkin (1993), Farley (2003), Jeffries (1997), MacKinnon (1993), and Raymond (1998). For a discussion of sex workers' agency and rights see E. Bernstein (2007), Cabezas (2004), Cheng (2004), Kempadoo and Doezema (1998), Law (2000), Leigh (2004), McClintock (1993), and Wright (2004). Wendy Chapkis offers a concise analysis of the ways these arguments took shape during the "sex wars" of the 1980s (1997: 11–32). As far as Filipina migrants in Japan are concerned, a number of scholars have suggested that these women are victims of poverty or a trafficking of women that has forced them

into the sex industry or correspondence marriages (DeDios 1990, 1992; Iyori 1987; Matsui 1997; Rimban 1997; Yamatani 1985/1990, 1992). Others have maintained that these women are agents who aspire to help their families through their employment and strategically come to Japan for adventure or to escape gendered surveillance and sexual violence in the Philippines (Ballescas 1992; Suzuki 2002a; Tyner 2004).

2. See Brennan (2004), Cabezas (2004), Chapkis (1997), Constable (2003), Law (1997, 2000), Kulick (1998), Schaeffer-Grabiel (2006), Wardlow (2006), and Wilson (2004).

3. Practice theory is often associated with the work of Pierre Bourdieu (1977) and Anthony Giddens (1986). Sherry Ortner (1996) offers an important feminist reworking of their ideas in which she opens up spaces for resistance and transformation within binary structure-agency relationships, as I hope to do here. See also Ahearn's development of Ortner's ideas in Ahearn (2001).

4. See Massey (1999).

5. As I later discuss, the mama-san greets customers and oversees the bar and the hostesses, taking customer requests, assigning women to tables, and making sure customers are happy; in smaller bars, she may also do other managerial jobs, such as handling customers' checks, paying bills, and overseeing the kitchen.

6. For a clear, but not unproblematic, rundown on different categories of *mizu shōbai* (literally, the water trades, a term used to refer to bars, clubs, and sex businesses) during the 1980s and early 1990s, see Bornoff (1991).

7. It is important to note that prostitution in Japan is legally defined only in terms of vaginal penetration; other forms of paid sexual contact are not necessarily illegal. Also, prostitution laws are not always enforced.

8. Allison (1994).

9. Allison (1994: 8).

10. According to Miriam Silverberg (1998), the job of a hostess in some ways recuperates elements of that of the prewar *jokyū* (café waitress), who was displaced by the regulation and scarcity of the wartime era; however, the postwar economic system that supports hostess bars also distinguishes them from prewar coffeehouses. Detailed histories of the establishment of hostess bars can be found in Chung (2004) and Iwamoto and Kuniyasu (2000). Discussions of café waitresses and sex work in prewar Japan as they relate to the development of hostess bars are in Garon (1993) and Silverberg (1998).

11. See Allison (1994) for a critical feminist discussion of *settai* and of the role of hostess bars as a setting for them during the 1980s. Iwamoto and Kuniyasu (2000) offer sensationalized discussions of hostess bars in Ginza as dramatic settings for an elite social scene beginning in the mid-1950s.

12. In contrast to prewar café waitresses, who held blue-collar jobs before waitressing, some Japanese women working at exclusive bars in Tokyo come from middle-class families. These women have elected to work as hostesses because it offers a higher standard of living than the other more prestigious jobs for which they are eligible; it is one of the few higher-paying jobs women can get without having specialized training or skills (Jackson 1976). John Mock interviewed Japanese women working as hostesses in Sapporo, who work at bars considered lower class by virtue of their location in a provincial city. He explains

that many came from small towns, small cities, and rural areas. Many also had difficult childhoods and migrated to the city to distance themselves from their families and the social environments in which they were raised. According to Mock, hostessing offered these women financial security and a modern lifestyle. Hostesses at elite bars, like the one where Allison worked, tend to be young; hostessing, like modeling, has an age ceiling, and one rarely finds a Japanese woman at a top bar hostessing beyond, or even into, her late thirties. For discussions of what women do when they leave bar work see Mock (1996).

13. Women from the United States, Britain, Australia, New Zealand, and other countries generally identified in Japan as "Western" also work in hostess bars. However, at the time of my research, they tended to work in higher-status clubs that catered to a more elite clientele than in those where Filipina women worked. Haeng-ja Chung (2004) also discusses the longstanding roles that resident Koreans have played in these bars. Because many of these women "pass" as Japanese, classifying the bars that hire them is difficult.

14. In August 1999, the Japanese government created a new criminal offense called "unlawful stay" that made entering and residing in Japan without legal documents punishable by imprisonment, a fine of up to ¥300,000 (about $2750 at the time), and a minimum of a five-year period for refusal of reentry to Japan. This policy took effect in February 2000. In May 2004, the Japanese government raised the fines for residing in Japan without a legal visa to ¥3,000,000 (about $26,780 at the time) and raised the potential period for refusal of reentry to ten years. Also, as I discuss in the epilogue, in March 2005, the government enforced stricter requirements for entering Japan on an entertainer visa.

15. Town officials in Central Kiso whom I spoke with during my primary fieldwork and also in 2006 and 2007 suggested that the region was facing problems on account of these policies. See Onishi (2007) for a discussion of the effects of these policies in Hokkaido. Rozman (1999) also has analyzed some of the failures of decentralization (as it stood in the 1990s) in other rural areas.

16. Bello et al. (2005).

17. Geisha were trained in classical Japanese music and arts and served as unmarried companions for elite male patrons. For an ethnography of geisha see Dalby (1983).

18. The Makio Dam project was the first in which large-scale machinery was used. See Hirata (1999) and Yamashita (2000) for discussions of the project and others in Central Kiso. See McCormack (2001) and Hein (1990) for discussions of hydroelectric dams and the postwar Japanese national economy.

19. See Yamashita (2000: 106–7).

20. Masaharu Sawada, whose photos of the region some have credited with helping inspire the Kisoji Boom, was one such worker (Sawada 1996; Tate 1996). Longtime Central Kiso residents spoke of many men coming to the region during this time to do such work.

21. Discussions of bars in Okinawa can be found in Sturdevant and Stoltzfus (1992). For problems caused by and critiques of the U.S. military presence in Okinawa, also see Johnson (2000).

22. According to Yamada-san, relations between Filipina and Japanese hostesses were good. She recalled that some of the older women took the Filipina

women under their wing, inviting them to their homes for Japanese meals and social visits.

23. Yamada-san had hired Taiwanese and Rumanian women on a couple of occasions several years back. However, she found Filipina women easier to work with, and hiring women from these other countries never became a trend in the area. Toward the end of my fieldwork, a large new snack bar along the highway began to advertise Koreans, Japanese, and Filipina women working together.

24. One finds Filipina women in the position of mama-san at bars throughout Japan. For example, the sister of one Filipina woman in Central Kiso ran a pub in Chiba, and I have heard of Filipina women running bars in other parts of Japan as well. However, such a high concentration of Filipina-managed clubs in one area is unusual. For measure, none of the Filipina bars in Agematsu, the next town over, were run by Filipina women.

25. See DeDios (1990, 1992), Enloe (2001), Sturdevant and Stoltzfus (1992), and Tyner (1996). Following Truong (1990), I differentiate sex tourism from prostitution around military bases, although there are linkages between the two.

26. Official Web site of the Bayanihan National Folk Dance Company, www .bayanihannationaldanceco.ph/nationaltreasure.htm (accessed November 12, 2007).

27. See, for example, Alejandro (1998) and official Web sites of other dance troupes in the Philippines, such as the Leyte Kalipayan Dance Company, www .kalipayan.org/about_history.htm (accessed November 6, 2008).

28. I thank Patrick Alcedo for helping me piece together this history of Philippine cultural dance performance (pers. comm., March 4, 2001, and March 24, 2001).

29. I take the expression "authorative modernization" from Bello, Kinley, and Elinson (1982).

30. Basch, Glick Schiller, and Szanton Blanc (1994: 231), Bello and Broad (1987), Bello, Kinley, and Elinson (1982), Chant and McIlwaine (1995), Hawes (1987), Lindsey (1987), and Schirmer and Shalom (1987).

31. Bello and Broad (1987) and Hawes (1987).

32. Boyce (1993).

33. For example, between 1971 and 1985, the percentage of rural households identified as living in poverty rose from 48 percent to 64 percent (Chant and McIlwaine 1995).

34. Tadiar (2004).

35. Perpiñan (1987).

36. Many studies have discussed Marcos's policies on overseas labor migration. See Bello et al. (2005), Chant and McIlwaine (1995), Rodriguez (2002), Tadiar (2004), and Schirmer and Shalom (1987). Robyn Rodriguez (1999) and James Tyner (2004) have pointed to the central role the Philippine state has played in brokering and regulating labor migration from the country.

37. For a discussion of the experiences of these men, see Margold (1995).

38. Neumann (1987).

39. These tours became popular leisure activities for Japanese businessmen as early as the mid-1960s when travel agencies began offering packaged tours to Taiwan and "*kisaeng* tours" to South Korea; both countries were former

colonies of Japan where Japanese was still understood (Bornoff 1991; Murata 1995). However, as currencies in these countries became more expensive, the destination of Japanese men on sex tours shifted toward the Philippines and Thailand.

40. Eviota (1992), Raquisa (1987), and A. Santos (1991).

41. Public outcry gathered steam in 1979 when Casio Electronics sent two hundred top customers to the Philippines on a group sex tour at a first-class hotel. Then, in 1981, when Japanese Prime Minister Zenko Suzuki visited the Philippines, Japanese and Filipina feminists united in the center of Manila and demonstrated against sex tours (Yamatani 1992; Matsui 1997).

42. Matsui (1997).

43. JNATIP and F-GENS (2005).

44. Cruz and Repetto (1992) and Chant and McIlwaine (1995).

45. Boyce (1993) and Chant and McIlwaine (1995).

46. Boyce (1993).

47. Potter (1996) and Sellek (2001).

48. Although large-scale Filipina migration to Japan as entertainers began during the Marcos administration, the largest increases in numbers of Filipina women coming to Central Kiso (and to Japan more generally) occurred during the Aquino administration, in 1987, 1990, and 1991 (Tyner 2004). To encourage labor migration, Aquino declared that overseas workers were the Philippines' *bagong bayani,* its new national heroes. According to statistics provided by local and prefectural governments (see Appendix A), between 1981 (the first year for which local governments began keeping statistics of foreign residents) and 1984, there were between 5 and 7 Philippine nationals registered in Kisofukushima each year. Presumably, these were the women working at Yamada-san's bar. In 1985 and 1986, there were 11 Philippine nationals in Kisofukushima, as well as 3 in surrounding villages—women who had married Japanese men and were now registered through their husbands' residences. In 1987, the numbers of Philippine nationals jumped to 36 and then 41 in 1988 and 1989. In 1990, there were 109 Philippine nationals in the county. Between 1991 and 1999, the numbers ranged between 127 and 191 each year. These fluctuations may in part reflect the opening and closing of bars in the region. However, numbers of Filipina entertainers to Japan have also fluctuated in response to changes in entertainer visa requirements. Also, during some years, women may have been dissuaded from going to Japan by widespread media stories in the Philippines about Filipina entertainers who suffered serious abuse or were killed while working there.

49. For a moving depiction of the glamour and respect accorded Filipina cultural dancers in the United States, see the short story "The Day the Dancers Came" by Bienvenido Santos (1979).

50. Esguerra (1994: 42). The title "Overseas Performing Artist" (OPA) was adopted as part of the Philippine government's efforts to professionalize this work (see Tyner 2004). Philchime stands for Philippine Chamber of Industries in Music and Entertainment Foundation, Inc. Its member agencies include a range of governmental and professional (talent, entertainment, and performance) groups. Although formal licensing exams and training programs have been required for entertainers since at least the early 1980s, the standardized

training program was established in 1993 by a group of representatives from the Philippine Overseas Employment Administration (POEA), the National Manpower and Youth Council (NMYC), and the Philippine Overseas Entertainment Industry (Esguerra 1994).

51. For a discussion of the death of Maricris Sioson and the Philippine government's response, see Tyner (2004).

52. In Tagalog, *TNT* is an acronym for *tago ng tago*, literally "hiding and hiding," and refers to undocumented Filipina/o migrants. The term is a pun on the explosive TNT and implies that these Filipinas/os are in a dangerous and potentially explosive state. (I thank Jody Blanco for suggesting this explanation.) *Bilog* in Tagalog literally means "circle" and is also used to refer to undocumented Filipinas/os in Japan. Rimban suggests that the term is shorthand for "overstayers," or "O's" (1997).

53. Some women also enter Japan with counterfeit passports, often with the help of organized crime syndicates. While volunteering at NGOs in Tokyo that assist Filipina migrants, I spoke with some women who had done so, but I never met a woman in this situation in Central Kiso.

54. Ruby had special-ordered the piglet through Victoria's sister's Japanese husband in Matsumoto, whose friend ran a butcher shop in Okinawa. The animal, nearly three feet from snout to rear hooves, had been sent in a cooler by overnight mail from Naha to Kisofukushima at a total cost of ¥33,000 (about $277). Ruby had roasted it herself in the small cement walkway behind her home. (Unless otherwise specified, the dollar equivalence is figured as $1.00=¥113, roughly the average of what the exchange rate was during the twenty-three months of my fieldwork.)

55. Hochschild (2003: 7). According to Hochschild, emotional labor is "the management of feeling to create a publicly observable facial and bodily display" (2003: 7). As she tells us, these performances are not necessarily superficial; people also come to internalize them.

56. Fenella Cannell, in her work on *bakla* beauty pageants in Bicol, has written provocatively about the vulnerabilities that accompany "becoming beautiful" through an approximation of Western models of ideal femininity in the Philippines (1995, 1999). See also Manalansan (2003) for a discussion of the multiple meanings—ranging from one's appearance to one's state of mind—that gay Filipino men in New York City ascribe to *biyuti* (beauty).

57. Discussions of the role and significance of beauty pageants in the Philippines can be found in Cannell (1995, 1999), Griffiths (1988), and Manalansan (2003).

58. See Mock (1996) for a discussion of Japanese women who open bars with the assistance of wealthy patrons.

59. I take the expression "social drama" from Victor Turner (1974).

60. Allison (1994: 134).

61. For a thoughtful discussion of the complicated ways that Japanese men married to Filipina women in urban areas perceive their wives see N. Suzuki (2007). In some ways their interests in Filipina women were consistent with those of men I met in Central Kiso; however, differences also exist on account of their residence in urban areas and class backgrounds.

62. Laura Miller (2006) has written extensively about beauty and fashion trends, including tanning, among high school girls in urban parts of Japan. Contrary to this man's perception, according to Miller these fashion trends can be interpreted as strategic means by which these girls crafted identities and engaged in forms of resistance.

63. For a discussion of such attitudes, see Knight (1995), Lebra (1984), and N. Suzuki (2007).

64. See also Faier (2007).

CHAPTER 2

1. A number of scholars have argued that attention be given not only to the ways that macrostructural contexts and intermediate institutional relationships shape transmigrants' lives but also to them as subjects with complex dreams, needs, and agendas. See Constable (1997, 1999), Espiritu (2003), Law (2001), Manalansan (2003), McKay (2003), Nakamatsu (2003), Parreñas (2001), G. Pratt (2004), Roces (2003), and N. Suzuki (2002a, 2002b, 2004).

2. For explorations of the ways that emotional attachments and political-economic considerations are intertwined in the lives of marriage migrants see Constable (2003) and Piper and Roces (2003).

3. Steedly (1993).

4. James Clifford (1997) discusses how peoples' lives take shape through forms of travel and dwelling. Many studies of the Philippine diaspora have focused on tensions between home and abroad in migrants' lives, documenting how longings for home combined with the marginality and struggles of living abroad prompt experiences of displacement and dislocation (Manalansan 2003; Constable 1999; Espiritu 2003; Parreñas 2001; G. Pratt 2004).

5. Carlos Bulosan's *America is in the Heart* (1973) is one well-known example of such narratives, which are also commonly found in films and television dramas. Recent films that deal with contemporary interpretations of such themes, primarily in terms of middle-class migrants, include *Anak* (2000), *Dubai* (2005), and *Milan* (2004).

6. See Ballescas (1992), Lauby and Stark (1988), and Sellek (1996).

7. See Berner (1997) for a discussion of life in squatter areas in the Philippines and government policy toward them. Berner suggests that while squatters are a seriously marginalized group of urban poor, they are not the poorest or most marginalized segment of the urban population: they have managed to acquire some land to squat upon and work collectively with NGOs for their rights.

8. For example, Nobue Suzuki (2002a) argues that some Filipina wives of Japanese men in Tokyo left the Philippines to escape forms of gendered violence. I did not hear any such stories in Central Kiso; however, it is possible that such experiences also influenced some Filipina women's decisions there as well.

9. Vicente Rafael has discussed the place of shopping malls in Philippine life today, and especially of their role in containing mass politics by substituting a "consumerist ethos" for "the communal exhilaration and confrontational politics of EDSA and Mendiola" (2000a: 180–81).

10. The suffix -*san* denotes respect and is frequently added in Japanese. I noticed that Filipinas/os (speaking Tagalog, Japanese, or English) often omitted it.

11. Yamatani's book is one of many that came out in the 1980s with accounts of Filipina migrants and other foreign women working in the sex industry in Japan. See Nakamatsu (2005), Satake and Da-anoy (2006), and N. Suzuki (2002b) for critical reviews of this literature.

12. For accounts of the lives and experiences of *karayukisan* see Tomoko Yamazaki (1975, 1999) and the film *Sandakan No. 8*

13. Ligaya's family, which identifies as firmly middle class and is financially stable in large part because of the employment of men in the family in the Middle East, suggested they were puzzled by her sudden decision to have an arranged marriage with a Japanese man she had just met.

14. Rafael (2000b). For discussions of attitudes toward *balikbayan* in the Philippines and the role of the state in developing a tourism industry around them, see Rafael (2000b: 206–9).

15. The quotation is Yen Le Espiritu's (2003: 71). For discussions of the brutality of U.S. presence in the Philippines see Broad and Cavanagh (1993), Ileto (1979), Salman (2001), and Tadiar (2004).

16. Cannell (1995: 225).

17. Choy (2003). Choy explains that during the Spanish and U.S. American colonial periods, studying and working abroad was primarily a means by which elite families reproduced their class standing by sending their children to Europe or the United States. In the 1960s, large numbers of Filipina women began to go to the United States as nurses, and studying and working abroad became a respectable means by which middle-class and professional Filipina women might not only achieve upward class mobility and professional advancement but also travel abroad.

18. In particular, bell hooks (1992) argues that travel is a form of movement tied to centers of Western power and overdetermined by colonialist and capitalist forms of exploitation. Other feminist scholars who have written about travel as a form of mobility shaped by inequalities of gender, race, class, and sexuality include Grewal (1996), Kaplan (1996), Luibhéid (2002), Massey (1992), G. Pratt (2004), M. L. Pratt (1992), Tsing (1993), and Visweswaran (1994).

19. According to T. J. Pempel (1997), after the Second World War, the Japanese government focused its foreign policy attention on the United States. Its involvement in Asia tended to take the forms of reparations, trade, and foreign aid. Most reparations and aid were tied to the purchase of Japanese goods and services, and in effect served to open markets in these countries to Japanese companies. After the oil shock of the 1970s, the Japanese government faced pressures to liberalize its markets. Foreign direct investment became more important, and the Japanese government also came under pressure from citizen groups who were concerned with pollution tied to industry. Beginning in the mid-1970s, Japan began to export manufacturing, including some of its dirtiest industries, to other parts of Asia.

20. Ventura (1992: 165–66).

21. Ventura (1992: 165, italics added).

22. See Parreñas (2001) for some of the disappointments Filipina migrants confront in the United States.

23. Rofel (2007: 14).

24. Steedly (1993: 23).

25. See, for example, Clifford (1997).

CHAPTER 3

1. See Anderson (1998) for the discussion of nationalism and the "spectre of comparisons." The short quotation is from Anderson (1998: 229), who is drawing on Rizal's famous novel *Noli Me Tángere* (1887/1996).

2. Anderson (1998: 229).

3. Those who have considered hegemonic discourses of race, ethnicity, culture, and nationality in Japan include Dower (1986), Lie (2001), Morris-Suzuki (1998), Oguma (2002), Robertson (2001, 2002), Siddle (1996), M. Weiner (1997a), and Yoshino (1992). See Ching (2001), Christy (1993), Douglass and Roberts (2000), Linger (2001), Roth (2002), Ryang (1997, 2000), and Tsuda (2003) for studies of the effects of these discourses on ethnic minority or colonized populations.

4. See Kelsky (2001), Kondo (1997), Lie (2001), Ivy (1995), Robertson (1998a), and Russell (1996).

5. For an excellent discussion of the history of speech patterns, gender, and class identities in Japan, see Inoue (2006).

6. See Chung (2004), Field (1993a), Ryang (1997, 2000), M. Weiner (1989, 1997c), Wender (2005), and Yoneyama (1995) for discussions of the struggles of, and discrimination faced by, resident Koreans in Japan.

7. Sachiko's comment suggests that the interactions through which people in Japan have come to know themselves as "Japanese" through cultural encounters have been going on for quite some time.

8. Launched in 1987 and a flagship kokusaika endeavor, the JET program invited English teachers, primarily from the United States, Canada, New Zealand, and Australia, to work as assistant English-language teachers in public schools. A cultural analysis of the JET program can be found in McConnell (2000).

9. The coordinator position focuses on organizing local and prefectural kokusaika events and teaching English part-time to county officials.

10. For critical discussions of kokusaika and nationalism in Japan, see Creighton (1997), Ehara (1992), Ivy (1995), Ogata (1992), and Robertson (1998a).

11. Discussions of the West as a standard of modernity in Japan can be found in Creighton (1997), Kelsky (2001), and Lie (2001). Discussions of kokusaika and education in Japan can be found in Goodman (2007) and McConnell (2000).

12. Marilyn Ivy has argued that the Japanese state-sponsored version of kokusaika has tended toward the "domestication of the foreign." In her words, "kokusaika is a conservative policy that reflects the other side of a renewed sense

of Japanese national pride, if not nationalism" (1995: 3). Similarly, Judy Yoneoka has pointed out that the Japanese university students she surveyed viewed kokusaika less in terms of adopting an affective (for example, open-minded or empathetic) disposition toward people from other countries as much as learning to speak English and acquiring certain forms of knowledge about other parts of the world *and* about oneself as a Japanese. She connects the project to a revived nationalism on the basis that these students identified the acquisition of "knowledge of Japan" as an integral part of being a *kokusaijin*, an international or cosmopolitan person. She points out that the kokusaika introduced in school curriculum has centered around "the development of awakening as a Japanese" just as much as the introduction of other parts of the world (2000: 9). Other critiques of kokusaika can be found in Lie (2001), Robertson (1998a), and Russell (1998).

13. Kelly (1990: 219).

14. I borrow this phrase from Yoneoka (2000).

15. Bourdieu (2007) has written extensively of the ways that cultural capital and markers of distinction both reflect and are converted into material gain.

16. Karen Kelsky (2001) also situates kokusaika within other related discourses of the global or cosmopolitan by focusing on the experiences of what she calls "internationalist Japanese women" and by exploring the ways that the discourses of cosmopolitanism engaged by these women are shaped by gender, race, class, and sexuality.

17. See Sassen (1991, 1994) for a discussion of "global cities" and of Tokyo as one in particular.

18. Robertson (1998a).

19. Robertson (1998a: 128), and see also Ivy (1995).

20. Both Marilyn Ivy (1995) and Mariko Tamanoi (1998) discuss such discourses of rural Japan.

21. The Kiso region prospered under the Tokugawa Shogunate on account of the *sankin kōtai* system, an alternate attendance system that typically required domain lords to live in Edo every other year and keep their first wives and heirs in residence there. After the fall of the Shogunate, the Kiso Valley became a regional periphery of interest to the new national government primarily for its rich cypress forests and the hydroelectric potential of the Kiso River. Before bus routes went directly to the base of Mt. Ontake, groups of Ontakekyō (Ontake religion) followers would stop in the town on their way to the sacred mountain. However, it was not until the mid-1970s and into the early 1980s that the Kiso Valley became a popular destination for tourists. For an idiosyncratic history of the rediscovery of the tourist potential of the region, see Sawada (1996).

22. The Kisoji Boom was related to the Discover Japan campaign about which Marilyn Ivy (1995) has written, as well as to a renewed wave of interest in the Edo. For discussions of the Edo as figure of a traditional Japanese past against which Japan defines its modernity, see Gluck (1998).

23. Kisofukushima residents first learned to see the landscape through the eyes of urban outsiders, and to privilege such a perspective, during the Kisoji Boom. Throughout my fieldwork, an expensive hardcover retrospective book of

Sawada Masaharu's photographs, *Kisoji futatabi: Sawada Masaharu shashin-chō, 1919–1992* (Revisiting the Kisoji: The Photographs of Sawada Masaharu, 1919–1992), was on display in bookstores and shops throughout the town. Sawada was an itinerant construction worker who came to Kiso from Tokyo in 1958 to work on one of the many postwar dam projects aimed at modernizing the country. Taking up photography as a hobby, Sawada decided that by photographing the Kiso landscape he might reclaim its illustrious history: "The Kisoji is one of Japan's highways with a long history and unique character. It is a famous highway that must be remembered not in the name only of Japanese, but of the global history of folk customs" (1996: 219). Sawada was an outsider, an urban subject with a camera, who identified the region as significant to both Japan and the world. Some claimed that he was responsible for rediscovering the Kisoji and thus for the tourism craze that followed.

24. For discussions of rural Japan as a destination for domestic tourism, see Ivy (1995), Kelly (1986), Knight (2000), Martinez (1990), Moon (1997), and Siegenthaler (1999, 2003).

25. I deliberately used the term *gaikokujin* instead of *gaijin* as the latter can carry the nuance of "white foreigners."

26. Furusato Kōza were semimonthly lectures offered at the local community center in which experts were invited to introduce interested residents to various aspects of the town's history, geography, industry, and culture.

27. Ōtaki and Kaida were two villages adjacent to the town of Kiso-fukushima that were up in the mountains and farther from the train line and main highway.

28. I adapt "affluent Japan" from Sen and Stivens (1998), who write of "affluent Asia."

29. Kären Wigen (1995) has described how the peripheralization of the Shimoina Valley during the late nineteenth and early twentieth centuries enabled Japan to emerge as a new and privileged core within Asia as it undermined local autonomy and accumulation within the region. While during the Edo period the Kiso Valley figured as something of a foil to Shimoina, in the years that followed the Meiji Restoration, and especially in the decades after the end of the Second World War, similar peripheralizing processes in Central Kiso have discouraged economic self-sufficiency, undermined local accumulation, and created dependency relationships between the region and Japan's urban centers (and also places like the Philippines). For example, Ligaya's husband, who had lived his life in a nearby village, described how in the 1950s and 1960s the self-sufficiency of hamlets, which had for generations maintained themselves through circuits of exchange, was undermined when residents were forced to look for waged employment in town to accumulate cash for membership dues in agricultural cooperatives and other national organizations.

30. See Knight (2000) for a discussion of postwar reforestation campaigns, the decline of forestry in mountainous areas, and efforts to make forests into destinations for tourism. See Dauvergne (1997) for a discussion of Japanese forestry policy in Southeast Asia after the Second World War.

31. See Ivy (1995), Robertson (1988), and Tamanoi (1998) for excellent discussions of such discourses.

32. See Matsui (1989) and Shukuya (1988) for related arguments that parallel the trenchant critique that feminists in the United States—such as Shellee Colen (1995), bell hooks (2000), and Chandra Mohanty, Ann Russo, and Lourdes Torres (1991)—have made about the ways that socioeconomic privileges enjoyed by middle-class white women since the 1970s have been achieved at the expense of women of color.

33. See Lie (2001).

CHAPTER 4

1. For discussion of these discourses, see Befu (2001), Dale (1986), Ivy (1989), Howell (1996), Lee (2006), Lie (2001), and Oguma (2002).

2. Ivy (1995).

3. See G. Bernstein (1983), Jolivet (1997), Kelsky (2001), Knight (1995), and K. Suzuki (1995) for discussions of Japanese women's changing attitudes toward marriage and life in rural areas.

4. Haraway (1997). Haraway is building from David Schneider's (1980) critique of biologically based notions of kinship.

5. Anderson (1991) was one of the first to point out the similarities between nationalism and kinship. Now a large body of work exists that explores the relationships between kinship, gender, and nationalism. See Buckley (1993), Burns (1998), Chatterjee (1989, 1993), Delaney (1995), Fujitani (1996), Mani (1987), Miyake (1991), Nolte and Hastings (1991), Parker et al. (1992), Rofel (1994), Sand (1998, 2003), Silverberg (1998), Tamanoi (1998), Uno (1993), and Visweswaran (1994).

6. Sylvia Yanagisako (1985) first put Schneider's critique of kinship (1980) into historical perspective, illustrating how kinship meanings change over time. More recently, scholars have focused on the ways that new reproductive technologies prompt shifts in how kinship is reckoned. See Franklin (1997), Franklin and McKinnon (2001), Kahn (2000), and Strathern (1992).

7. See Borneman (1992), Chatterjee (1989), Delaney (1995), Moeller (1993), Tamanoi (1998), and Visweswaran (1994).

8. Scholars have argued that unlike the nuclear family, the ie was historically organized around a set of positions oriented toward household succession. See Bachnik (1983), Befu (1963), Fukutake (1982), Hamabata (1991), Kitaoji (1971), Kondo (1990), Lebra (1984), and Nakane (1967).

9. Kondo (1990) and Sand (2003).

10. Nolte and Hastings (1991), Uno (1993), Sand (2003), and Tamanoi (1998).

11. Fujitani (1996).

12. Sand (2003).

13. In some surrounding villages, responsibilities toward *tonarigumi* included assisting with preparations and visitors during events such as funerals and weddings. At one time, and even on occasion during the years just before I conducted my fieldwork, these obligations included arriving with soba-making boards on one's back to help make soba for guests at a wake.

14. Being a yome is famously a difficult and trying time of a woman's life. G. Bernstein (1983), Dore (1978), Hamabata (1991), Knight (1995), Kondo

(1990), and Lebra (1984) offer additional discussions of the role of the yome as a worker and of tensions between brides and their mothers-in-law.

15. For example, I was told that a Japanese woman who had been raised in a farming community would be expected to have the knowledge and skills necessary to manage everything properly when she married into another farming household in the same community. However, Japanese women who came from households different from their affines' or who married outside their natal communities were expected to, at least initially, need more instruction.

16. Lest we think that training courses for foreign-born brides are exclusive to Japan: The USO Bride School linked to U.S. military bases in South Korea similarly provides guidance to new Korean brides of U.S. military servicemen on everything from military terminology to cooking "American-style" breakfasts; see the documentary *The Women Outside* (Takagi and Park 1995).

17. Nagaoka-san and Itoh-san arranged for the county community center to provide a room for the class to meet, and two retired elementary school teachers volunteered to teach it. Before beginning the class, the teachers consulted Filipina women in the region about what they wanted to learn and accompanied them to ongoing classes in a nearby city. Generous and committed, perhaps more so than some of their students, the teachers continued to teach the class even when, by its fourth year, regular attendance had dropped to only a few members. Like many Filipina women with whom I spoke, I was touched by the Japanese teachers' sincere interest in the lives of these women and their commitment to helping them. My Filipina friends trusted the teachers and appreciated their efforts to include their voices in the community. When I asked Filipina women in the region why they had stopped going to the class, they told me that as the economy had worsened they had become too busy with work. Some felt that their Japanese was sufficient. Some also suggested that they did not attend because they had interpersonal tensions with other Filipina women in the class. However, I also noticed that the teachers romanticized these women's plight and infantilized them. They ran the group like a third-grade classroom, often beginning by singing children's songs and playing children's games. No doubt their pedagogy was influenced by years of teaching elementary school, the generational gap between the Filipina women in the class (most of whom were in their twenties and thirties) and the teachers (who were in their sixties), and the teachers' desires to familiarize the women with what their children were exposed to in local schools. However, this strategy also, in effect, positioned Filipina women as children who required proper guidance and instruction, and may have put off some Filipina women in the region.

18. See Hendry (1986) for meanings of the word *shitsuke* and the ways scholars have discussed it in Japan.

19. Discussions of Japanese national identity and food culture can be found in Bestor (1999, 2004), Lie (2001), and Ohnuki-Tierney (1993). A mention of discussions of the uniqueness of Japanese bodies and their abilities to digest only certain foods can be found in Dale (1986).

20. For example, Ligaya's efforts at teaching Filipino cooking classes at her village community center were much appreciated by her community as contributing to *"mura okoshi"* (village-revival projects). Similarly, Filipina women

I knew received overwhelmingly positive reactions when they organized a Filipino food stand at another village festival and in a grassroots cultural exchange group that a local nursery school teacher organized. These efforts were seen as reflecting the women's commitment to encouraging international exchange in their local communities.

21. Rather than viewing the exception as marking out those who are denied protection, Ong focuses on the exception as "an extraordinary departure in policy that can be deployed to include as well as to exclude" (2006: 5). See Agamben (1998, 2005) for discussions of the "state of exception" and its place in biopolitical organizations of power.

22. Critiques of Japanese women can be found in newspapers and on television in Japan. For a sampling in English, see the special issue of *Japan Echo*, "The Graying Society" (1996).

23. Such moralizing critiques ignore the social and political-economic conditions that inform the choices that these women are making—the lack of domestic help that working men in Japan are able (or choose) to provide, the high cost of living and childrearing, and women's desires for careers or other kinds of relationships. Jolivet (1997) and Kelsky (2001) have discussed these issues in depth.

24. See Migiya (1998), Shukuya (1988), and N. Suzuki (2003). These studies have focused on farming regions (often the Tohoku region or Niigata) in which local government administrations and professional marriage agencies have brokered marriages between local Japanese men and women from other parts of Asia (including not only the Philippines, but also Korea, China, and Sri Lanka). These studies have stressed the need in these areas to find heirs to inherit farmland and maintain village life more generally. This body of work importantly draws attention to ways that gender and political-economic inequalities shape relationships between Filipina women and rural Japanese men. Yet such arguments tend to stress that these marriages differ from "modern" marriages that center on "love" or "individual choice." They thus overlook the ways that love is itself a social and cultural product shaped by relations of power (Abu-Lughod 1986, 1990a, 1990b; Ahearn 2001; Brennan 2004; Faier 2007; Povinelli 2006; Rebhun 1999). They also do not account for the way that the "modern family" is itself based in systematic and patriarchal relationships with the state. Finally, they situate rural Japan as a place that is not yet modern in comparison with urban areas. For a discussion of the ideal of a modern Western family as an ideological construct, see Collier, Rosaldo, and Yanagisako (1997).

25. I, of course, borrow the term interpellate from Louis Althusser (1971), who uses it to refer to the way that individuals are "hailed" by ideological forms of power and thus are compelled to respond, producing themselves as subjects in the process.

26. Discussions of assimilation in the Japanese empire can be found in Ching (2001), Christy (1993), Howell (2004), and Uchida (2005a, 2005b).

27. Oguma (2002).

28. Ching (2001).

29. Here, Central Kiso residents' critiques of Japanese women find earlier precedent in popular agrarianisms of the 1920s when middling farmers in Nagano produced an alternative discourse of "rural modernity" that criticized

women who eschewed farming and aspired to urban ways. Mariko Tamanoi (1998) discusses these discourses in depth. However, while contemporary discourses of Filipinas brides as ideal oyomesan in some ways echo these earlier discourses of an alternative rural Japanese modernity, they also differ in their glorification of *foreign* women as ideal brides.

30. Ivy (1995), Kelly (1986), Robertson (1988, 1998a), and Tamanoi (1998).

31. The linguist J. L. Austin (1975) was the first to theorize the performative. His ideas were reworked by Jacques Derrida (1988) and later Judith Butler (1993, 1999), who developed a performative theory of gender. Building on Butler, Stuart Hall (1996) discusses more general processes of identification as performative. Here I draw most directly on him.

32. Butler (1993) and Hall (1996).

CHAPTER 5

1. I am, again, working here from Bakhtin's argument (1981a) that all meaning is situated and emerges dialogically.

2. At least 20 percent, and likely more, of the Filipina women married to Japanese men in Central Kiso had children in the Philippines from previous relationships with Filipino or Japanese men. In most cases, their mothers or siblings were caring for these children. Many Filipina women in Central Kiso were reluctant to talk about this. In some cases, as I discuss in the epilogue, some husbands of Filipina women in Central Kiso did later adopt these women's children from previous relationships.

3. Many women worked at local Filipina bars (about 30 percent of them, as I mentioned earlier). Others did janitorial work at pachinko parlors or worked in ballpoint pen and *annin dōfu* (a packaged dessert made with almond gelatin) factories. A few worked in their families' businesses. Tessie did piecework at home. In this regard, these Filipina women were similar to marriage migrants in other parts of the world: Their identities as wives were not easily separated from their identities as workers (Piper and Roces 2003).

4. The notion of double-consciousness is famously W. E. B. DuBois's (1989). See also Gilroy (1993).

5. Manalansan (2003).

6. Foucault (1976, 1977b).

7. According to the Ministry of Justice, a foreign national married to a Japanese citizen can become eligible for permanent residency after a minimum of three years of continuous residence in Japan. (Single foreign nationals must have ten years of continuous residence to become eligible.) However, although men from the United States, Australia, or western Europe who are married to Japanese women may receive permanent residency after three years (Brophy 2006), I never met a Filipina woman married to a Japanese man in Central Kiso who received her permanent residency this quickly. During my primary fieldwork, these women more commonly waited closer to ten years, even if they had children who were Japanese nationals.

8. Permanent residents in Japan are technically also eligible if they have contributed to a pension fund for the requisite number of years.

9. A *koseki* is a family register in which births, marriages, and deaths within a household are recorded. The modern koseki system was established with the Family Registration Law of 1871 (Matsushima 1997). It has been a source of controversy in contemporary Japan because koseki have been used to trace household residence and lineages for discriminatory purposes.

10. See Constable (1999) and Parreñas (2001) for discussions of how Filipina migrants in other parts of the world gain status in their families in the Philippines by becoming breadwinners.

11. A number of scholars have discussed the politics of "home," including Blunt (2005), Constable (1999), Espiritu (2003), Grewal (1996), Halberstam (2005), Manalansan (2003), G. Pratt (2004), McClintock (1995), and Rose (1993).

12. Manalansan (2003).

13. I borrow this definition from Lim (2004: 66). A babaeng martir is literally a woman martyr.

14. Many of these women saw their families in Japan and the Philippines as independent kinship units. When I asked them to list the "members of their family," they would respond, "Which one?"

15. Shiraishi (2006).

16. Fenella Cannell (1999) has suggested that *awa* is an idiom through which people throughout the Philippines express their vulnerabilities and struggles within hierarchies of power. She stresses that while the term resonates with Christian ideology it cannot be reduced to it; we must also attend to local translations and interpretations of Christian belief (also see Rafael 1988).

17. Of the women whose situations were known in some detail (fifty-nine of sixty-five women), approximately twenty-nine lived, or had lived, with their in-laws and sixteen other women had in-laws who lived nearby and with whom they had regular contact. Seven women were known not to have contact with their in-laws and seven women's in-law situation was unknown to my friends.

18. At the time I was conducting my primary fieldwork, Tessie's daily routine went something like this: She awoke around 7:00 A.M. to prepare breakfast for her husband and children and to get her children dressed and ready for school. About 7:30 her husband came down, ate breakfast, and helped with last-minute school preparations. Fifteen minutes later he left for work with the children, whom he dropped off at school along his way. Once the house was empty, Tessie began a rotating cleaning routine. She would dust the house, vacuum the floors, or clean the kitchen, toilet, and bathroom depending on the day. Occasionally she would do special projects like cleaning out closets or the refrigerator. Tessie would accomplish as much cleaning as possible before 11:00 or 11:30 A.M., when she began to prepare lunch for her husband, who came home for lunch between 12:00 and 12:10 P.M. every day. Tessie would eat with him, and after he returned to work, she would clean up the dishes and finish the housework. Then she would do a few hours of piecework before it was time to pick up her children from school. Sometimes in the afternoon, Tessie would make a trip to the supermarket and occasionally she would leave in the morning to shop with other Filipina friends at discount stores in Shiojiri. Sometimes friends, including me, would come over during the day, and we would sit around the table

and chat while she was doing piecework. Tessie's children got out of school at 3:00 P.M. She would pick them up, take them home, and get them cleaned up, changed, and settled in front of the television. She would then begin dinner preparation. After washing the dinner dishes, Tessie would give her children a bath. Sometimes Tessie's husband would bathe the children while she finished her piecework or began ironing the laundry. After bathing, Tessie would usually spend time with her children before bedtime. After they went to bed, she would finish up the laundry and other chores or plan for a prayer meeting or other parties and events for Filipina women in the area.

19. Hollnsteiner (1973: 76); also cited in Cannell (1999: 29).

20. Migiya (1998) and Takahashi, Hasumi, and Yamamoto (1992).

21. See Reader and Tanabe's work (1998) on religion as a set of ritual practices in Japan aimed at practical everyday benefit.

22. To my knowledge, most Filipina women's Japanese families respected the women's religious faith. The family of only one of these women, which belonged to Sōka Gakkai, a "new religion" in Japan, expected her to convert. She told me that she had not been an especially observant Catholic and so she heeded their wishes, but around Christmastime she also told me that she missed celebrating the holiday.

23. Practices of making offerings to deceased ancestors are often troped as Buddhist (or tied to Confucianism) in Japan. Robert Smith (1983) argues that while such practices can be associated with the ie, they are not necessarily. Rather, he suggests that they precede the popular adoption of the ie following its codification with the Meiji civil code. He also notes that when he conducted research in the early 1960s, sentimental relationships, as opposed to the dutiful worship of ie ancestors, inspired some people to maintain memorial tablets on a *butsudan*.

24. Jimenez (1983: 96).

25. Ocampo (1983).

26. There is a long history in Japan of using climatological and geomorphic features of the country to define Japanese culture. See, for example, Watsuji (1961).

27. Ruby had a very different perspective on her behavior. While she expressed remorse over the breakup of her relationship with her husband, she also told me that she felt like "a dog that had finally been let off its leash."

28. Griesemer and Star (1989: 393). In their work on the Museum of Vertebrate Zoology at UC Berkeley, Griesemer and Star offer the term "boundary objects" to examine how amateurs, professionals, administrators, and others negotiate collaborations by developing boundary objects that can translate between different viewpoints (1989). Boundary objects are those scientific objects—such as museums and scientific publications—that are "simultaneously concrete and abstract, specific and general, conventionalized and customized" (1989: 408). With the notion of boundary objects, Griesemer and Star demonstrate that a consensus of meaning is not necessary for collaboration.

29. Bell and Valentine (1997), and Law (2001).

30. Hall (1996: 14).

31. Butler (1993, 1999).

32. Hall (1996: 14).

33. Butler (1993) uses the phrase "come to matter" with a double inflection to mean both to materialize through processes of discursive construction and to become significant in a hierarchically differentiated social order.

34. I borrow the notion of cross talk from Tsing (1993) and Stewart (1996). Saba Mahmood (2005) and Kamari Clarke (2004) have also suggested that performances of compliance do not necessarily involve subordination, but can also reflect different ways of enacting appropriate behavior.

CHAPTER 6

1. See Hisada (1989), Kawabata (1995), Kuwayama (1995), Satake and Da-anoy (2006), and N. Suzuki (2003). Also, Yea (2004) and Constable (1997, 2003) discuss Filipina women who ran away from employers or husbands in, respectively, South Korea, Hong Kong, and the United States.

2. My use of the term *gaps* both builds on and differs from that put forth by Anna Tsing (2005), who tells us that gaps are not transcendent, transhistorical spaces of difference but critical sites for emergent dreams that develop "in the seams" of hegemonic projects. For Tsing, gaps are sites of unspeakability within recognized or acceptable languages. Here I use the term to refer to those spaces where different genealogies of meaning and desire misalign.

3. Foucault (1990). See also Certeau (1984) and Scott (1985).

4. Basch, Glick Schiller, and Szanton Blanc (1994), Constable (1997, 1999), Espiritu (2003), Gilroy (1993), Linger (2001), Manalansan (2003), Ong (2003), Parreñas (2001), and Tsuda (2003).

5. Strategies scholars have documented for Filipina migrants in particular include participating in cultural and self-help groups (N. Suzuki 2002b); joining or soliciting the assistance of activist organizations (Kuwayama 1995; Nakamatsu 2003); producing art and poetry (Tadiar 2004); pursuing legal cases (Constable 1997); accumulating social capital (Burgess 2004); and making jokes, secretly circumventing household rules, or having romantic affairs (Constable 1997; Kuwayama 1995; Parreñas 2001; N. Suzuki 2003).

6. Abu-Lughod (1990a).

7. For feminist critiques of notions of resistance, see Abu-Lughod (1990a), Kondo (1990), Mahmood (2005), Ortner (1995), and Tsing (1993). Recently, Saba Mahmood has encouraged us to pay attention to those dimensions of human action that do not easily map only to logics of resistance. She argues for an analysis of agency that is not framed in terms of obedience/rebellion, compliance/resistance, and submission/subversion but that attends to "the grammar of concepts within which a set of actions are located" (2005: 180). This task, as I understand it here, involves paying attention not only to different modalities of agency but also to the different dynamics of social relationships, and the possibilities and constraints out of which women build their lives.

8. For a discussion of the chronotope, see Bakhtin (1981b). I thank Kamari Clarke for suggesting it to evoke this dynamic.

9. See, for example, Tadiar (2004) and Ileto (1997).

10. Tadiar (2004: 114).

11. See Appadurai (1996) for a discussion of the "social life of things." Cruikshank (1998) extends this idea to narratives.

12. See Barad (2003, 2007), Cruikshank (2005), Haraway (2003), Mahmood (2005), and Whatmore (2002).

13. The expression "processes of identification" is from Stuart Hall (1996).

14. Some help line and shelter staff told me that since the Domestic Violence Prevention Law took effect in 2001, some Filipina women have had more success getting custody of their children in part because they have been able to get social welfare assistance.

15. In recent years, I have heard from shelter staff that Filipina women have had an easier time getting custody of their Japanese children. Those who do get custody have been successful in receiving these visas.

16. For discussions of domestic violence in Japan, see Babior (1993) and Piper (1997).

17. I have figured the exchange rate here at $1.00=¥105, roughly what it was at the time Sharyn and I visited the lawyer.

18. Parreñas (2001).

19. Curtin (2002).

20. While some parallels may exist in the reasons Filipina and Japanese women run away from their husbands, the similarities of their situations should not be overstated. Unlike Filipina women, Japanese women who want to leave their husbands do not risk losing spousal visas, and do not face the possibility of deportation and international separation from their children. Filipina women and Japanese women who want to leave their husbands face different religious, cultural, and familial pressures, all of which may inform or complicate their decisions; employment, educational, cultural, and language barriers are also different. Finally, Japanese women are not subject to the same racial discrimination that Filipina women often are, and are not obvious targets of racial profiling by police.

21. Mankekar (1999), Tamanoi (1998), and Visweswaran (1994).

22. Coutin (2005).

23. See also Law (1997) for a discussion of Filipina women's ambivalence about bar work.

24. Tessie and some others changed their minds after they saw the video of Sharyn's husband and his girlfriend at a love hotel.

25. Harding (1975) and Wolf (1972, 1974, 1985).

26. Discussions of the role of gossip in the Philippines and the Philippine diaspora can be found in Manalansan (2003), Parreñas (2001), and Rafael (2000b).

27. Rafael (2000b).

28. For discussions of labor migration as a means of what might be called "running away" from difficult or painful situations in the Philippines, see Parreñas (2005), Constable (1999), and N. Suzuki (2002a).

EPILOGUE

1. U.S. State Department, 2004, *Trafficking in Persons Report*, June, www
.state.gov/g/tip/rls/tiprpt/2004 (accessed November 10, 2008).

2. These numbers are based on statistics available on Japan's Ministry of Foreign Affairs Web site, www.mofa.go.jp/mofaj/toko/tokei/hakkyu/index.html (accessed April 16, 2008).

3. In addition to the decline in the number of Filipina women coming to Central Kiso on entertainer visas, the few Filipina women I knew who had been working in local bars without government-issued visas had left the region. Since 2000, police officers throughout Japan have been intensifying their crackdown on undocumented migrant workers, conducting more raids on hostess bars. The Japanese government has both criminalized residing in Japan without a visa and increased the penalties of doing so. The few undocumented Filipina women I had known in Central Kiso either had surrendered to Immigration and returned to the Philippines or had gone to stay with friends and relatives in urban areas, where they hoped to more easily hide.

4. According to this information sheet, which was issued by the Nagano prefectural government, in May 2005 there were 218 Philippine nationals registered in Kiso County, accounting for 48 percent of foreign residents in the county—by far the largest percentage. (As I mentioned, in 1999 there were 189 Philippine nationals registered in the region of Kiso County that I call Central Kiso, and 191 in all of Kiso County. At the time, they accounted for 45 percent of all foreign nationals in the region. About 60 of those registered were wives of Japanese men, and the overwhelming remainder, I presume, were Filipina women on entertainer visas. A few may have been Philippine nationals on temporary visas visiting family members; however, I never met a Filipino man with a government-issued visa in the region.)

Bibliography

Abu-Lughod, Lila. 1986. *Veiled Sentiments: Honor and Poetry in a Bedouin Society.* Berkeley: University of California Press.

———. 1990a. The Romance of Resistance: Tracing Transformations of Power through Bedouin Women. *American Ethnologist* 17(1): 41–55.

———. 1990b. Shifting Politics in Bedouin Love Poetry. In *Language and the Politics of Emotion,* ed. L. Abu-Lughod and C. Lutz, 24–45. New York: Cambridge University Press.

———. 1993. *Writing Women's Worlds.* Berkeley: University of California Press.

Agamben, Giorgio. 1998. *Homo Sacer: Sovereign Power and Bare Life.* Trans. D. Heller-Roazen. Stanford, CA: Stanford University Press.

———. 2005. *States of Exception.* Trans. K. Attell. Chicago: University of Chicago Press.

Ahearn, Laura. 2001. *Invitations to Love: Literacy, Love Letters, and Social Change in Nepal.* Ann Arbor: University of Michigan Press.

Alejandro, Reynaldo Gamboa. 1998. Letter from the Philippines. *Dance Magazine* (Online) 72 (1): 40. www.thefreelibrary.com/Letter+from+the+Philippines.-a020183121 (accessed April 18, 2008).

Alexander, M. Jacqui, and Chandra Talpade Mohanty, eds. 1997. *Feminist Genealogies, Colonial Legacies, Democratic Futures.* New York: Routledge.

Allison, Anne. 1994. *Nightwork: Sexuality, Pleasure, and Corporate Masculinity in a Tokyo Hostess Club.* Chicago: University of Chicago Press.

———. 2000. *Permitted and Prohibited Desires: Mothers, Comic, and Censorship in Japan.* Berkeley: University of California Press.

———. 2006. *Millennial Monsters: Japanese Toys and the Global Imagination.* Berkeley: University of California Press.

Althusser, Louis. 1971. Ideology and Ideological State Apparatuses: Notes toward an Investigation. In *Lenin and Philosophy and Other Essays,* 127–86. New York: Monthly Review Press.

Anderson, Benedict. 1991. *Imagined Communities: Reflections on the Origin and Spread of Nationalism*. London: Verso.

——. 1998. *The Spectre of Comparisons: Nationalisms, Southeast Asia, and the World*. New York: Verso.

Anzaldúa, Gloria. 1987. *Borderlands/La Frontera: The New Mestiza*. San Francisco: Aunt Lute Books.

Appadurai, Arjun. 1986. Introduction: Commodities and the Politics of Value. In *The Social Life of Things: Commodities in Cultural Perspective*, ed. A. Appadurai, 3–63. Cambridge: Cambridge University Press.

——. 1996. *Modernity at Large: Cultural Dimensions of Globalization*. Minneapolis: University of Minnesota Press.

Austin, J. L. 1975. *How to Do Things with Words*. Cambridge, MA: Harvard University Press.

Babior, Sharman. 1993. Women of a Tokyo Shelter: Domestic Violence and Sexual Exploitation in Japan. PhD diss., Department of Anthropology, UCLA.

Bachnik, Jane. 1983. Recruitment Strategies for Household Succession: Rethinking Japanese Household Organisation. *Man* 18:160–82.

Bakhtin, Mikhail. 1981a. Discourse in the Novel. In *The Dialogic Imagination*, ed. M. Holquist, 259–422. Austin: University of Texas Press.

——. 1981b. Forms of Time and of the Chronotope in the Novel. In *The Dialogic Imagination*, ed. M. Holquist, 84–258. Austin: University of Texas Press.

Bakrania, Falu. 2004. Re-fusing Identities: British Asian Youth and the Cultural Politics of Popular Music. PhD diss, Department of Anthropology, Stanford University.

Ballescas, Ma. Rosario. P. 1992. *Filipino Entertainers in Japan: An Introduction*. Quezon City, Philippines: Foundation for Nationalist Studies.

Barad, Karen. 2003. Posthumanist Performativity: Toward an Understanding of How Matter Comes to Matter. *Signs* 28 (3): 801–32.

——. 2007. *Meeting the Universe Halfway: Quantum Physics and the Entanglement of Matter*. Durham, NC: Duke University Press.

Barry, Kathleen. 1979. *Female Sexual Slavery*. New York: New York University.

Basch, Linda, Nina Glick Schiller, and Cristina Szanton Blanc. 1994. *Nations Unbound: Transnational Projects, Postcolonial Predicaments, and Deterritorialized Nation-States*. Langhorne, PA: Gordon and Breach.

Basu, Amrita, Inderpal Grewal, Caren Kaplan, and Liisa Malkki. 2001. Editorial. *Signs* 26 (4): 943–47.

Battistella, Graziano, and Anthony Paganoni, eds. 1992. *Philippine Labor Migration: Impact and Policy*. Quezon City, Philippines: Scalabrini Migration Center.

Baty, S. Paige. 1995. *American Monroe: The Making of a Body Politic*. Berkeley: University of California Press.

Befu, Harumi. 1963. Patrilineal Descent and Personal Kindred in Japan. *American Anthropologist* 65 (6): 1328–41.

——. 1993. Nationalism and Nihonjinron. In *Cultural Nationalism in East Asia: Representation and Identity*, ed. H. Befu, 107–35. Berkeley: University of California Institute of East Asian Studies Research Papers and Policy Studies.

———. 2001. *Hegemony of Homogeneity: An Anthropological Analysis of Nihonjinron*. Melbourne: Trans Pacific.

Bell, David, and Gill Valentine. 1997. *Consuming Geographies: We Are Where We Eat*. New York: Routledge.

Bello, Walden, and Robin Broad. 1987. The International Monetary Fund in the Philippines. In *The Philippines Reader: A History of Colonialism, Neocolonialism, Dictatorship, and Resistance*, ed. D. B. Schirmer and S. R. Shalom, 261–66. Boston: South End.

Bello, Walden, Marissa De Guzman, Mary Lou Malig, and Herbert Docena. 2005. *The Anti-Development State: The Political Economy of Permanent Crisis in the Philippines*. London: Zed Books.

Bello, Walden, David Kinley, and Elaine Elinson. 1982. *Development Debacle: The World Bank in the Philippines*. San Francisco: Institute for Food and Development Policy.

Berner, Erhard. 1997. *Defending a Place in the City: Localities and the Struggle for Urban Land in Metro Manila*. Quezon City, Philippines: Ateneo de Manila University Press.

Bernstein, Elizabeth. 2007. *Temporarily Yours: Intimacy, Authenticity, and the Commerce of Sex*. Chicago: University of Chicago Press.

Bernstein, Gail Lee. 1983. *Haruko's World: A Japanese Farm Woman and Her Community*. Stanford, CA: Stanford University Press.

Bestor, Theodore. 1999. Constructing Sushi: Food Culture, Trade, and Commodification in a Japanese Market. In *Lives in Motion*, ed. S. O. Long, 151–90. Cornell East Asia Series, Monograph 106. Ithaca, NY: East Asia Program, Cornell University.

———. 2004. *Tsukiji: The Fish Market at the Center of the World*. Berkeley: University of California Press.

Bhabha, Homi. 1990. Introduction: Narrating the Nation. In *Nation and Narration*, ed. H. Bhabha, 1–7. New York: Routledge.

———. 1994. *The Location of Culture*. New York: Routledge.

———. 1996. Culture's In-Between. In *Questions of Cultural Identity*, ed. S. Hall and P. DuGay, 53–60. Thousand Oaks, CA: Sage.

Blunt, Alison. 2005. *Domicile and Diaspora: Anglo-Indian Women and the Spatial Politics of Home*. Malden, MA: Blackwell.

Borneman, John. 1992. *Belonging in the Two Berlins: Kin, State, Nation*. Cambridge: Cambridge University Press.

Bornoff, Nicholas. 1991. *The Pink Samurai: Love, Marriage and Sex in Contemporary Japan*. New York: Simon and Schuster.

Bourdieu, Pierre. 1977. *Outline of a Theory of Practice*. Trans. R. Nice. Cambridge: Cambridge University Press.

———. 2007. *Distinction: A Social Critique of the Judgement of Taste*. Trans. R. Nice. Cambridge, MA: Harvard University Press.

Boyce, James K. 1993. *The Philippines: The Political Economy of Growth and Impoverishment in the Marcos Era*. Honolulu: University of Hawaii Press.

Brah, Avtar. 1996. *Cartographies of Diaspora: Contesting Identities*. New York: Routledge.

Brennan, Denise. 2004. *What's Love Got to Do with It? Transnational Desires and Sex Tourism in the Dominican Republic.* Durham, NC: Duke University Press.

Broad, Robin, and John Cavanagh. 1993. *Plundering Paradise: The Struggle for the Environment in the Philippines.* Berkeley: University of California Press.

Brophy, Barry. 2006. Permanent Residency Can Relieve Pension Pain. *Japan Times Online,* October 6. http://search.japantimes.co.jp/cgi-bin/fl20061003zg.html (accessed November 2, 2008).

Brown, Jacqueline Nassy. 2005. *Dropping Anchor, Setting Sail: Geographies of Race in Black Liverpool.* Princeton, NJ: Princeton University Press.

Buckley, Sandra. 1993. Altered States: The Body Politics of "Being-Women." In *Postwar Japan as History,* ed. A. Gordon, 347–72. Berkeley: University of California Press.

Bulosan, Carlos. 1973. *America Is in the Heart.* Seattle: University of Washington Press.

Burgeson, Suzanne. 2001. Political Economy Discourses of Globalization and Feminist Politics. *Signs* 26 (4): 983–1005.

Burgess, Chris. 2004. (Re)constructing Identities: International Marriage Migrants as Potential Agents of Social Change in Globalising Japan. *Asian Studies Review* 28 (3): 223–42.

Burns, Susan. 1998. Bodies and Borders: Syphilis, Prostitution, and the Nation in Japan, 1860–1890. English Supplement. *U.S.-Japan Women's Journal* 15:3–30.

Butler, Judith. 1987. *Subjects of Desire: Hegelian Reflections in Twentieth-Century France.* New York: Columbia University Press.

———. 1993. *Bodies That Matter: On the Discursive Limits of Sex.* New York: Routledge.

———. 1997a. "Conscience Doth Make Subjects of Us All": Althusser's Subjection. In *The Psychic Life of Power: Theories in Subjection,* 106–31. Stanford, CA: Stanford University Press.

———. 1997b. *The Psychic Life of Power: Theories in Subjection.* Stanford, CA: Stanford University Press.

———. 1999. *Gender Trouble: Feminism and the Subversion of Identity.* New York: Routledge.

———. 2000. *Antigone's Claim: Kinship between Life and Death.* New York: Columbia University Press.

Cabezas, Amalia. 2004. Between Love and Money: Sex, Tourism, and Citizenship in Cuba and the Dominican Republic. *Signs* 29 (4): 988–1015.

Cannell, Fenella. 1995. The Power of Appearances: Beauty, Mimicry, and Transformation in Bicol. In *Discrepant Histories: Translocal Essays on Filipino Cultures,* ed. V. Raphael, 223–58. Philadelphia, PA: Temple University Press.

———. 1999. *Power and Intimacy in the Christian Philippines.* New York: Cambridge University Press.

Castañeda, Claudia. 2002. *Figurations: Child, Bodies, Worlds.* Durham, NC: Duke University Press.

Castree, Noel. 2003. Environmental Issues: Relational Ontologies and Hybrid Politics. *Progress in Human Geography* 27 (2): 203–11.

Certeau, Michel de. 1984. *The Practice of Everyday Life*. Trans. S. Rendall. Berkeley: University of California Press.

Chakrabarty, Dipesh. 2000. *Provincializing Europe: Postcolonial Thought and Historical Difference*. Princeton, NJ: Princeton University Press.

Chant, Sylvia, and Cathy McIlwaine. 1995. *Women of a Lesser Cost: Female Labour, Foreign Exchange, and Philippine Development*. East Haven, CT: Pluto.

Chapkis, Wendy. 1997. *Live Sex Acts: Women Performing Erotic Labor*. New York: Routledge.

Chatterjee, Partha. 1989. Colonialism, Nationalism, and Colonized Women: The Contest in India. *American Ethnologist* 16 (4): 622–33.

———. 1993. *The Nation and Its Fragments: Colonial and Postcolonial Histories*. Princeton, NJ: Princeton University Press.

Cheng, Sealing. 2004. Interrogating the Absence of HIV/AIDS Prevention for Migrant Sex Workers in South Korea. *Health and Human Rights* 7 (2): 193–204.

Ching, Leo T. S. 2001. *Becoming "Japanese": Colonial Taiwan and the Politics of Identity Formation*. Berkeley: University of California Press.

Chow, Rey. 1993. *Writing Diaspora: Tactics of Intervention in Contemporary Cultural Studies*. Durham, NC: Duke University Press.

Choy, Catherine Ceniza. 2003. *Empire of Care: Nursing and Migration in Filipino American History*. Durham, NC: Duke University Press.

Christy, Alan. 1993. The Making of Imperial Subjects in Okinawa. *positions: east asia cultures critique* 1 (3): 607–39.

Chung, Haeng-ja. 2004. *Performing Sex, Selling Heart: Korean Nightclub Hostesses in Japan*, PhD diss., Department of Anthropology, UCLA.

Clarke, Kamari Maxine. 2004. *Mapping Yoruba Networks: Power and Agency in the Making of Transnational Communities*. Durham, NC: Duke University Press.

———. 2007. Transnational Yoruba Revivalism and the Diasporic Politics of Heritage. *American Ethnologist* 34 (4): 721–34.

———. 2009. *The International Criminal Court and the Fictions of Justice: Challenges of Legal Pluralism in Sub-Saharan Africa*. New York: Cambridge University Press.

Clifford, James. 1988. *The Predicament of Culture: Twentieth-Century Ethnography, Literature, and Art*. Cambridge, MA: Harvard University Press.

———. 1997. *Routes: Travel and Translation in the Late Twentieth Century*. Cambridge, MA: Harvard University Press.

Clifford, James, and James E. Marcus, eds. 1986. *Writing Culture: The Poetics and Politics of Ethnography*. Berkeley: University of California Press.

Colen, Shellee. 1995. "Like a Mother to Them": Stratified Reproduction and West Indian Childcare Workers and Employers in New York. In *Conceiving the New World Order: The Global Politics of Reproduction*, ed. F. Ginsburg and R. Rapp, 78–102. Berkeley: University of California Press.

Collier, Jane, Michelle Rosaldo, and Sylvia Yanagisako. 1997. Is There a Family? New Anthropological Views. In *The Gender/Sexuality Reader: Culture,*

History, and Political Economy, ed. R. N. Lancaster and M. Di Leonardo, 71–81. New York: Routledge.

Comaroff, John, and Jean Comaroff. 1991. *Of Revelation and Revolution: Christianity, Colonialism, and Consciousness in South Africa.* Chicago: University of Chicago Press.

Constable, Nicole. 1997. *Maid to Order in Hong Kong: Stories of Filipina Workers.* Ithaca, NY: Cornell University Press.

———. 1999. At Home, But Not at Home: Filipina Narratives of Ambivalent Returns. *Cultural Anthropology* 14 (2): 203–28.

———. 2002. Sexuality and Discipline among Filipina Domestic Workers in Hong Kong. In *Filipinos in Global Migration: At Home in the World?* ed. F. V. Aguilar, 237–68. Quezon City: Philippine Migration Research Network and the Philippine Social Science Council.

———. 2003. *Romance on a Global Stage: Pen Pals, Virtual Ethnography, and "Mail-Order" Marriages.* Berkeley: University of California Press.

Constantino, Renato, and Constantino Letizia. 1978. *The Philippines: The Continuing Past.* Quezon City, Philippines: Foundation for Nationalist Studies.

Cooper, Frederick, and Ann Laura Stoler, eds. 1997. *Tensions of Empire: Colonial Cultures in a Bourgeois World.* Berkeley: University of California Press.

Coutin, Susan Bibler. 2003. *Legalizing Moves: Salvadoran Immigrants' Struggle for U.S. Residency.* Ann Arbor: University of Michigan Press.

———. 2005. Being En Route. *American Anthropologist* 107 (2): 195–206.

Creighton, Millie. 1997. Soto Others and Uchi Others: Imaging Racial Diversity, Imagining Homogeneous Japan. In *Japan's Minorities: The Illusion of Homogeneity,* ed. M. Weiner, 211–38. New York: Routledge.

Cruikshank, Julie. 1998. *The Social Life of Stories: Narrative and Knowledge in the Yukon Territory.* Lincoln: University of Nebraska Press.

———. 2005. *Do Glaciers Listen? Local Knowledge, Colonial Encounters, and Social Imagination.* Vancouver: University of British Columbia Press.

Cruz, Wilfrido, and Robert Repetto. 1992. *The Environmental Effects of Stabilisation and Structural Adjustment Programs: The Philippine Case.* Washington DC: World Resources Institute.

Curtin, J. Sean. 2002. International Marriages in Japan: Part Two; Impact of 17 October 2002 Supreme Court Decision on International Marriages. *Social Trends* 14 (October 28). www.glocom.org/special_topics/socialtrends/20021028_trends_s14/index.html (accessed November 2, 2008).

Dalby, Liza. 1983. *Geisha.* Berkeley: University of California Press.

Dale, Peter N. 1986. *The Myth of Japanese Uniqueness.* New York: St. Martin's.

Dauvergne, Peter. 1997. *Shadows in the Forest: Japan and the Politics of Timber in Southeast Asia.* Cambridge, MA: MIT Press.

de Genova, Nicholas. 2005. *Working the Boundaries: Race, Space, and "Illegality" in Mexican Chicago.* Durham, NC: Duke University Press.

DeDios, Aurora Javate. 1990. The Case of the Japayuki-san and the Hanayome-san: A Preliminary Inquiry into the Culture of Subordination. In *Women's Springbook: Readings on Women and Society,* ed. M. M. Evasco, A. J. DeDios, and F. Caagusan, 35–41. Quezon City, Philippines: Women's

Resource and Research Center and the Katipunan ng Kababaihan para sa Kalayaan.

———. 1992. Japayuki-san: Filipinas at Risk. In *Filipino Women Overseas Contract Workers . . . At What Cost?* ed. R. P. Beltran and A. J. DeDios, 39–58. Manila: Goodwill Trading.

Delaney, Carol. 1995. Father State, Motherland, and the Birth of Modern Turkey. In *Naturalizing Power: Essays in Feminist Cultural Analysis,* ed. S. J. Yanagisako and C. Delaney, 177–200. New York: Routledge.

Derrida, Jacques. 1981. *Dissemination.* Chicago: University of Chicago Press.

———. 1988. Signature Event Context. In *Limited Inc,* ed. G. Graft, 1–21. Chicago: Northwestern University Press.

Dirks, Nicholas. 1990. History as a Sign of the Modern. *Public Culture* 2:25–32.

Doi, Takeo. 1973. *The Anatomy of Dependence.* Trans. J. Bester. San Francisco: Kodansha International.

Dore, Ronald P. 1978. *Shinohata: A Portrait of a Japanese Village.* New York: Pantheon Books.

Douglass, Mike, and Glenda S. Roberts. 2003. Japan in an Age of Global Migration. In *Japan and Global Migration: Foreign Workers and the Advent of a Multicultural Society,* ed. M. Douglass and G. S. Roberts, 3–37. Honolulu: University of Hawaii Press.

Dower, John W. 1986. *War without Mercy: Race and Power in the Pacific War.* New York: Pantheon Books.

DuBois, W. E. B. 1989. *The Souls of Black Folk.* New York: Bantam.

Dumont, Jean-Paul. 1992. *Visayan Vignettes: Ethnographic Traces of a Philippine Island.* Chicago: University of Chicago Press.

Durkheim, Emile. 1979. *Suicide: A Study in Sociology.* Trans. J. A. Spaulding and G. Simpson. New York: Free Press.

———. 1982. *Rules of the Sociological Method.* Trans. W. D. Halls. New York: Free Press.

———. 2001. *The Elementary Forms of Religious Life.* Trans. C. Cosman. New York: Oxford University Press.

Dworkin, Andrea. 1993. Prostitution and Male Supremacy. *Michigan Journal of Gender and Law* 1:1–12.

Ehara, Takekazu. 1992. The Internationalization of Education. In *The Internationalization of Japan,* ed. G. D. Hook and M. Weiner, 269–83. New York: Routledge.

Enloe, Cynthia. 2001. *Bananas, Beaches, and Bases: Making Feminist Sense of International Politics.* Berkeley: University of California Press.

Enriquez, Virgilio G. 1992. *From Colonial to Liberation Psychology: The Philippine Experience.* Quezon City: University of the Philippines Press.

Esguerra, Lawrence A., ed. 1994. *Philchime Career Manual for Overseas Performing Artists.* Manila: Philchime.

Espiritu, Yen Le. 2003. *Home Bound: Filipino American Lives across Cultures, Communities, and Countries.* Berkeley: University of California Press.

Evans-Pritchard, E. E. 1990. *Kinship and Marriage among the Nuer:* Oxford University Press.

Eviota, Elizabeth. 1992. *The Political Economy of Gender: Women and the Sexual Division of Labour in the Philippines.* Atlantic Highlands, NJ: Zed Books.

Faier, Lieba. 2007. Filipina Migrants in Rural Japan and Their Professions of Love. *American Ethnologist* 34 (11): 148–62.

Fajardo, Kale Bantigue. 2004. Filipino Cross Currents: Seafaring, Masculinities, and Globalization. PhD diss., Department of Anthropology, UC Santa Cruz.

Farley, Melissa, ed. 2003. *Prostitution, Trafficking, and Traumatic Stress.* New York: Haworth Maltreatment and Trauma Press.

Field, Norma. 1993a. Beyond Envy, Boredom, and Suffering: Toward an Emancipatory Politics for Resident Koreans and Other Japanese. *positions: east asia cultures critique* 1 (3): 640–70.

———. 1993b. *In the Realm of a Dying Emperor.* New York: Vintage Books.

———. 1997. *From My Grandmother's Bedside: Sketches of Postwar Tokyo.* Berkeley: University of California Press.

Foucault, Michel. 1976. Two Lectures. In *Power/Knowledge: Selected Interviews and Other Writings, 1972–1977,* ed. C. Gordon, 78–108. New York: Pantheon Books.

———. 1977a. Nietzsche, Genealogy, History. In *Language, Counter-Memory, Practice: Selected Essays and Interviews,* ed. D. F. Bouchard, 139–64. Ithaca, NY: Cornell University Press.

———. 1977b. Truth and Power. Interview by Alessandro Fontana and Pasquale Pasquino. In *Power/Knowledge: Selected Interviews and Other Writings, 1972–1977,* ed. C. Gordon, 109–33. New York: Pantheon Books.

———. 1990. *The History of Sexuality.* Trans. R. Hurley. New York: Vintage Books.

Fowler, Edward. 1996. *San'ya Blues: Laboring Life in Contemporary Japan.* Ithaca, NY: Cornell University Press.

Franklin, Sarah. 1997. *Embodied Progress: A Cultural Account of Assisted Conception.* New York: Routledge.

Franklin, Sarah, and Susan McKinnon, eds. 2001. *Relative Values: Reconfiguring Kinship Studies.* Durham, NC: Duke University Press.

Fujime, Yuki. 1997. The Licensed Prostitution System and the Prostitution Abolition Movement in Modern Japan. *positions: east asia cultures critique* 5 (1): 135–70.

Fujitani, Takashi. 1992. Electronic Pageantry and Japan's "Symbolic Emperor" *Journal of Asian Studies* 51 (4): 824–50.

———. 1993. Inventing, Forgetting, Remembering: Toward a Historical Ethnography of the Nation-State. In *Cultural Nationalism in East Asia: Representation and Identity,* ed. H. Befu, 77–106. Berkeley: University of California Institute of East Asian Studies Research Papers and Policy Studies.

———. 1996. *Splendid Monarchy: Power and Pageantry in Modern Japan.* Berkeley: University of California Press.

Fukutake, Tadashi. 1980. *Rural Society in Japan.* Tokyo: University of Tokyo Press.

———. 1982. *The Japanese Social Structure.* Trans. R. P. Dore. Tokyo: University of Tokyo Press.

Furusawa, Mei. 1992. *Firipinjin hanayome to Nihon no nōson kazoku: bunka-jinruigakuteki kōsatsu*. PhD diss., Department of International Studies, Rikkyō University, Tokyo, Japan.

Garon, Sheldon. 1993. The World's Oldest Debate? Prostitution and the State in Imperial Japan, 1900–1945. *American Historical Review* 98 (3): 710–32.

Ghosh, Amitav. 2005. *The Shadow Lines*. New York: Mariner Books.

Gibson-Graham, J. K. 1996. *The End of Capitalism (As We Knew It): A Feminist Critique of Political Economy*. Malden, MA: Blackwell.

———. 2006. *A Postcapitalist Politics*. Minneapolis: University of Minnesota Press.

Giddens, Anthony. 1986. *The Constitution of Society: Outline of the Theory of Structuration*. Berkeley: University of California Press.

Gill, Tom. 2001. *Men of Uncertainty: The Social Organization of Day Laborers in Contemporary Japan*. Albany, NY: SUNY Press.

Gilroy, Paul. 1993. *The Black Atlantic: Modernity and Double Consciousness*. Cambridge, MA: Harvard University Press.

Ginsburg, Faye, and Anna Tsing. 1990. Introduction. In *Uncertain Terms*, 1–16. Boston: Beacon.

Gluck, Carol. 1998. The Invention of Edo. In *Mirror of Modernity*, 262–84. Berkeley: University of California Press.

Goodman, Roger. 2007. The Concept of Kokusaika and Japanese Educational Reform. *Globalisation, Societies, and Education* 5 (1): 71–87.

Gopinath, Gayatri. 2005. *Impossible Desires: Queer Diasporas and South Asian Public Cultures*. Durham, NC: Duke University Press.

Gordon, Avery. 1997. *Ghostly Matters: Haunting and the Sociological Imagination*. Minneapolis: University of Minnesota Press.

Graying Society. 1996. Special Issue, *Japan Echo* 23.

Grewal, Inderpal. 1996. *Home and Harem: Nation, Gender, Empire and the Cultures of Travel*. Durham, NC: Duke University Press.

Grewal, Inderpal, and Caren Kaplan. 1994. Introduction: Transnational Feminist Practices and Questions of Postmodernity. In *Scattered Hegemonies: Postmodernity and Transnational Feminist Practices,* ed. I. Grewal and C. Kaplan, 1–36. Minneapolis: University of Minnesota Press.

Griesemer, James R. and Susan Leigh Star. 1989. Institutional Ecology, "Translations" and Boundary Objects: Amateurs and Professionals in Berkeley's Museum of Vertebrate Zoology, 1907–1939. *Social Studies of Science* 19 (3): 387–420.

Griffiths, Stephan. 1988. *Emigrants, Entrepreneurs, and Evil Spirits*. Honolulu: University of Hawaii Press.

Guha, Ranajit, and Gayatri Spivak, eds. 1988. *Selected Subaltern Studies*. New York: Oxford University Press.

Gupta, Akhil. 1992. The Song of the Non-aligned World: Transnational Identities and the Reinscription of Space in Late Capitalism. *Cultural Anthropology* 7 (1): 63–79.

Gupta, Akhil, and James Ferguson. 1997. Culture, Power, Place: Ethnography at the End of an Era. In *Culture, Power, Place: Explorations in Critical Anthropology,* ed. A. Gupta and J. Ferguson, 1–32. Durham, NC: Duke University Press.

Gutiérrez, David G. 1999. Migration, Emergent Ethnicity, and the "Third Space": The Shifting Politics of Nationalism in Greater Mexico. *Journal of American History* 86 (2): 481–517.

Halberstam, Judith. 2005. *In a Queer Time and Place: Transgender Bodies, Subcultural Lives*. New York: New York University Press.

Hall, Stuart. 1990. Cultural Identity and Diaspora. In *Identity: Community, Culture, Difference*, ed. J. Rutherford, 222–37. London: Lawrence and Wishart.

———. 1996. Introduction: Who Needs Identity. In *Questions of Cultural Identity*, ed. S. Hall and P. DuGay. 1–17. Thousand Oaks, CA: Sage.

Hamabata, Matthews Masayuki. 1991. *Crested Kimono: Power and Love in the Japanese Business Family*. Ithaca, NY: Cornell University Press.

Hamada, Tomoko. 1997. Absent Fathers, Feminized Sons, Selfish Mothers and Disobedient Daughters: Revisiting the Japanese Ie Household. JPRI Working Paper 33. Cardiff, CA: Japan Policy Research Institute.

Haraway, Donna. 1997. *Modest_Witness@Second_Millennium.FemaleMan©_Meets_Oncomouse™: Feminism and Technoscience*. New York: Routledge.

———. 2003. *The Companion Species Manifesto: Dogs, People, and Significant Otherness*. Chicago: Prickly Paradigm.

Harding, Susan. 1975. Women and Words in a Spanish Village. In *Toward an Anthropology of Women*, ed. R. Reiter, 283–308. New York: Monthly Review.

———. 2000. *The Book of Jerry Falwell: Fundamentalist Language and Politics*. Princeton, NJ: Princeton University Press.

Hawes, Gary. 1987. *The Philippine State and the Marcos Regime: The Politics of Export*. Ithaca, NY: Cornell University Press.

Hein, Laura. 1990. *Fueling Growth: The Energy Revolution and Economic Policy in Postwar Japan*. Cambridge, MA: Harvard Council on East Asian Studies.

Hendry, Joy. 1981. *Marriage in Changing Japan*. New York: St. Martin's.

———. 1986. *Becoming Japanese: The World of the Preschool Child*. Honolulu: University of Hawaii Press.

Higurashi, Takanori. 1989. *"Mura" to "ore" no kokusai kekkon*. Tokyo: Jōhō Kikaku Shuppan.

Hirata, Toshio, ed. 1999. *Kisodani no rekishi*. Tokyo: Rindoren Kenkyūsha.

Hisada, Megumi. 1989. *Firipina o ai shita otokotachi*. Tokyo: Bungei Shunjū.

Ho, Engseng. 2006. *The Graves of Tarim: Genealogy and Mobility across the Indian Ocean*. Berkeley: University of California Press.

Hobsbawm, Eric. 1983. Introduction: Inventing Traditions. In *The Invention of Tradition*, ed. E. Hobsbawm and T. O. Ranger, 1–14. New York: Cambridge University Press.

Hochschild, Arlie. 2003. *The Managed Heart: Commercialization of Human Feeling*. Berkeley: University of California Press.

Hollnsteiner, Mary R. 1973. Reciprocity in the Lowland Philippines. In *Four Readings in Philippine Values*, ed. F. Lynch and A. De Guzman II, 69–91. Quezon City, Philippines: Ateneo de Manila Press.

Hōmushō Daijin Kanbō Shihō Hōseibu [Judicial System Department, Minister's Secretariat, Ministry of Justice], ed. 2005. *Dai-44 shutsunyūkoku kanri tōkei nenpō* [Annual Report of Statistics on Legal Migrants]. Tokyo: Hōmushō Daijin Kanbō Shihō Hōseibu.

————, ed. 2006. *Dai-45 shutsunyūkoku kanri tōkei nenpō* [Annual Report of Statistics on Legal Migrants]. Tokyo: Hōmushō Daijin Kanbō Shihō Hōseibu.

————, ed. 2007. *Dai-46 shutsunyūkoku kanri tōkei nenpō* [Annual Report of Statistics on Legal Migrants]. Tokyo: Hōmushō Daijin Kanbō Shihō Hōseibu.

hooks, bell. 1992. *Black Looks: Race and Representation*. Boston: South End.

————. 2000. *Feminist Theory: From Margin to Center*. Cambridge, MA: South End.

Howell, David. 1996. Ethnicity and Culture in Contemporary Japan. *Journal of Contemporary History* 31 (1): 171–90.

————. 2004. Making "Useful Citizens" of Ainu Subjects in Early Twentieth-Century Japan. *Journal of Asian Studies* 63 (1): 5–29.

Ileto, Reynaldo Clemena. 1979. *Pasyon and Revolution: Popular Movements in the Philippines, 1840–1910*. Quezon City, Philippines: Ateneo de Manila University Press.

Inda, Jonathan Xavier, and Renato Rosaldo. 2002. Introduction: A World in Motion. In *The Anthropology of Globalization: A Reader*, ed. J. X. Inda and R. Rosaldo, 1–34. Malden, MA: Blackwell.

Inoue, Miyako. 2006. *Vicarious Language: Gender and Linguistic Modernity in Japan*. Berkeley: University of California Press.

Ivy, Marilyn. 1989. Critical Texts, Mass Artifacts: The Consumption of Knowledge in Postmodern Japan. In *Postmodernism and Japan*, ed. H. D. Harootunian and M. Miyoshi, 21–46. Durham, NC: Duke University Press.

————. 1995. *Discourses of the Vanishing: Modernity, Phantasm, Japan*. Chicago: University of Chicago Press.

Iwamoto, Jun, and Rin Kuniyasu. 2000. *Ginza no onna, Ginza no kyaku: shūkan shinchō kurabu tsūshinbu hatsu*. Tokyo: Shinchōsha.

Iyori, Naoko. 1987. The Traffic in Japayuki-san. *Japan Quarterly* 34 (1): 84–88.

Jackson, Laura. 1976. Bar Hostesses. In *Women in Changing Japan*, ed. J. Lebra, J. Paulson, and E. Powers, 133–56. Stanford, CA: Stanford University Press.

Jeffries, Sheila. 1997. *The Idea of Prostitution*. Melbourne: Spinifex.

Jimenez, Ma. Carmen C. 1983. Masculinity/Femininity Concepts of the Filipino Man and Woman. In *Developments in Philippine Psychology*, ed. Leah Montes and Gina Ylaya, 91–99. Diliman, Quezon City, Philippines, Psychological Association of the Philippines. Paper presented at the Twentieth Annual Convention of the Psychological Association of the Philippines, Manila, August 16–18.

JNATIP [Japan Network against Trafficking in Persons] and F-GENS [Ochanomizu University Frontiers of Gender Studies]. 2005. *"Nihon ni okeru jinshinbaibai no higai ni kan suru chosa kenkyū" hōkokusho*. Tokyo: JNATIP and F-GENS.

John, Mary. 1996. *Discrepant Dislocations: Feminism, Theory, and Postcolonial Histories*. Berkeley: University of California Press.

Johnson, Chalmers. 2000. *Blowback: The Costs and Consequences of American Empire*. New York: Henry Holt.

Jolivet, Muriel. 1997. *Japan, the Childless Society? The Crisis of Motherhood*. New York: Routledge.

Kahn, Susan Martha. 2000. *Reproducing Jews: A Cultural Account of Assisted Conception in Israel*. Durham, NC: Duke University Press.

Kang, Laura. 1997. Si(gh)ting Asian/American Women as Transnational Labor. *positions: east asia cultures critique* 5 (2): 403–37.

Kaplan, Caren. 1996. *Questions of Travel: Postmodern Discourses of Displacement.* Durham, NC: Duke University Press.

Kawabata, Mayumi. 1995. Imported Brides: A Case of a Runaway Filipina. In *NGO's Report on the Situation of Foreign Migrant Women in Japan and Strategies for Improvement,* ed. Migrant Women Worker's Research and Action Committee. Fourth World Conference on Women, Beijing, September 4–15, 1995.

Kelly, William. 1986. Rationalization and Nostalgia: Cultural Dynamics of New Middle-Class Japan. *American Ethnologist* 13 (4): 603–18.

———. 1990. Regional Japan: The Price of Prosperity and the Benefits of Dependency. *Daedalus* 119 (3): 209–27.

Kelsky, Karen. 2001. *Women on the Verge: Japanese Women, Western Dreams.* Durham, NC: Duke University Press.

Kempadoo, Kamala, and Jo Doezema, eds. 1998. *Global Sex Workers: Rights, Resistance, and Redefinition.* New York: Routledge.

Kitaoji, Hironobu. 1971. The Structure of the Japanese Family. *American Anthropologist* 73:1036–57.

Knight, John. 1995. Municipal Matchmaking in Rural Japan. *Anthropology Today* 11 (2): 9–17.

———. 2000. From Timber to Tourism: Recommoditizing the Japanese Forest. *Development and Change* 31 (1): 341–59.

Kondo, Dorinne. 1990. *Crafting Selves: Power, Gender, and Discourses of Identity in a Japanese Workplace.* Chicago: University of Chicago Press.

———. 1997. *About Face: Performing Race in Fashion and Theater.* New York: Routledge.

Koshiro, Yukiko. 1999. *Trans-Pacific Racisms and the U.S. Occupation of Japan.* New York: Columbia University Press.

Kulick, Don. 1998. *Travesti: Sex, Gender, and Culture among Brazilian Transgendered Prostitutes.* Chicago: University of Chicago Press.

Kuwayama, Norihiko. 1995. *Sutoresu to kokusai kekkon.* Tokyo: Akashi Shoten.

Lauby, Jennifer, and Oded Stark. 1988. Individual Migration as a Family Strategy: Young Women in the Philippines. *Population Studies* 42:473–86.

Law, Lisa. 1997. Dancing on the Bar: Sex, Money, and the Uneasy Politics of Third Space. In *Geographies of Resistance,* ed. S. Pile and M. Keith, 107–23. New York: Routledge.

———. 2000. *Sex Work in Southeast Asia: The Place of Desire in a Time of AIDS.* New York: Routledge.

———. 2001. Home Cooking: Filipino Women and Geographies of the Senses in Hong Kong. *Ecumene* 8 (3): 264–83.

Lebra, Takie Sugiyama. 1984. *Japanese Women: Constraint and Fulfillment.* Honolulu: University of Hawaii Press.

Lee, Soo im. 2006. The Cultural Exclusiveness of Ethnocentrism: Japan's Treatment of Foreign Residents. In *Japan's Diversity Dilemmas: Ethnicity, Citizenship, and Education,* ed. S. i. Lee, S. Murphy-Shigematsu, and H. Befu, 100–125. New York: iUniverse.

Leigh, Carol. 2004. *Unrepentant Whore: The Collected Works of Scarlot Harlot*. San Francisco: Last Gasp.

Levi-Strauss, Claude. 1969. *The Elementary Structures of Kinship*. Trans. J. H. Bell and J. R. Von Sturmer. Boston: Beacon.

Lie, John. 2001. *Multiethnic Japan*. Cambridge, MA: Harvard University Press.

Lim, Bliss Cua. 2004. Cult Fiction: Himala and Bakya Temporality. *Spectator* 24 (2): 61–72.

Lindsey, Charles W. 1987. Foreign Investment in the Philippines. In *The Philippines Reader: A History of Colonialism, Neocolonialism, Dictatorship, and Resistance*, ed. D. B. Schirmer and S. R. Shalom, 230–34. Boston: South End.

Linger, Daniel Touro. 2001. *No One Home: Brazilian Selves Remade in Japan*. Stanford, CA: Stanford University Press.

Lorde, Audre. 1984. *Sister Outsider: Essays and Speeches*. New York: Quality Paperback Book Club.

Lowe, Lisa. 2006. The Intimacies of Four Continents. In *Haunted by Empire: Geographies of Intimacy in North American History*, ed. A. L. Stoler, 191–212. Durham, NC: Duke University Press.

Luibhéid, Eithne. 2002. *Entry Denied: Controlling Sexuality at the Border*. Minneapolis: University of Minnesota Press.

MacKinnon, Catherine. 1993. Prostitution and Civil Rights. *Michigan Journal of Gender and Law* 1:13–31.

Maher, John C., and Gaynor MacDonald, eds. 1995. *Diversity in Japanese Culture and Language*. New York: Kegan Paul International.

Mahmood, Saba. 2005. *Politics of Piety: The Islamic Revival and the Feminist Subject*. Princeton, NJ: Princeton University Press.

Manalansan, Martin F. 2003. *Global Divas: Filipino Gay Men in the Diaspora*. Durham, NC: Duke University Press.

Mani, Lata. 1987. Contentious Traditions: The Debate on Sati in Colonial India. *Cultural Critique* (Fall): 119–56.

Mankekar, Purnima. 1999. *Screening Culture, Viewing Politics: An Ethnography of Television, Womanhood, and Nation in Postcolonial India*. Durham, NC: Duke University Press.

Marcus, George E., and Michael M. J. Fischer. 1986. *Anthropology as Cultural Critique: An Experimental Moment in the Human Sciences*. Chicago: University of Chicago Press.

Margold, Jane. 1995. Narratives of Masculinity and Transnational Migration: Filipino Workers in the Middle East. In *Bewitching Women, Pious Men: Gender and Body Politics in Southeast Asia*, ed. A. Ong and M. Peletz, 274–98. Berkeley: University of California Press.

Martinez, D. P. 1990. Tourism and the Ama: The Search for a Real Japan. In *Unwrapping Japan: Society and Culture in Anthropological Perspective*, ed. E. Ben-Ari, B. Moeran, and J. Valentine, 97–116. Manchester, England: Manchester University Press.

Massey, Doreen. 1992. A Place Called Home? In *Space, Place, and Gender*, 157–73. Minneapolis: University of Minnesota Press.

———. 1999. *Power-Geometries and the Politics of Space-Time: Hettner-Lecture 1998.* Heidelberg, Germany: Department of Geography, University of Heidelberg.

Matsui, Yayori. 1989. *Women's Asia.* New Jersey: Zed Books.

———. 1997. Asian Migrant Women in Japan. Opening address at the Conference on International Trafficking in Women, New York, October 22–23, 1988. In *Broken Silence: Voices of Japanese Feminism,* ed. S. Buckley, 143–55. Berkeley: University of California Press.

Matsushima, Yukiko. 1997. Japan: What Has Made Family Law Reform Go Astray? In *International Survey of Family Law,* ed. A. Bainham, 193–206. The Hague: Kluwer Law International.

McClintock, Anne. 1993. Sex Workers and Sex Work: Introduction. *Social Text* 37 (Winter): 1–10.

———. 1995. *Imperial Leather: Race, Gender, and Sexuality in the Colonial Conquest.* New York: Routledge.

McConnell, David L. 2000. *Importing Diversity: Inside Japan's JET Program.* Berkeley: University of California Press.

McCormack, Gavan. 2001. *The Emptiness of Japanese Affluence.* Armonk, NY: Sharpe.

McKay, Deirdre. 2003. Filipinas in Canada: De-skilling as a Push toward Marriage. In *Wife or Worker? Asian Women and Migration,* ed. N. Piper and M. Roces, 23–51. Lanham, MD: Rowman and Littlefield.

Meyler, Bernadette. 1997. Bakhtin's Irony. *Pacific Coast Philology* 32 (1): 105–20.

Migiya, Risa. 1998. Kokusai kekkon kara miru konnichi no Nihon nōson shakai to "ie" no henka. *Shien* 59 (1): 72–92.

Miller, Laura. 2006. *Beauty Up: Exploring Contemporary Japanese Body Aesthetics.* Berkeley: University of California Press.

Miyake, Yoshiko. 1991. Doubling Expectations: Motherhood and Women's Factory Work under State Management in Japan in the 1930s and 1940s. In *Recreating Japanese Women, 1600–1945,* ed. G. L. Bernstein, 267–95. Berkeley: University of California Press.

Mock, John. 1996. Mother or Mama: The Political Economy of Bar Hostesses in Sapporo. In *Re-imaging Japanese Women,* ed. A. E. Imamura, 177–91. Berkeley: University of California Press.

Moeller, Robert G. 1993. *Protecting Motherhood: Women and the Family in the Politics of Postwar West Germany.* Berkeley: University of California Press.

Mohanty, Chandra Talpade. 2003. *Feminism without Borders: Decolonizing Theory, Practicing Solidarity.* Durham, NC: Duke University Press.

Mohanty, Chandra Talpade, Ann Russo, and Lourdes Torres, eds. 1991. *Third World Women and the Politics of Feminism.* Bloomington: Indiana University Press.

Moon, Okpyo. 1997. Marketing Nature in Rural Japan. In *Japanese Images of Nature: Cultural Perspectives,* ed. P. J. Asquith and A. Kalland. Richmond, UK: Curzon.

Moraga, Cherrie, and Gloria Anzaldúa, eds. 1981. *This Bridge Called My Back: Writings by Radical Women of Color.* Albany: Kitchen Table.

Morris-Suzuki, Tessa. 1993. Rewriting History: Civilization Theory in Contemporary Japan. *positions: east asia cultures critique* 1 (2): 526–49.

———. 1998. *Re-inventing Japan: Time, Space, Nation.* Armonk, NY: Sharpe.

Mouer, Ross, and Yoshio Sugimoto. 1986. *Images of Japanese Society: A Study in the Structure of Social Reality.* New York: Kegan Paul International.

Murata, Noriko. 1995. The Trafficking of Women. *AMPO: Japan-Asia Quarterly Review* 25 (4): 63–65.

Nader, Laura. 1972. Up the Anthropologist—Perspectives Gained from Studying Up. In *Reinventing Anthropology*, ed. D. H. Hymes, 284–311. New York: Pantheon Books.

Nagano Nippō. 1999. Kekkon mondai no kakehashi ni: Hiyoshi no Watazawa-san Chūgoku ryūgaku. November 11.

Nakamatsu, Tomoko. 2003. International Marriage through Introduction Agencies: Social and Legal Realities of "Asian" Wives of Japanese Men. In *Wife or Worker? Asian Women and Migration*, ed. N. Piper and M. Roces, 181–201. Lanham, MD: Rowman and Littlefield.

———. 2005. Faces of "Asian Brides": Gender, Race, and Class in the Representations of Immigrant Women in Japan. *Women's Studies International Forum* 28:405–17.

Nakamura, Karen. 2003. Deaf Shock and the Hard of Hearing: Japanese Deaf Identities at the Borderlands. In *Many Ways to be Deaf*, ed. L. Monaghan, K. Nakamura, C. Schmaling, and G. Turner, eds. Washington DC: Gallauded University Press.

———. 2006. *Deaf in Japan: Signing and the Politics of Identity.* Ithaca, NY: Cornell University Press.

Nakane, Chie. 1967. *Kinship and Economic Organization in Rural Japan.* New York: Humanities.

Narayan, Uma. 1997. *Dislocating Cultures: Identities, Traditions, and Third-World Feminism.* New York: Routledge.

Ness, Sally Ann. 1992. *Body, Movement, and Culture: Kinesthetic and Visual Symbolism in a Philippine Community.* Philadelphia: University of Pennsylvania Press.

Neumann, A. Lin. 1987. Tourism Promotion and Prostitution. In *The Philippines Reader: A History of Colonialism, Neocolonialism, Dictatorship, and Resistance*, ed. D. B. Schirmer and S. R. Shalom, 182–87. Boston: South End.

Niigata Nippōsha Gakugeibu, ed. 1989. *Mura no kokusai kekkon.* Akita City, Japan: Mumyōsha Shuppan.

Nolte, Sharon H., and Sally Ann Hastings. 1991. The Meiji State's Policy toward Women, 1890–1910. In *Recreating Japanese Women, 1600–1945*, ed. G. L. Bernstein, 151–74. Berkeley: University of California Press.

Ocampo, Alicia R. 1983. Discussion. In *Developments in Philippine Psychology*, ed. Leah Montes and Gina Ylaya, 109–112. Diliman, Quezon City, Philippines. Psychological Association of the Philippines. Paper presented at the Twentieth Annual Convention of the Psychological Association of the Philippines, Manila, August 16–18.

Ogata, Sadako. 1992. Interdependence and Internationalization. In *The Internationalization of Japan*, ed. G. D. Hook and M. Weiner, 63–71. New York: Routledge.

Oguma, Eiji. 2002. *A Genealogy of "Japanese" Self-Images*. Trans. D. Askew. Melbourne: Trans Pacific.

Ohnuki-Tierney, Emiko. 1993. *Rice as Self: Japanese Identities through Time*. Princeton, NJ: Princeton University Press.

Ong, Aihwa. 1999. *Flexible Citizenship: The Cultural Logics of Transnationality*. Durham, NC: Duke University Press.

———. 2003. *Buddha Is Hiding: Refugees, Citizenship, and the New America*. Berkeley: University of California Press.

———. 2006. *Neoliberalism as Exception: Mutations in Citizenship and Sovereignty*. Durham, NC: Duke University Press.

Ong, Aihwa, and Donald Nonini, eds. 1997. *Ungrounded Empires: The Cultural Politics of Modern Chinese Transnationalism*. New York: Routledge.

Onishi, Norimitsu. 2007. Tokyo Cuts Aid, and Hinterland Withers in Japan. *New York Times Online*, January 27. www.nytimes.com/2007/01/27/world/asia/27japan.html?scp=1&sq=onishi%20norimitsu%20tokyo%20cuts%20aid&st=cse (accessed November 12, 2008).

Ortiz, Fernando. 1995. *Cuban Counterpoint: Tobacco and Sugar*. Trans. H. De Onis. Durham, NC: Duke University Press.

Ortner, Sherry. 1995. Resistance and the Problem of Ethnographic Refusal. In *Recapturing Anthropology in Working in the Present*, ed. R. G. Fox, 163–90. Santa Fe, NM: School of American Research.

———. 1996. *Making Gender: The Politics and Erotics of Culture*. Boston: Beacon.

Parker, Andrew, Patricia S. Yaeger, Doris Sommer, and Mary Russo, eds. 1992. *Nationalisms and Sexualities*. New York: Routledge.

Parreñas, Rhacel. 2001. *Servants of Globalization: Women, Migration, and Domestic Work*. Stanford, CA: Stanford University Press.

———. 2005. *Children of Global Migration: Transnational Families and Gendered Woes*. Stanford, CA: Stanford University Press.

Pateman, Carole. 1988. *The Sexual Contract*. Stanford, CA: Stanford University Press.

Pempel, T. J. 1997. Transpacific Torii: Japan and the Emerging Asian Regionalism. In *Network Power: Japan and Asia*, ed. Peter J. Katzenstein and Takashi Shiraishi, 47–82. Ithaca, NY: Cornell University Press.

Perpiñan, Sr. Mary Soledad. 1987. Philippine Women and Transnational Corporations. In *The Philippines Reader: A History of Colonialism, Neocolonialism, Dictatorship, and Resistance*, ed. D. B. Schirmer and S. R. Shalom, 234–43. Boston: South End.

Pflugfelder, Gregory. 1999. *Cartographies of Desire: Male-Male Sexuality in Japanese Discourse*. Berkeley: University of California Press.

Piper, Nicola. 1997. International Marriage in Japan: "Race" and "Gender" Perspectives. *Gender, Place, Culture* 4 (3): 321–38.

Piper, Nicola, and Mina Roces, eds. 2003. *Wife of Worker? Asian Women and Migration*. Lanham, MD: Rowman and Littlefield.

Potter, David M. 1996. *Japan's Foreign Aid to Thailand and the Philippines.* New York: St. Martin's.

Povinelli, Elizabeth A. 1993. *Labor's Lot: The Power, History, and Culture of Aboriginal Action.* Chicago: University of Chicago Press.

———. 2006. *The Empire of Love: Toward a Theory of Intimacy, Genealogy, and Carnality.* Durham, NC: Duke University Press.

Pratt, Geraldine. 1999. From Registered Nurse to Registered Nanny: Discursive Geographies of Filipina Domestic Workers in Vancouver, BC. *Economic Geography* 75 (3): 215–36.

———. 2004. *Working Feminism.* Philadelphia, PA: Temple University Press.

Pratt, Mary Louise. 1992. *Imperial Eyes: Travel Writing and Transculturation.* New York: Routledge.

Rafael, Vicente. 1988. *Contracting Colonialism: Translation and Christian Conversion in Tagalog Society under Early Spanish Rule.* Manila: Ateneo de Manila Press.

———. 1995. Writing Outside: On the Question of Location. In *Discrepant Histories: Translocal Essays on Filipino Cultures,* ed. V. Raphael, xii-xxvii. Philadelphia, PA: Temple University Press.

———. 2000a. *White Love and Other Events in Filipino History.* Durham, NC: Duke University Press.

———. 2000b. "Your Grief Is Our Gossip": Overseas Filipinos and Other Spectral Presences. In *White Love and Other Events in Filipino History,* 204–28. Durham, NC: Duke University Press.

Raquisa, Tonette. 1987. Prostitution: A Philippine Experience. In *Third World, Second Sex.* ed. M. Davies, 218–24. London: Zed Books.

Raymond, Janice. 1998. Prostitution as Violence against Women: NGO Stonewalling in Beijing and Elsewhere. *Women's Studies International Forum* 21:1–9.

Reader, Ian, and George J. Tanabe Jr. 1998. *Practically Religious: Worldly Benefits and the Common Religion of Japan.* Honolulu: University of Hawaii Press.

Rebhun, L. A. 1999. *The Heart Is Unknown Country.* Stanford, CA: Stanford University Press.

Rimban, Luz. 1997. Risky Vows. *"i," the Investigative Reporting Magazine* 3 (4): 30–33.

Rizal, José. 1887/1996. *Noli Me Tángere.* Trans. M. S. Lacson-Locsin. Manila: Ateneo de Manila Press.

Robertson, Jennifer. 1988. Furusato Japan: The Culture and Politics of Nostalgia. *Politics, Culture, and Society* 1 (4): 494–518.

———. 1991. *Native and Newcomer: Making and Remaking a Japanese City.* Berkeley: University of California Press.

———. 1998a. It Takes a Village: Internationalization and Nostalgia in Postwar Japan. In *Mirror of Modernity,* ed. S. Vlastos, 110–32. Berkeley: University of California Press.

———. 1998b. *Takarazuka: Sexual Politics and Popular Culture in Modern Japan.* Berkeley: University of California Press.

———. 2001. Japan's First Cyborg? Miss Nippon, Eugencis and Wartime Technologies of Beauty, Body and Blood. *Body and Society* 7 (1): 1–34.

———. 2002. Blood Talks: Eugenic Modernity and the Creation of New Japanese. *History and Anthropology* 13 (3): 191–216.

Roces, Mina. 2003. Sisterhood Is Local: Filipino Women in Mount Isa. In *Wife or Worker? Asian Women and Migration,* ed. N. Piper and M. Roces, 73–100. Lanham, MD: Rowman and Littlefield.

Rodriguez, Robyn. 1999. Outline of a Theory of the Labor-Sending State: The State and Migration. *Philippine Sociological Review* 47:101–16.

———. 2002. Migrant Heroes: Nationalism, Citizenship, and the Politics of Filipino Migrant Labor. *Citizenship Studies* 6 (3): 341–56.

Rofel, Lisa. 1994. Yearnings: Televisual Love and Melodramatic Politics in Contemporary China. *American Ethnologist* 21 (4): 700–22.

———. 1999. *Other Modernities: Gendered Yearnings in China after Socialism.* Berkeley: University of California Press.

———. 2007. *Desiring China: Experiments in Neoliberalism, Sexuality, and Public Culture.* Durham, NC: Duke University Press.

Rosaldo, Renato. 1993. *Culture and Truth: The Remaking of Social Analysis.* Boston: Beacon.

Rose, Gillian. 1993. *Feminism and Geography: The Limits of Geographical Knowledge.* Minneapolis: University of Minnesota Press.

Roth, Joshua Hotaka. 2002. *Brokered Homeland: Japanese Brazilian Migrants in Japan.* Ithaca, NY: Cornell University Press.

Rouse, Roger. 1995. Questions of Identity: Personhood and Collectivity in Transnational Migration to the United States. *Cultural Anthropology* 15 (4): 351–80.

Rozman, Gilbert. 1999. Backdoor Japan: The Search for a Way Out via Regionalism and Decentralization. *Journal of Japanese Studies* 25 (1): 3–31.

Rubin, Gayle. 1975. The Traffic in Women: Notes on the "Political Economy" of Sex. In *Toward an Anthropology of Women,* ed. R. Reiter. 157–210. New York: Monthly Review.

Russell, John G. 1996. Race and Reflexivity: The Black Other in Contemporary Japanese Mass Culture. In *Contemporary Japan and Popular Culture,* ed. J. W. Treat, 17–40. Honolulu: University of Hawaii Press.

———. 1998. Consuming Passions: Spectacle, Self-Transformation, and the Commodification of Blackness in Japan. *positions: east asia cultures critique* 6 (1): 113–77.

Ryang, Sonia. 1997. *North Koreans in Japan: Language, Ideology, and Identity.* Boulder, CO: Westview.

———. 2000. *Koreans in Japan: Critical Voices from the Margins.* New York: Routledge.

Sahlins, Marshall. 1981. *Historical Metaphors and Mythical Realities: Structure in the Early History of the Sandwich Islands Kingdom.* Ann Arbor: University of Michigan Press.

———. 1985. *Islands of History.* Chicago: University of Chicago Press.

Sakai, Naoki. 1997. *Translation and Subjectivity: On "Japan" and Cultural Nationalism.* Minneapolis: University of Minnesota Press.

Salman, Michael. 2001. *The Embarrassment of Slavery: Controversies over Bondage and Nationalism in the American Colonial Philippines*. Berkeley: University of California Press.

Sand, Jordan. 1998. At Home in the Meiji Period: Inventing Japanese Domesticity. In *Mirror of Modernity: Invented Traditions of Modern Japan*, ed. S. Vlastos, 191–207. Berkeley: University of California Press.

———. 2003. *House and Home in Modern Japan: Architecture, Domestic Space, and Bourgeois Culture 1880–1930*. Cambridge, MA: Harvard University Press.

Santos, Aida F. 1991. Do Women Really Hold Up Half the Sky? Notes on the Women's Movement in the Philippines. In *Essays on Women*, ed. S. M. J. Mananzan, 36–51. Manila: Institute on Women's Studies, St. Scholastica's College.

Santos, Bienvenido N. 1979. *Scent of Apples: A Collection of Stories*. Seattle: University of Washington Press.

Sassen, Saskia. 1991. *The Global City: New York, London, Tokyo*. Princeton, NJ: Princeton University Press.

———. 1994. *Cities in a World Economy*. Thousand Oaks, CA: Pine Forge.

Satake, Masaaki, and Mary Angeline Da-anoy. 2006. *Firipin-Nihon kokusai kekkon: tabunka kyōsei to ijū* [Filipina-Japanese intermarriages: Migration, settlement, and multicultural coexistence]. Tokyo: Mekong.

Sato, Takao. 1989. *Mura to kokusai kekkon*. Tokyo: Nihon Hyōronsha.

Sawada, Masaharu. 1996. Kisoji no kokoro. In *Kisoji futatabi: Sawada Masaharu shashinchō, 1919–1992*, ed. Kisofukushima Kankōkai, 218–20. Matsumoto, Japan: Kyōdō Shuppansha.

Schaeffer-Grabiel, Felicity. 2006. Planet-Love.com: Cyberbrides in the Americas and the Transnational Routes of U.S. Masculinity. *Signs* 31 (2): 331–56.

Scheiner, Irwin. 1998. The Japanese Village: Imagined, Real, Contested. In *Mirror of Modernity: Invented Traditions of Modern Japan*, ed. S. Vlastos, 67–78. Berkeley: University of California Press.

Schirmer, Daniel B, and Stephen Rosskamm Shalom, eds. 1987. *The Philippines Reader: A History of Colonialism, Neocolonialism, Dictatorship, and Resistance*. Boston: South End.

Schneider, David M. 1980. *American Kinship: A Cultural Account*. 2nd ed. Chicago: University of Chicago Press.

Scott, James C. 1985. *Weapons of the Weak: Everyday Forms of Peasant Resistance*. New Haven, CT: Yale University Press.

Sellek, Yoko. 1996. Female Foreign Migrant Workers in Japan: Working for the Yen. *Japan Forum* 8 (2): 159–75.

———. 2001. *Migrant Labour in Japan*. New York: Palgrave.

Sen, Krishna, and Maila Stivens. 1998. *Gender and Power in Affluent Asia*. London: Routledge.

Shiraishi, Takashi. 2006. The Third Wave: Southeast Asia and Middle-Class Formation in the Making of a Region. In *Beyond Japan: The Dynamics of East Asian Regionalism*, ed. T. Shiraishi and P. J. Katzenstein, 237–72. Ithaca, NY: Cornell University Press.

Shukuya, Kyoko. 1988. *Ajia kara kita hanayome: mukaeru gawa no ronri.* Tokyo: Akashi Shoten.

Siddle, Richard. 1996. *Race, Resistance and the Ainu of Japan.* New York: Routledge.

———. 1997. Ainu: Japan's Indigenous People. In *Japan's Minorities: The Illusion of Homogeneity,* ed. M. Weiner, 17–49. New York: Routledge.

Siegenthaler, Peter. 1999. Japanese Domestic Tourism and the Search for National Identity. *CUHK Journal of Humanities* 3:178–95.

———. 2003. Creation Myths for the Preservation of Tsumago Post-Town. *Planning Forum* 9:29–45.

Silverberg, Miriam. 1991. The Modern Girl and Militant. In *Recreating Japanese Women: 1600–1945,* ed. G. Bernstein, 239–66. Berkeley: University of California Press.

———. 1998. The Cafe Waitress Serving Modern Japan. In *Mirror of Modernity: Invented Traditions of Modern Japan,* ed. S. Vlastos, 208–25. Berkeley: University of California Press.

Smith, Robert. 1983. Ancestor Worship in Contemporary Japan. *Bulletin of the Nanzan Institute for Religion and Culture* 7:30–40.

Soja, Edward W. 1996. *Thirdspace: Journeys to Los Angeles and Other Real-and-Imagined Places.* Malden, MA: Blackwell.

Spivak, Gayatri. 1993. Marginality in the Teaching Machine. In *Outside in the Teaching Machine,* 53–76. New York: Routledge.

Steedly, Mary Margaret. 1993. *Hanging without a Rope: Narrative Experience in Colonial and Postcolonial Karoland.* Princeton, NJ: Princeton University Press.

Stewart, Kathleen. 1996. *A Space on the Side of the Road.* Princeton, NJ: Princeton University Press.

Stoler, Ann Laura. 1995. *Race and the Education of Desire: Foucault's History of Sexuality and the Colonial Order of Things.* Durham, NC: Duke University Press.

———. 2002. *Carnal Knowledge and Imperial Power.* Berkeley: University of California Press.

———. 2006. *Haunted by Empire: Predicaments of the Tactile and Unseen,* ed. A. L. Stoler, 1–23. Durham, NC: Duke University Press.

Strathern, Marilyn. 1992. *Reproducing the Future: Anthropology, Kinship, and the New Reproductive Technologies.* New York: Routledge.

Sturdevant, Saundra, and Brenda Stoltzfus, eds. 1992. *Let The Good Times Roll: Prostitution and the U.S. Military in Asia.* New York: New Press.

Suzuki, Kazue. 1995. Women Rebuff the Call for More Babies. *Japan Quarterly* 42 (1): 14–20.

Suzuki, Nobue. 2000. Between Two Shores: Transnational Projects and Filipina Wives in from Japan. *Women's Studies International Forum* 23 (4): 431–44.

———. 2002a. Gendered Surveillance and Sexual Violence in Filipina Premigration Experiences to Japan. In *Gender Politics in Asia Pacific: Agencies and Activisms,* ed. B. Yeoh, P. Teo, and S. Huang, 99–119. New York: Routledge.

———. 2002b. Women Imagined, Women Imagine: Re/presentations of Filipinas in Japan since the 1980s. In *Filipinos in Global Migrations: At Home in the*

World? ed. F. V. Aguilar, 176–203. Quezon City: Philippine Migration and Research Network and Philippine Social Science Council.

———. 2003. Transgressing "Victims": Reading Narratives of "Filipina Brides" in Japan. *Critical Asian Studies* 35 (3): 399–420.

———. 2004. Inside the Home: Power and Negotiation in Filipina-Japanese Marriages. *Women's Studies* 33 (4): 481–506.

———. 2007. Marrying a Marilyn of the Tropics: Manhood and Nationhood in Filipina-Japanese Marriages. *Anthropology Quarterly* 80 (2): 427–54.

Tadiar, Neferti Xina M. 2004. *Fantasy-Production: Sexual Economies and Other Philippine Consequences for the New World Order.* Quezon City, Philippines: Ateneo de Manila University Press.

Takagi, J. T., and Hye Jung Park. 1995. *The Women Outside: Korean Women and the U.S. Military.* VHS. New York: Third World News Reel.

Takahashi, Akiyoshi, Otohiko Hasumi, and Eiji Yamamoto, eds. 1992. *Nōson shakai no henbō to nōmin ishiki: 30-nenkan no hendō bunseki.* Tokyo: Tokyo Daigaku Shuppankai.

Tamanoi, Mariko Asano. 1990. Women's Voices: Their Critique of the Anthropology of Japan. *Annual Review of Anthropology* 19:17–37.

———. 1998. *Under the Shadow of Nationalism: Politics and Poetics of Rural Japanese Women.* Honolulu: University of Hawaii Press.

Tanaka, Stephen. 1993. *Japan's Orient: Rendering Pasts into History.* Berkeley: University of California Press.

Tate, Hideo. 1996. Kisoji to Sawada Masaharu-san: sabishiki tabibito. In *Kisoji futatabi: Sawada Masaharu shashinchō, 1919–1992,* ed. Kisofukushima Kankōkai, 228–33. Matsumoto: Kyōdō Shuppansha.

Taussig, Michael. 1987. *Shamanism, Colonialism, and the Wild Man: A Study in Terror and Healing.* Chicago: University of Chicago Press.

Taylor, Jean. 1984. *The Social World of Batavia: European and Eurasian in Dutch Asia.* Madison: University of Wisconsin Press.

Thomas, Nicholas. 1991. *Entangled Objects: Exchange, Material Culture, and Colonialism in the Pacific.* Ithaca, NY: Cornell University Press.

Tobin, Joseph J., ed. 1992. *Re-Made in Japan: Everyday Life and Consumer Taste in a Changing Society.* New Haven, CT: Yale University Press.

Trask, Haunani-Kay. 1999. *From a Native Daughter: Colonialism and Sovereignty in Hawai'i.* Honolulu: University of Hawaii Press.

Trinh, Minh-ha. 1989. *Woman, Native, Other.* Bloomington: Indiana University Press.

Truong, Thanh-Dam. 1990. *Sex, Money, and Morality: Prostitution and Tourism in Southeast Asia.* London: Zed Books.

Tsing, Anna. 1993. *In the Realm of the Diamond Queen.* Princeton, NJ: Princeton University Press.

———. 2000a. The Global Situation. *Cultural Anthropology* 15 (3): 327–60.

———. 2000b. Inside the Economy of Appearances. *Public Culture* 12 (1): 115–44.

———. 2005. *Friction: An Ethnography of Global Connection.* Princeton, NJ: Princeton University Press.

Tsuda, Takeyuki. 2003. *Strangers in the Ethnic Homeland.* New York: Columbia University Press.

Turner, Victor. 1974. *Dramas, Fields, and Metaphors: Symbolic Action in Human Society*. Ithaca, NY: Cornell University Press.

Tyner, James A. 1996. Constructions of Filipina Migrant Entertainers. *Gender, Place, Culture* 3 (1): 77–93.

———. 2004. *Made in the Philippines: Gendered Discourses and the Making of Migrants*. London: Routledge.

Uchida, Jun. 2005a. Brokers of Empire: Japanese and Korean Business Elites in Colonial Korea. In *Settler Colonialism in the Twentieth Century: Projects, Practices, Legacies*, ed. C. Elkins and S. Pedersen, 153–70. New York: Routledge.

———. 2005b. "Brokers of Empire": Japanese Settler Colonialism in Korea, 1910–1937. Cambridge, MA: Harvard University Press.

Ueno, Chizuko. 1987. Genesis of the Urban Housewife. *Japan Quarterly* 34 (April–June): 130–42.

Uno, Kathleen. 1993. The Death of "Good Wife, Wise Mother"? In *Postwar Japan as History*, ed. A. Gordon, 293–324. Berkeley: University of California Press.

Usuki, Keiko. 1988. Jápayukisan genshō o miru. *Gendai no esupuri (japayukisan no ima, gaikoku rōdōsha o meguru mondaiten)* 4 (249):85–99.

Van der Veer, Peter. 2001. *Imperial Encounters: Religion and Modernity in India and Britain*. Princeton, NJ: Princeton University Press.

Ventura, Rey. 1992. *Underground in Japan*. London: Jonathan Cape.

Visweswaran, Kamala. 1994. *Fictions of Feminist Ethnography*. Minneapolis: University of Minnesota Press.

Wardlow, Holly. 2006. *Wayward Women: Sexuality and Agency in a New Guinea Society*. Berkeley: University of California Press.

Watsuji, Tetsuro. 1961. *A Climate: A Philosophical Study*. Trans. G. Bownas. Tokyo: Japanese Government Printing Bureau.

Weiner, Annette B. 1983. *Women of Value, Men of Renown: New Perspectives in Trobiand Exchange*. Austin: University of Texas Press.

Weiner, Michael. 1989. *The Origins of the Korean Community in Japan, 1910–1923*. Atlantic Highlands: Humanities.

———. 1994. *Race and Migration in Imperial Japan*. New York: Routledge.

———. 1997a. The Invention of Identity: "Self" and "Other" in Pre-war Japan. In *Japan's Minorities: The Illusion of Homogeneity*, ed. M. Weiner, 1–16. New York: Routledge.

———, ed. 1997b. *Japan's Minorities: The Illusion of Homogeneity*. New York: Routledge.

———. 1997c. The Representation of Absence and the Absence of Representation: Korean Victims of the Atom Bomb. In *Japan's Minorities: The Illusion of Homogeneity*, ed. M. Weiner, 79–107. New York: Routledge.

Wender, Melissa. 2005. *Koreans in Japan, 1965–2000*. Stanford, CA: Stanford University Press.

Whatmore, Sarah. 2002. *Hybrid Geographies: Natures, Cultures, Spaces*. London: Sage.

Wigen, Kären. 1995. *The Making of a Japanese Periphery, 1750–1920*. Berkeley: University of California Press.

Williams, Brackette. 1989. A Class Act: Anthropology and the Race to Nation across Ethnic Terrain. *Annual Review of Anthropology* 18:401–44.

Wilson, Ara. 2004. *The Intimate Economies of Bangkok: Tomboys, Tycoons, and Avon Ladies in the Global City.* Berkeley: University of California Press.

Winichakul, Thongchai. 1994. *Siam Mapped: A History of the Geo-Body of a Nation.* Honolulu: University of Hawaii Press.

Wolf, Margery. 1972. *Women and the Family in Rural Taiwan.* Stanford, CA: Stanford University Press.

———. 1974. Chinese Women: Old Skills in a New Context. In *Woman, Culture, and Society,* ed. M. Z. Rosaldo and L. Lamphere, 157–72. Stanford, CA: Stanford University Press.

———. 1985. *Revolution Postponed: Women in Contemporary China.* Stanford, CA: Stanford University Press.

Wright, Melissa. 2004. From Protests to Politics: Sex Work, Women's Worth, and Ciudad Juarez Modernity. *Annals of the Association of American Geographers* 94 (2): 369–86.

Yamanaka, Keiko. 1993. New Immigration Policy and Unskilled Foreign Workers in Japan. *Pacific Affairs* 66 (1): 72–90.

Yamashita, Seiroku, ed. 2000. *Kiso no Shōwashi.* Matsumoto, Japan: Kyōdō Shuppansha.

Yamatani, Tetsuo. 1985/1990. *Japayukisan.* Tokyo: Jōhō Sentā.

———. 1992. *Japayukisan: onnatachi no Ajia.* Tokyo: Kōdansha.

Yamazaki, Tomoko. 1975. Sandakan No. 8 Brothel. *Bulletin of Concerned Asian Scholars* 7 (4): 52–60.

———. 1999. Sandakan Brothel No. 8: An Episode in the History of Lower-Class Japanese Women. Trans. K. Colligan-Taylor. Armonk, NY: Sharpe.

Yanagisako, Sylvia Junko. 1985. *Transforming the Past: Tradition and Kinship among Japanese Americans.* Stanford, CA: Stanford University Press.

———. 2002. *Producing Culture and Capital: Family Firms in Italy.* Princeton, NJ: Princeton University Press.

Yea, Sallie. 2004. Runaway Brides: Anxieties of Identity for Trafficked Filipinas in South Korea. *Singapore Journal of Tropical Geography* 25 (2): 180–97.

Yoneoka, Judy. 2000. Ten Years of Kokusaika: Has Progress Been Made? *The Language Teacher Online* 24 (10). www.jalt-publications.org/tlt/articles/2000/10/yoneoka (accessed November 13, 2007).

Yoneyama, Lisa. 1995. Memory Matters: Hiroshima's Korean Atom Bomb Memorial and the Politics of Ethnicity. *Public Culture* 7 (Spring): 499–527.

———. 1999. *Hiroshima Traces: Time, Space, and the Dialectics of Memory.* Berkeley: University of California Press.

Yoshino, Kosaku. 1992. *Cultural Nationalism in Contemporary Japan: A Sociological Inquiry.* New York: Routledge.

Index

Filipina women (*continued*)
49–50, 52–54; names/naming, 31–32;
not seen as contributors to cosmopolitanism in Central Kiso, 117; passports
and visas as topics of conversation
for, 95; permanent residency as goal
of, 94, 100, 165–67, 207, 211; presence as indicator of Central Kiso's
marginality, 121, 130–31; presence as
indicator of Japan's success, 130; rape
of, 67, 92, 202; reasons for coming to
Japan of, 36, 37, 74, 89, 90, 92; reservations about bar work of, 67–68; resistance to changing nationality by,
100; respect and care of elderly by,
176; sacrifices made by, 168–69, 170,
172, 173; stereotypes about, 17, 164,
165, 183, 203; support for family in
Philippines of, 87, 102, 135, 162,
167, 168–70, 181, 208, 209, 214; undocumented, 57, 58, 67, 233n52–53;
unspoken expectations of, 128; view
of Philippines of, 93–94; vision of
Japan as America of, 81; way of opening hostess bars of, 70–71. See also
entertainer visas; Filipina wives; hostesses; *shikkari*; names of individual
women
food/eating practices: Filipino foods
served in alternative spaces, 149,
185–86; as form of international exchange, 127, 241n20; identity and,
149, 185, 240n19; importance to Japanese of preparation and serving of,
147, 149, 153, 160, 161; as sites of
tension, 184–85
Foucault, Michel, 35, 165, 193, 221n5,
228n2
Fujitani, Takashi, 141

gender: "backwards" ideas about in
rural Japan, 154–55; changes in Japanese ideas about, 127, 128, 139; cultural encounters and, 11, 14; of
household division of labor, 143, 154,
180; inequality and, 140, 241n24;
jobs segregated by, 16; mass media
and production of, 9; in middle-class
Japanese ideals, 111; performativity,
187, 242n31; resonance between
Japan and Philippines in understandings of, 179, 180, 184, 188; sacrifice
and suffering in Philippines and,
168–69; taken for granted in Japanese
studies, 23
Ghosh, Amitav (*The Shadow Lines*), vii,
22

Giddens, Anthony, 229n3
Gilroy, Paul, 9
Gina (pseudo.), 56, 58, 59, 60, 66
global processes, 5, 13–14, 20
Gopinath, Gayatri, 10
Gordon, Avery, 29
gossip, 159; about runaways, 192, 196,
199, 202–6, 208–9; concern about, 84,
85; Filipina *mama-sans* as subject of,
71–72, 73, 181–83
Griesemer, James R., 184, 244n28

Hall, Stuart, 186–87, 242n31,
246n13
Haraway, Donna, 38, 137, 140, 226n63,
239n4
histories, converging, 21, 44, 79
Hochschild, Arlie, 61, 233n55
home, ambivalence and unequal relations
of, 168, 243n11
hooks, bell, 235n18
hostess bars: advertisements for, 39–40;
closing in Central Kiso of, 43, 212,
213, 215; Club Dream, 48; Club
Tomoko, 2, 3, 49; customers, 47, 49,
59–60; defined, 41–42; description of,
57; Filipina, 43–44, 47–49; historical
precursors of, 229n10; history of,
42–43, 46–49; Mass at, 71, 72; as
navigation landmarks, 17; replacement of Japanese women by Filipina
women in, 43, 47, 74, 76, 77; role to
Japanese men of, 74–76; rural elite
Japanese negative opinion of, 55–56;
Sampagita, 43, 55–60, 67–70, 71, 73,
94, 146, 150–51, 212; Santo Niño
statues in, 67–68, 69; as sites of
encounter for Japanese men and
Filipina women, 20, 36, 41, 44, 50,
54, 56, 61, 64, 74, 75, 78, 79, 80–81,
120, 190; as sites of masculinity and
class-based identity, 75. See also
mama-sans
hostesses: becoming beautiful as part of
job, 65; dealing with lecherous men
by, 66–67; *dōhan* (accompaniment)
of, 62–64, 67; drink-back quotas for,
61; as job category, 223–24n42;
looked down upon by some Japanese,
126, 148, 159, 165; marriage to customers by, 2, 36, 41, 64–65, 80–81,
82, 86; as modern-day derivative of
geisha, 45; perform sexualized labor,
42; practices of, 60–67; pressure to
have sexual relations with customers,
44, 60, 67; relationships with customers of, 60–67; request quotas for,